T0294207

The Making of the

FIFA WORLD CUP

The Making of the

75 of the Most Memorable,
Celebrated, and Shocking Moments
in the History of Football's
Greatest Tournament

Jack Davies

First published by Pitch Publishing, 2022

Pitch Publishing
9 Donnington Park,
85 Birdham Road,
Chichester,
West Sussex,
PO20 7AJ
www.pitchpublishing.co.uk
info@pitchpublishing.co.uk

© 2022, Jack Davies

Every effort has been made to trace the copyright.
Any oversight will be rectified in future editions at the
earliest opportunity by the publisher.

All rights reserved. No part of this book may be reproduced,
sold or utilised in any form or transmitted in any form or by
any means, electronic or mechanical, including photocopying,
recording or by any information storage and retrieval system,
without prior permission in writing from the Publisher.

A CIP catalogue record is available for this book
from the British Library.

ISBN 978 1 80150 166 8

Typesetting and origination by Pitch Publishing
Printed and bound in Great Britain by TJ Books, Padstow

Contents

With massive thanks to my supportive family, and to Jade and Elsa, who couldn't care less about this book

Introduction

'I'm sure sex isn't as rewarding as winning the World Cup. It's not that good, but the World Cup is every four years and sex is not.'
Brazil's Ronaldo Luís Nazário de Lima

There are very few spectacles that can capture the imagination of planet Earth quite like the World Cup can. For one month every four years, this superbly unique football tournament sits front and centre in the minds of hundreds of millions around the globe. Or billions, even – FIFA estimates the audience for the 2018 World Cup Final reached over 1.1 billion people. These sensational numbers make it comfortably the most watched sporting event in the world, eclipsing even the Olympic Games.

Ask any football fan when they first really started getting excited about the sport, and the chances are they'll cite watching the World Cup on TV as a key reason. There's a magic surrounding the tournament that no other competition in football can compare to, giving it that special edge to captivate hardened fans and first-time followers alike. Maybe it's the chance to see the world's best players ply their trade in pursuit of that ultimate prize. Maybe it's the knowledge that it only comes around once every four years. Or maybe it's just because there's nothing else on telly.

Whatever you think explains the World Cup's monumental popularity, there's one thing that's undeniable: it's bloody entertaining. Try finding another event that can deliver such drama, excitement, shock, rage and ecstasy. It is those moments of extreme emotion that make the World Cup the ever-growing behemoth that it is today, and keep us coming back every four years to do it all over again.

This is the story of the World Cup, told through those pivotal, awe-inspiring, downright sensational moments on – and sometimes off – the pitch. From the tournament's beginnings as one man's idea to bring the world of football together at the first competition in Uruguay, to the biggest stars, most remarkable matches, inexplicable flashpoints, controversial decisions, and all the way through to that record-breaking final in 2018, this is your ultimate guide to why the World Cup is sport's greatest tournament.

1930: A Very Important Boat Trip

Friday, 20 June 1930–Friday, 4 July 1930
SS *Conte Verde*
Atlantic Ocean

Nowadays, the majority of professional international footballers lead lives of uninterrupted comfort and luxury when travelling abroad with their national teams. They stay in only the best hotels, are provided with top-class training facilities and get to travel all over the world on grand private jets and team coaches so hi-tech they wouldn't look out of place in a *Star Wars* movie.

Back in 1930, though, things were a little different. International football was in something of a fledgling state. The first international match – a 0-0 draw between England and Scotland – had been played in 1872, but in the nearly 60 years that had passed since, nations had predominantly stuck to playing the countries nearest to them geographically in exhibition matches and small regional tournaments, such as the British Home Championship.

A big step towards a major international competition was taken at the London Olympics in 1908, when eight teams from seven nations (France also fielded a 'B' team) contested the first official Olympic football tournament, organised by the English Football Association. But the sides involved comprised exclusively amateur players, with no professionals allowed to compete. This stayed the same until the 1924 Games in France, when for the first time players were paid for appearing. FIFA, formed in 1904, had since taken over the running of Olympic football, and made the rule change to allow higher-quality players to take part; in what became a recurring theme, the British football associations opposed the change and felt they knew best, withdrawing from the tournament.

The success of these first professional competitions in 1924 and 1928 (both won by Uruguay) led FIFA to believe that they could go it on their own and host a standalone football tournament separate to the Olympics. The organisation's president, Jules Rimet, was determined that this time, after a few failed attempts and false starts, a footballing world championship would flourish. Uruguay was chosen as the host country to honour the national team's status as defending Olympic champions, with the capital Montevideo scheduled to host every match, and a date was set for summer 1930.

The FIFA World Cup started out life as an experiment, and Rimet was keen to just get as many established footballing nations involved as possible, with the hope of persuading 16 teams to take part. An open invite was sent out to the football associations of all countries that had a relatively good playing standard. Rimet's experiment was not as popular as he had hoped it would be, however. In May 1930, with just two months to go before the tournament's start, only nine teams had entered – all from the Americas.

This was a disastrous blow to Rimet's hopes of staging a proper intercontinental tournament. It would be difficult for FIFA to dub the competition a world championship if teams from only South and North America took part. They were desperate to secure some European participants. England were invited on more than one occasion, but the chances of persuading the FA to support the World Cup were slim given that all of the British nations had resigned from FIFA following the disagreement over Olympic football. They preferred instead to focus on the British Home Championship, which they felt was more prestigious.

Rimet had a bigger problem still than the British teams throwing their dummies out of the pram: the location. International travel in the 1930s was not what it is today. Similarly, national football teams were yet to have the astronomical funding that many of them enjoy in the 21st century. So, for the European teams, crossing the Atlantic and travelling south beyond the equator to get to Uruguay was always going to be a big ask.

FIFA relied on the connections of senior officials to persuade some European teams to make the trip. France reluctantly agreed at the behest of Rimet, himself a Frenchman, but both the team's coach and star player declined to travel. FIFA's vice-president, Rudolf Seedrayers, used his links at the Belgian FA to ensure his nation was represented. Meanwhile, in Romania, football-loving monarch King Carol II ordered his country to play, and even went as far as to select the squad himself. It was Carol who also persuaded the fourth and final European entrants, Yugoslavia, to take part, bringing the total number of teams for the inaugural World Cup up to 13. And it was down to an Italian ocean liner – built just outside Glasgow – to ensure that the full 13 were present in Uruguay in time for the tournament's start date.

When the SS *Conte Verde* set sail from Genoa on 20 June, the Romanian team were already on board, having endured a two-day train journey simply to get to the port. The vessel was a passenger ship, so they were joined by plenty of non-footballing civilians making their own voyages. The French team were next to board just outside of Nice, before the Belgians joined at Barcelona. Yugoslavia also tried to travel on the *Conte Verde* but ended up having to make their own way to Uruguay; the ship was fully booked by the time they had decided to participate.

Also joining the footballers for the trip were three European referees and Jules Rimet himself. He even had the now-iconic trophy – named after him in 1950 – packed in his suitcase. A huge portion of the key elements needed for the tournament to actually go ahead were on that ship; the organisers would be forgiven for being on tenterhooks for the duration of the journey.

And that journey was by no means a short one. It would ultimately take over two weeks for those departing from Europe to reach Montevideo, limiting the players' preparation for the competition. France's Lucien Laurent, who would go on to book his own place in football history as the first man to score a goal in the World Cup, remembered, 'There was no talk of tactics or anything like that, no coaching. It was just running about the boat on deck.'

Far from the rival teams keeping one another at arm's length, a spirit of camaraderie was fostered aboard the *Conte Verde*. Laurent spoke of how the journey 'was like a holiday camp'. After their short bouts of physical training, the players would eat together and be entertained by comedy acts and string quartets.

The Brazilian team were also picked up by the *Conte Verde* when the boat reached South America, joining their European counterparts for the final leg of the journey. On 4 July, after over a fortnight at sea, the ship docked in Montevideo, well in time for the tournament's opening game nine days later. Ultimately, those who had travelled on the *Conte Verde* only had short stays in the tournament. All four teams were knocked out in the group stages, in a format that saw only the four group winners progress straight to the semi-finals. But they had played an integral part.

The travel problems that hampered participation in the first World Cup would remain throughout the 1934 and 1938 tournaments, which were both staged on European soil and saw limited numbers of non-European teams compete. But, like in 1930, a handful did make transatlantic journeys to take part, and those tournaments also saw the debuts of teams from Africa and

Asia. That voyage of the *Conte Verde* had set the precedent for worldwide participation, and the World Cup never looked back.

1930: The First World Cup Final
Wednesday, 30 July 1930
Estadio Centenario
Montevideo, Uruguay

While FIFA mightn't have had as many teams taking part as they'd have liked, the first World Cup had been an understated success. Attendances were high, and the tournament had been lit up by some stunning performances and memorable matches.

That said, there were two teams who stood out from the rest as being at a level above: hosts and reigning Olympic champions Uruguay, and Argentina, their neighbours and fierce rivals. The two South American nations had led eerily similar campaigns. Both had slightly laboured to 1-0 wins in their respective opening group games before going on runs where they exhibited their dominant attacking prowess, sweeping aside the teams who faced them with ease.

They had even both won their semi-final matches by the same unlikely scoreline of 6-1. Argentina were first up, romping past an unfancied United States team who had been something of a surprise package in their group. Uruguay, meanwhile, faced a very capable Yugoslavia side in a match not lacking in controversy. With the scores at 1-1, the Yugoslavs went behind to a goal that stands to this day as one of the most bizarre ever scored in the World Cup. A wayward ball drifted out of play during a Uruguay counter attack, only for a uniformed policeman at the side of the pitch to boot it back in. The (hopefully) oblivious referee allowed play to continue. Striker Peregrino Anselmo latched on to the ball, surged beyond the Yugoslavian defence and made it 2-1. Dubious goal aside, Uruguay had four more goals up their sleeve and ultimately rampaged into the final with little fuss.

Their star man was Pedro Cea. At 29, the forward was one of the oldest members of the Uruguay team, and a seasoned veteran who had helped the country win back-to-back Olympic golds. He was his country's top scorer in the tournament and even bagged a hat-trick in that semi-final rout.

Argentina also had a leading light who shone even brighter than Cea. Guillermo Stábile must go down as one of the happiest accidents in international football. The 25-year-old went to the 1930 World Cup having never played a game for the national side, and was taken largely as backup to Roberto Cerro, star striker for Boca Juniors (at the time Argentina's biggest and most successful club). Stábile sat out his country's opening game against France and, in the days before substitutes were allowed, was expected to do the same for the rest of the competition.

Fate would carve out a different path for him. Cerro had a bad reaction to some anti-anxiety medication and was unavailable for Argentina's second fixture, against Mexico, while another forward, Manuel Ferreira, had to sit the match out because he had a law exam to take back in Buenos Aires. Out of these unorthodox circumstances Stábile got his chance, and made sure to grab it with both hands. In that game against Mexico – his international debut – he scored a hat-trick as Argentina ran out 6-3 winners. He'd score four more in their next two games to help fire his team into the final.

The scene was set for a magnificent footballing occasion. Two great rivals – who had two years prior played each other in the gold medal match of the 1928 Olympics – facing off in the kind of centrepiece that organisers would have dreamed of. FIFA now put the number at 80,000 but reports at the time suggested up to 100,000 supporters crammed inside Montevideo's Estadio Centenario, which had been built specially for the World Cup. Thousands of these were Argentina fans who had crossed the River Plate to attend the match, ensuring their team was well represented in the stands.

The opposing supporters made for a tense, hostile atmosphere. There'd been reports of death threats made to some of the Argentina players, and fans were searched for weapons upon entry to the stadium. With no separated seating sections, many Argentina fans who were not in larger groups of their compatriots found themselves surrounded by Uruguayans. Francisco Varallo, who played for Argentina in the final, remembered, 'My father was in the stands and he had to leave the stadium disguised with a Uruguayan flag because some Uruguayans ... were trying to find the Argentinians to punch them.'

There was plenty of hostility between the players themselves, too. In a somewhat farcical episode, the kick-off was actually delayed because the two teams couldn't agree on which ball to use. Both had been allowed to provide their own balls for every game that they'd played in the tournament up to that point. But now that they were facing each other it seemed one side would be left disappointed. John Langenus, the experienced Belgian referee officiating the match, had the solution: the first half would be played with Argentina's ball, the second with Uruguay's.

The hosts took the lead in the 12th minute, with Argentina looking erratic in possession and nervy without it. The goal they had conceded seemed to calm them though, and eight minutes later they were level. Largely in control, they took the lead through a sleek, angled shot from Stábile shortly before half-time. It was the striker's eighth goal of the tournament, ensuring he finished three clear of Cea as the World Cup's first top scorer (amazingly, this was his last game for Argentina, with his four appearances and eight goals for his country all coming during the tournament).

Uruguay, now playing with their own ball, rallied in the second half. The Centenario had become a deadly bear pit and the home team surged forward relentlessly. Twelve minutes in, Cea tapped in an equaliser. From that moment on, Argentinian heads dropped and mistakes were rife. In the 68th minute, Uruguay winger Santos Iriarte scored with a low, driven shot that seemed to take Argentina keeper Juan Botasso completely by surprise, the stopper flailing helplessly in the direction of the ball long after it had travelled past him and into the net.

At 3-2, Argentina threw everything they had at Uruguay in search of an equaliser but came up against a rigid, regimented team that was drilled to perfection. The match was clinched with a fourth goal a minute from full time, when the one-armed Héctor Castro rose high in the box to rifle a header past Botasso. Fans spilled on to the pitch to celebrate Uruguay's triumph as maiden champions of the world.

Post-game, Argentinian media suggested that their players' confidence had been shot by threats they had received before the match, and the Uruguayan consulate in Buenos Aires was pelted with rocks. The *Daily Herald* reported that the feeling was so strong, women seen flying the Uruguayan flag in the Argentinian capital were stoned. Uruguay, meanwhile, declared the day after their victory a national holiday. Even with the tournament in its infancy, a World Cup win there was deemed significant enough for a full day of celebration.

Despite their fervour, Uruguay would become the only champions in the competition's history to not defend their title. They boycotted the next edition – the 1934 World Cup in Italy – protesting against the lack of European attendance at their own tournament. They withdrew from the 1938 tournament in France too, angry at FIFA for picking two European countries in a row to host. Still, the passion and appetite of the fans for a football world championship had shown FIFA and the wider footballing community that maybe, the World Cup was an idea they could run with.

1934: Mussolini's Refereeing Puppets and the Fascist World Cup

Friday, 1 June 1934
Stadio Giovanni Berta
Florence, Italy

Ask anyone with a GCSE in History to give you an example of sport being politicised, and the chances are they'll point to the 1936 Olympics in Berlin, when Adolf Hitler and Nazi Party propaganda loomed large over the event. But two years earlier, it was Italian dictator Benito Mussolini who first seized his opportunity to promote fascism through sport when his country hosted the second World Cup.

Naturally, choosing Italy to host was controversial. FIFA executives met no fewer than eight times to decide between the fascist country and Sweden, the other nation bidding to host the tournament. Ultimately, they felt Mussolini's regime stood the best chance of success in organising the first European edition of the World Cup. Knowing that its member nations would likely disagree, FIFA went ahead and selected Italy for the tournament without holding any kind of ballot. They argued that it was a decision made purely for footballing reasons, pointing to the success of the country's recently revamped league, Serie A, as an example of how the Italians could organise an immensely popular competition. With the World Cup still in its infancy, they wanted to maximise the tournament's exposure, and the country's high-capacity stadia and good transport links would allow for large numbers of travelling fans to attend from across Europe.

While FIFA may have wanted to put Italy's divisive politics aside, Mussolini certainly wasn't going to miss the chance to put his own stamp on proceedings. This was a huge opportunity to show off Italian fascism, and he involved himself at every stage of organising the tournament, even having a special trophy made to be awarded alongside the existing prize. The Coppa del Duce (which Mussolini modestly named after himself – he was known as *Il Duce* in Italy) was six times the size of the World Cup trophy, just to ensure it would tower over FIFA's award.

Italian hopes of ensuring that that gigantic new trophy would stay in the country were complicated by the fact that they had to qualify first, to this day the only World Cup hosts to ever have to do so. The successful tournament of 1930 led to much increased interest in the 1934 edition, and 32 teams entered the 16-team competition. As such, a first batch of World Cup qualifiers would be needed.

Italy were drawn against Greece in a two-legged play-off, the winners of which would play in the finals. The Italians ran out comfortable 4-0 victors in the home leg, and ahead of their trip to Athens for the second fixture there was no real danger of them throwing their commanding lead away. Still, it was a gruelling journey that the team would have to make just four weeks before the finals were due to start, despite the result essentially being a formality.

But then something rather odd happened. The Greeks, having already sold 20,000 tickets for the game, pulled out. Italy, now formally qualified, were able to enjoy an uninterrupted month preparing for the tournament that Mussolini was so desperate for them to win, and the second leg's cancellation was chalked up as a team essentially conceding defeat. Decades later, reports emerged alleging that the Italian FA pressured Greece into withdrawing from the match, and purportedly paid off senior figures in Greek football for their silence.

Mussolini was determined to give the Italian team as many advantages as he possibly could. In the days before strict rules on representing more than one national team, a timely reversal of a ban on foreign players in Serie A welcomed global stars to Italy and allowed them to poach players with dubious Italian heritage from other nations, particularly Argentina. Seven of Italy's 22-man squad for the tournament were born on foreign soil, four of those from Argentina (midfielder Luis Monti had even played in the 1930 World Cup Final for the Argentines). *Il Duce* went further still; he actually hand-picked the referees who would be officiating at the tournament, as well as personally selecting the individual refs who would oversee Italy's games and wining and dining them at extravagant dinners. This was his World Cup in every way possible.

For the 1934 tournament, the group stages that were used in 1930 were discarded in favour of a pure knockout format. Italy's first match was against the USA, who they steamrollered 7-1 to advance to the quarter-finals. There they would face Spain, who would provide a much sterner test.

On 31 May in Florence the two played out a ferocious clash that wouldn't have looked out of place on a battlefield. Players from both sides flew into brutally dangerous challenges, the worst of which saw Italian midfielder Mario Pizziolo have his leg broken. The match ended 1-1 after extra time. With penalty shoot-outs not arriving for another 40 years, a replay was scheduled for the following day.

While Pizziolo undoubtedly suffered the worst injury, it was the Spanish who found themselves most depleted on 1 June, having to make an eye-watering seven changes due to injuries sustained in the original match. When the sides took to the field again they were heading into one of the most controversial games in World Cup history.

The officiating on the day of the replay was shamelessly one-sided, in Italy's favour of course. In front of Mussolini and the fascist hierarchy, Swiss referee René Mercet – who *Il Duce* had selected for Italy's first game against the USA too – made a series of bizarre decisions that incensed the Spanish. With Italy 1-0 up through a Giuseppe Meazza goal, Mercet deemed a would-be Spain equaliser offside in dubious circumstances. An even more surreal decision was to come. The Spanish again put the ball in the Italy net, and again the goal was chalked off, on this occasion with Mercet recalling play for a free kick actually in Spain's favour. The match stayed at 1-0 and Italy progressed to the semi-finals.

The fallout from the game was astronomical. Spanish newspapers were understandably incensed, and not only lambasted the referee for the two goals they had ruled out, but also suggested that the Italy goal had been the result of a foul on Spain's goalkeeper. Reaction in Mercet's home country was just as critical. The *Basler National-Zeitung* asserted that he had 'favoured the Italians in a most shameful manner'. FIFA took note; Mercet was banned from ever officiating an international match again. Upon his return to Switzerland, he was also suspended by the country's FA, so ashamed were they of his performance in the Italy-Spain game.

Meanwhile, Italy would go on to reach the final in Rome, where they faced a strong Czechoslovakia side. The match was not, as Mussolini hoped, a glorious show of Italian strength; for much of the game their opponents dominated. Extra time was needed with the scores at 1-1 after 90 minutes. But *Il Duce* did get his ultimate wish. He was in the stands along with senior representatives from communist Czechoslovakia and Nazi Germany to see Angelo Schiavio score the goal that would make Italy champions and allow Mussolini to present the trophy named after him to his own team.

To this day, sections of Spanish media point to their quarter-final replay and suggest that it should have been them contesting that final, not Italy. The Italians would be tarnished with the accusation that they were false world champions. If they were to really prove their prowess, they'd have to do it in circumstances where their leader couldn't stack the odds in their favour.

1938: The Battle of Bordeaux

Sunday, 12 June 1938
Stade du Parc Lescure
Bordeaux, France

By the time the World Cup rolled into France in 1938, the tournament was starting to gather pace. FIFA were getting plenty of interest from nations wanting to both participate in and host the competition. However, the sticking point regarding the difficulty of international travel remained. Argentina had been particularly vocal about wanting to host the tournament, so when FIFA picked France, they raged that it was unfair to select two European nations in a row and subsequently withdrew. Uruguay followed suit. That left Brazil as the sole representatives of South America. Their performance in one game in particular at the 1938 World Cup was hardly the kind to make their continent proud, and a million miles from the silky, flamboyant style the Brazil teams of later years were known for.

Brazil qualified automatically for the tournament thanks to their South American counterparts refusing to compete, so their first chance to prove that they deserved to be there was in their opening match. This was against Poland, World Cup debutants with an amateur squad that had only been able to meet up and train together a week before the competition kicked off. While Brazil in the 1930s were not the force they would later become, they were strongly fancied to cruise past Poland and into the quarter-finals (FIFA had, for the second and last time, plumped for a straight knockout format for the 1938 tournament).

Instead, the Polish gave as good as they got in what remains one of the greatest games in World Cup history. Brazil triumphed 6-5 after extra time. They were through, but they'd been humbled by the Poles, and more importantly their defence had been breached five times in the process.

When their quarter-final arrived, the Brazilians were determined not to be so leaky at the back. Their opponents, Czechoslovakia, would make this an even harder task; they were a strong, physical side who had of course made it all the way to the final against Italy four years earlier.

A crowd of 22,000 packed inside the Stade du Parc Lescure in Bordeaux on a Sunday afternoon. At the time, this was an impressively large attendance for a match not involving the host nation, in no small part down to the fact that the ground, formerly a cycle track, had recently been rebuilt for the World Cup, and this was to be its first football match. Czechoslovakia and Brazil made it abundantly clear as soon as the game kicked off that it was going to be a baptism of fire for the revamped arena.

From the first minute Brazil indicated that they would not be as much of a soft touch in defence as they had been against Poland. The opening exchanges of the match saw them using their physicality as much as possible, crunching into some questionable tackles. Czechoslovakia, meanwhile, took this as their cue to respond in kind. Hungarian referee Pál von Hertzka found himself struggling to control the game as both sides committed foul after foul.

The first big flashpoint arrived in the 14th minute. Brazil midfielder Zezé Procópio clattered into a high challenge on forward Oldřich Nejedlý, who had won the Golden Boot four years earlier in Italy. Czechoslovakia's star man found himself winded in a heap on the floor, and von Hertzka instantly dismissed Zezé Procópio. Not even 15 minutes in and Brazil were already a man down.

The referee dismissing a player so early on did nothing to stop the brutality on the pitch, and the South Americans in particular continued to play in the ruthless fashion in which they had started. Now without one of their key men, they adopted a long-ball style of play which paid off on the half-hour mark. Eventual Golden Boot winner Leônidas put them 1-0 up, prompting complaints from the Czechoslovakians about the manner in which Brazil were playing. With their protests falling on deaf ears, they instead opted to inject even more aggression into their own play, and shortly after the goal Leônidas found himself on the end of a dreadful off-the-ball challenge that left him needing lengthy treatment before the game could carry on.

At half-time, von Hertzka spoke at length to both captains in the hope of regaining control of the match. This was to no avail. After a Brazilian handball in the box allowed Nejedlý to equalise from the penalty spot in the 65th minute, the game descended into a savage nadir. Shortly after his goal, Nejedlý was for the second time hit with diabolical challenge. This time he wouldn't play on; the forward had suffered a broken leg. A few more minutes passed before things got even worse for Czechoslovakia. Their captain and talismanic goalkeeper František Plánička broke his arm mid-save. He bravely continued for the rest of the match, but it would be the last time he played for his country.

The combative drama continued until the very end of normal time. Both Czechoslovakia (Jan Říha) and Brazil (Machado) had men sent off in the final few minutes. The two had swung punches at each other to spark a chaotic melee involving most of the players on the pitch before receiving their marching orders. It was the first time in World Cup history that three dismissals had happened in the same game.

After a significantly less raucous period of extra time, with the teams weary and low on numbers, the match ended 1-1. A replay contested two days later saw a gigantic 14 changes made in total, so battered and bruised were the players who featured in the original fixture. Brazil ran out 2-1 winners in a game noted for its fair play and progressed to the semi-finals, where they were defeated by Italy.

As World Cups came and went, more infamous 'battles' would be added to the list of mean-spirited, dirty and downright vicious contests between teams who decided to abandon sportsmanship for 90 minutes. But that match in Bordeaux was the blueprint.

1938: The Blackshirts Reign Supreme
Sunday, 19 June 1938
Stade Olympique Yves-du-Manoir
Colombes, France

There was a big question mark over Italy going into the 1938 World Cup. Mussolini's dubious relationship with the referees four years earlier had, outside of the country, raised numerous doubts about the team's ability. Despite claiming gold at the Olympics two years later, the football world was still unsure about the Italians' prowess on the biggest stage of all. Had they really been as good as the title of 'world champions' suggested? Or had the path to victory been smoothed for them?

As such, the Italians went to France in 1938 with a renewed determination and a big point to prove. But a lot had changed in the four years since they'd first lifted the trophy. The tournament arrived in a summer that saw Europe teetering on all-out war. The fascist expansionism exhibited by both Italy in their war with

Ethiopia and Nazi Germany in their annexation of Austria was deeply unpopular across the continent, and the nations' football teams arrived at the tournament as the two most reviled sides in the international game.

The fans in France made that clear in the very first match of the tournament. Switzerland faced off against a Germany side that featured five Austrian players in the starting line-up who had been plucked straight from their own recently defunct national team and forced to join the Germany squad. The Germans were loudly booed throughout the 1-1 draw (Switzerland would be victorious in the replay, with the German coach accusing his Austrian imports of throwing the game).

After this, Italy knew to expect a less-than-welcoming reception from the crowds as they headed into their own opening fixture, against Norway. In fact, they didn't even need to wait until the match itself; the team were reportedly welcomed into Marseille train station by 3,000 anti-fascist protestors.

As the teams lined up ahead of kick-off at the city's Stade Vélodrome, the Italian National Fascist Party's anthem was met with almost universal jeers from those in attendance. But that was nothing in comparison to the cacophony invoked when the team performed the fascist salute. Italy manager Vittorio Pozzo remembered that they were battered with a 'deafening barrage of whistles, insults and remarks' from the stands. Pozzo, who led his national side with military precision, was not one to be intimidated. When the noise had died down and his players had lowered their arms, he ordered them to perform the salute again, inciting even more vitriol from the crowd.

The match itself was a significantly less fearless display from the Italians, as a determined Norway side took them to extra time, in which Italy nicked a winner. *La Gazzetta dello Sport* ran with the headline 'Victory but not enough'. The team was going to need to do a whole lot more to show both the media back home and the rest of the football world that they were deserved champions four years prior.

Next up in the quarter-finals were the hosts, France. Like in Marseille, the crowd at the match in Paris was extremely hostile towards Italy. The teams, both ordinarily playing in blue, had drawn lots to decide who'd get to wear their home colours. France had won, so Italy instead prompted for a menacing all-black kit;

Mussolini's regime had ordered that the country's change strip should be this. Some 58,000 supporters watched on as the Italian team again gave the fascist salute in their Mussolini-approved uniforms, throwing the criticisms of them and their country back into the faces of those who made them. The photograph captured of this moment – the only time the Italians donned the black strip in the tournament and often wrongly attributed to having been taken ahead of the 1938 final – has become one of the most infamous images in football.

The roaring protestations from the French fans did nothing to dampen Italy's performance. Far from the laboured display against Norway, Pozzo's team looked energised and sharp. They surged into an early lead, and even when France replied with an equaliser a minute later, the match remained firmly in their control. They eventually ran out comfortable 3-1 winners, sending the host nation out and sending a strong message to their doubters that they were in the tournament for the long haul.

Another difficult test arrived for Italy in the semi-finals, and again they passed it. Brazil, fresh from their battle with Czechoslovakia, were their opponents. Italy progressed to the final thanks to a 2-1 win. With their detractors starting to dwindle, Hungary stood in the *Azzurri*'s way of proving unmistakably that they were the best football team in the world.

The importance of this opportunity was not lost on Mussolini. The dictator reportedly sent a telegram to the team ahead of the game that, translated into English, read, 'Win or die.' Whether this was meant literally or not has been questioned, although it's fair to say that the players perhaps wouldn't want to take the chance with someone as ruthless as *Il Duce*.

The final was held on Sunday, 19 June in the same stadium on the outskirts of Paris where Italy had defeated France a week earlier. And again, those inside the ground made no mistake in declaring their allegiances in the game's opening stages. Italy's opener – a close-range volley from striker Gino Colaussi in the sixth minute – was met with a chorus of boos and jeers. The pantomime continued two minutes later; Hungary's Pál Titkos booted in an equaliser after a period of atrocious Italian defending, prompting the crowd to explode with delight.

Their ecstasy was short-lived. It seemed Hungary's goal had injected the Italian players with the impetus to play their best football of the tournament. They bombarded the Hungarian goal with shots, twice striking the woodwork, before a glittering passage of laser-guided passing that would bring a tear to Pep Guardiola's eye scythed a gaping hole in the Hungary defence and allowed Silvio Piola to hammer Italy back in front after 16 minutes. The *Azzurri*'s dominance continued and 20 minutes later Colaussi struck his second of the match to make it 3-1 going into half-time.

The second half saw Hungary rally slightly and steal a goal back, but in truth the damage was done, and Italy never looked like relinquishing their grip on the game. Piola completed his brace with a sublime one-touch finish in the 82nd minute, reinstating Italy's two-goal lead and making certain that they would lift the World Cup for the second time in a row.

Mussolini was said to feel vindicated. He showered the team with accolades and prizes upon their return to Italy. Hungary's goalkeeper, Antal Szabó, felt things could have been very different, quipping after the match, 'I may have let in four goals, but at least I saved their lives.' It turns out this probably wasn't true; the Italy squad's last-surviving member, Pietro Rava, denied that Mussolini had ever sent the threatening telegram in the first place.

The Italian team never failed to court controversy at the 1938 World Cup. They defiantly represented their nation's despised fascist regime wherever they went and had a manager who seemed to take great pleasure in riling opposition fans. But they proved their point; they were undeniably the best football team on the planet and underlined that fact by becoming both the first team to defend a World Cup and the first team to win one on foreign soil. The spectres of doubt that loomed after 1934 had been vanquished.

1950: American Amateurs and English Embarrassment

Thursday, 29 June 1950
Estádio Independência
Belo Horizonte, Brazil

FIFA had gone to great lengths to ensure the success of the first three World Cups, but the future of the competition was thrown into uncertainty as the Second World War began in 1939. As the Nazis enjoyed initial successes in the war, there were worries that they might try and take ownership of any future tournaments. The 1942 edition was cancelled, and the trophy spent the 1940s in a shoebox hidden under the bed of a senior FIFA official, who was concerned that the Nazis may seize it from the bank in Rome where it was being kept.

The would-be 1946 competition was also cancelled as it was too soon after the conclusion of the war the year before for any country to be prepared to host it. FIFA pushed ahead with trying to organise a tournament in 1949, keen to as soon as possible regain the momentum they had built in the 1930s. But still they couldn't find a nation willing to host it. Finally Brazil stepped in, with the caveat that the tournament be played a year later, in 1950. With no other options, FIFA agreed.

While intercontinental travel was by now a lot easier, there was still some difficulty in persuading certain teams to enter. Reigning champions Italy in particular were reluctant. Much of their team had tragically died in an air disaster the year before. Eventually, the Italians were convinced, but elected to travel by ship instead.

Elsewhere, the British nations had in the intervening years put aside their dispute with FIFA and for the first time accepted the invitation to participate. That year's British Home Championship doubled up as a qualifying group, with the top two earning places at the tournament. England packed their bags for Brazil as winners of the group and jetted off to play in their debut World Cup. They were not, however, joined by their Scottish counterparts, who had qualified in second place; in a bizarre showing of pride, Scottish FA chairman George Graham refused to allow the team to travel unless they won the Home Championship, and they promptly withdrew.

English expectations for the competition were high. The home nations had turned their noses up at the 1930s tournaments, feeling that, as inventors of the game, their standard of football would naturally be higher than the rest of the world's. They were also considered to be one of the favourites for World Cup glory across the rest of the globe thanks to a glittering recent record that included big wins against some top European teams.

While England hardly ran riot in their first World Cup match – a 2-0 victory over Chile with goals from Stan Mortensen and Wilf Mannion – their win was comfortable enough to prompt bookies to lower their odds and make them outright favourites to win the competition. Match reports suggested that England had been sloppy and far from their best, but felt that there was a lot more to come from the side, pointing to the fact that star man Stanley Matthews had been left out of the team and that they would be facing much easier opposition in the shape of the USA in their next match.

That USA side had a considerably less comfortable opening fixture. Despite taking a surprise early lead against Spain, they went on to concede three times in the last ten minutes to lose 3-1. Still, that wasn't a bad showing for a team that were 500/1 rank outsiders and comprised entirely of amateur players that held down other jobs alongside their football careers (the team that faced England featured a postman, a teacher and – perhaps ominously – a hearse driver).

This was to be a mismatch of stratospheric proportions. The *Daily Express* was bullish about England's chances, claiming that the US would need a three-goal head start to stand any chance of getting a decent result. The United States' own coach, Bill Jeffrey, even wrote his team off, describing his players as 'sheep ready to be slaughtered'.

The US game plan was simple: damage limitation. American midfielder Walter Bahr remembered their mantra was 'keep the score respectable'. Bahr, who usually captained his national team, notably didn't have the armband against England. That honour was instead bestowed upon winger Ed McIlvenny, a Scotsman from Greenock who qualified to play for the States at the tournament because he intended to become a US citizen after the World Cup (although he never did). Bahr, knowing the special importance playing the English carried for McIlvenny, relinquished the captaincy and both men would go on to play a key role.

On England's part, they approached the game with their usual confidence that some might suggest bordered on arrogance. Matthews was again left out of the line-up; it was widely agreed that saving their talisman for the later stages of the tournament – when facing more difficult opposition – was a wise move.

The opening stages in Belo Horizonte were as one-sided as everyone anticipated. England took ownership of the ball for the vast majority of the first half and were only denied a goal by a defiant display from US goalkeeper Frank Borghi. Then, in the 38th minute, the unthinkable happened. A McIlvenny throw-in found Bahr on the edge of England's box. The midfielder let fly a speculative shot destined for the stands. But a young Haitian dishwasher by the name of Joe Gaetjens intervened. While no footage of the goal exists, those on the pitch that day report that Gaetjens flew towards the ball – which was careering out of play – head first. He didn't make a clean contact; rather, it brushed off the back of his head and rolled past the already diving England goalkeeper Bert Williams. The USA had scored first.

Even then, a goal up, the Americans didn't think their lead would last long. Defender Harry Keough remembered, 'We just hoped we could hold on until half-time.' That they did. In the second half, England again dominated, but resolute defending, spurned chances and more magnificent goalkeeping from Borghi saw the US claim a historic win.

Perhaps fortunately for England, press coverage of the result back home was overshadowed by the nation's cricket team suffering their first loss to the West Indies on the very same day. When the BBC radio broadcast read out the football result, listeners reportedly assumed the scoreline was an error. Similarly, in the USA, the *New York Times* didn't even report on the match, believing that the result wired across was a hoax.

Ultimately, both sides would exit the competition in the group stage. The US were thrashed by Chile in their next match, while England lost a pivotal game against Spain and were sent packing at the first hurdle in their debut World Cup. But that American victory over England – later dubbed 'The Miracle on Grass' and immortalised in the movie *The Game of Their Lives* – would go down as one of the biggest shock results in World Cup history.

1950: The Final That Wasn't

Sunday, 16 July 1950
Maracanã Stadium
Rio de Janeiro, Brazil

Football fever had well and truly swept across Brazil during the 1950 World Cup. An expectant crowd of 81,000 gathered in the newly built (and not-quite-finished) Maracanã for the team's opening match, a 4-0 rout of Mexico. The hosts finally had a team capable of competing with the footballing giants that dominated the 1930s. They had a fluid, fast, attractive style of play that promised goals galore; they'd plundered an eye-watering 46 goals across just eight matches while sweeping to Copa América glory the year before.

After that Mexican demolition, a draw and another win were enough to see Brazil top their group and head through to the final stage of the competition. In 1950, that didn't consist of the standard knockout system leading up to a showpiece, winner-takes-all final. Instead, the top team in each of the four opening groups would qualify for a final group stage. There, they'd face off in a round robin against each other, with the top team at the end of it all becoming world champions.

The three teams standing in Brazil's way of lifting the Jules Rimet Trophy before their adoring fans were Spain (who'd topped England's group), Sweden (who beat reigning champions Italy on the way to winning their group), and inaugural World Cup winners Uruguay. Thanks to some last-minute withdrawals, including France, who had initially been drawn in their group, Uruguay needed only to beat minnows Bolivia to advance to the final stage; they did so 8-0.

While Uruguay and Spain played out an entertaining 2-2 draw in the opening match of that championship group in São Paulo, Brazil steamrollered Sweden 7-1 in front of 140,000 at the Maracanã. The sensational Ademir, who won the tournament's Golden Boot, hit four goals as the cacophonous crowd bayed for Scandinavian blood. Even more were present there four days later as the Brazilians took Spain apart, beating them 6-1. Meanwhile, Uruguay struggled past Sweden after coming from behind twice to win 3-2.

Those results meant that going into the final pair of fixtures, only Uruguay and Brazil could still win the World Cup, with the two still to face each other. Effectively, their match became a World Cup Final in everything but name, with one key difference: thanks to their superior points tally, Brazil only needed a draw to become world champions, while Uruguay would need to win.

It's safe to say that confidence in Brazil was high. And not without reason. They possessed seemingly unstoppable goalscoring prowess, and their march to the Copa América title in 1949 had included a 5-1 battering of Uruguay. Brazilian fans knew that they had a team capable of not only beating any in world football, but destroying them.

This goes some way to explaining the remarkable events that led up to the 3pm kick-off on an eventful Sunday in Rio. A triumphant samba, entitled 'Brazil The Victors', had been composed, with the band inside the Maracanã that day instructed to launch straight into the bombastic number as soon as the match finished. Twenty-two gold medals, enough for each member of the Brazil squad, had been made up specially. The early edition of Brazilian newspaper *O Mundo* proclaimed 'These are the world champions' above a photo of the national side. An impromptu carnival broke out across the city, and the mayor of Rio delivered an emphatic speech addressing the team, 'You, players, who in less than a few hours will be hailed as champions by millions of compatriots! You, who I already salute as victors!'

The game was merely a formality. Ask anyone in Brazil that day. Anyone but the Uruguayans, whose enigmatic captain, centre-half Obdulio Varela, was incensed, particularly by *O Mundo*'s assertion that Brazil were already world champions. Ahead of the match, he took a copy into the dressing room with him and proceeded to urinate on it in front of his team-mates. He told them, 'We have to put our balls on the line to win this game.'

The Uruguay side that afternoon made their way into a Maracanã filled with over 200,000 spectators; still to this day the record attendance at a football match. Of that number, about 100 were supporting the away side. Suffice it to say, Uruguay had a mountain bigger than Everest to overcome.

Kick-off was akin to a starter's pistol for Brazil as they hurtled at their opposition with everything they had. It looked certain that Uruguay would become yet another side flattened by the dominant attacking might of the hosts, and it was clear that the *Seleção* weren't happy to just clinch the title with a draw. But Brazil just couldn't find the back of the net. In all, they registered a gigantic 17 efforts on the Uruguayan goal in the first half, but at the half-time whistle the match remained goalless.

Brazil began the second half in the same manner, and finally broke the deadlock just two minutes after the restart. Ademir released Friaça down the right wing, and his bobbling shot snuck into the bottom-left corner. Brazil had one hand and four fingers on the trophy, and the Maracanã exploded.

Varela didn't panic. Rather than rush to get the game restarted, he remonstrated extensively with English referee George Reader and his officiating team, arguing that the goal was offside. Varela later admitted that he knew the goal was legit; his lengthy protestations served as a way of delaying the game's restart until the vociferous Brazilian supporters had quietened down.

It was a masterstroke. Varela was a calming influence on his team in a situation that might have seen them suffer the same fate as Spain and Sweden. Instead, it was time for them to start playing. They mightn't have had the glittering attacking options that Brazil boasted, but Uruguay were still a formidable team. And, in their own minds, they had a title to preserve – Uruguay had boycotted the 1934 and 1938 World Cups, so this was their first chance to defend their 1930 crown.

Finally, they started to pose a threat to Brazil. The hosts' coach, Flávio Costa, indicated to his players to sit back a little more and defend what they had. Uruguay, however, possessed a key that perfectly fitted Brazil's lock in the shape of a rapid, fleet-footed winger named Alcides Ghiggia. After turning his man down the right-hand side, he fired the ball into the box and straight on to the foot of onrushing forward Juan Alberto Schiaffino. With 66 minutes gone, Uruguay were level, and the carnival atmosphere inside the stadium died down. The Brazil team were pinned back as Uruguay mounted more attacks. The unthinkable couldn't happen, could it?

The Maracanã held its breath. Finally, the home team advanced forward to try and kill the game. As they crept into the opposing half, a stray pass was intercepted. Uruguay surged forward in a flurry of laser-guided one-twos. That man Ghiggia chased a tantalising through ball and bore down on Moacir Barbosa in the Brazil goal. The keeper hesitated, and Ghiggia fired the ball low at Barbosa's near post. He didn't get down quick enough, and Uruguay had the lead.

They didn't relinquish it. The crowd fell silent from the moment Uruguay's second went in until the final whistle 11 minutes later. Brazil's party had become a funeral. There was to be no celebratory samba; no gold medals; no world championship.

While the Uruguayan players celebrated, hugging and kissing referee Reader, Brazil as a nation dealt with a collective national tragedy. There were allegedly two suicides in the ground after the match, and many more were reported across the country. Brazil wept and grieved as one. *O Mundo*'s succinct summary of the match was simply 'Drama, tragedy and farce', while revered Brazilian writer Nelson Rodrigues described the result as 'Our Hiroshima'. Fingers were pointed in every direction in a desperate attempt to explain this humiliation. Barbosa was made an unfortunate scapegoat, and even the kit was blamed. The white shirt with blue trim that was at the time Brazil's home strip was ditched in favour of the yellow and green shirt the team wear to this day.

In years to come, the game became known as the *Maracanazo* (which roughly translates as 'the great Maracanã blow'). Football was and still is linked intrinsically with national identity in Brazil, and this loss was felt so strongly as the 1950 World Cup was meant to signal the beginning of a prosperous new era for the country. Instead, they were eviscerated in front of football's largest crowd, in the expensive colosseum that was meant to be the jewel in their footballing crown. In mourning, the national team didn't play another match for almost two years.

Brazil's time would come, but the scars of *Maracanazo* would never fully heal.

1954: Scotland and the World Cup's Most Disastrous Debut

Saturday, 19 June 1954
St. Jakob Stadium
Basel, Switzerland

Back in 1950, the blazers at the Scottish FA had declined to travel as anything other than winners of the British Home Championship, so their second-placed finish wasn't enough. In 1954, however, the SFA were happy to accept their place at the World Cup in Switzerland after again finishing as runners-up in the Home Championship. Maybe that had something to do with the fact that Switzerland was a hell of a lot nearer and cheaper to get to than Brazil. Or maybe the SFA officials just really liked Toblerone.

Regardless, the Scots were finally going to play on the biggest stage of all. And it seemed those SFA officials who had so pointlessly deprived the national team of their World Cup debut four years prior were starting to change. They appointed Andy Beattie, who had just guided Huddersfield Town to third place in England's top flight, as the team's first manager, doing away with the old-fashioned selection committees that had picked the team up until then. It looked for all the world as though this was a national team that was modernising, preparing for a new era of football; an era that they intended to be key players in.

Looks can be deceiving. When it came to picking his squad for the tournament, Beattie was told by the SFA that he would have to make do with 13 players. The majority of teams at the competition took squads of 22, so Beattie was perplexed by this restriction. The reason became apparent when the small squad arrived to board the plane to Switzerland. As defender Tommy Docherty explained, 'The rest of the plane was filled with Scottish FA committee members and their wives.'

Even the 13 players at Beattie's disposal were unlikely to have been his first choices. Rangers refused to release any of their players to the national team as they were off on a tour of North America at the time of the World Cup, and Scottish league champions Celtic only consented to three of their players travelling to Switzerland. Scotland not only boasted the smallest squad at the tournament, but also one of the most inexperienced; only two of the 13 had played more than ten times for the national side.

Despite this, Scotland were still a nation with footballing resources that far eclipsed most others. As one of the founding fathers of football along with England, the SFA felt they were a cut above some of the other nations who didn't possess the same heritage in the game as them. Clearly, they hadn't learned from the dismal English display in Brazil.

Scotland were drawn in a group alongside Austria, Czechoslovakia and reigning champions Uruguay. FIFA had again tweaked the format for the 1954 World Cup; their latest ingenious idea was to have teams play only twice in the group stages. Two countries in each group were seeded, and the fixtures were always between a seeded team and an unseeded team. Scotland and Czechoslovakia were the unseeded teams in their group, meaning the Scots would face Austria and Uruguay.

Their maiden World Cup match, on 16 June in Zürich, was against the Austrians. Despite the 6pm kick-off, the blazing Swiss summer sun produced scorching heat. As the teams lined up, it became apparent the SFA had made another blunder. Whoever was in charge of deciding on the kits for the tournament had clearly put two and two together and come out with five, as the Scottish players trudged out in heavy, long-sleeved cotton shirts similar to old-fashioned rugby jerseys. It seemed no one had told the SFA that the Swiss mountains are really quite hot in the summer. 'The heat was incredible and we were drenched in sweat,' Docherty remembered. 'At half-time we had to get in a lukewarm bath to cool down. We just weren't prepared.'

That was an understatement. Even the boots Scotland had were wrong. While most sides donned fast, lightweight footwear, the Scottish players had hard, heavy-duty boots that were more suited to a wintry Glasgow mud bath than the lush greenery of the pitches in Switzerland.

Ultimately, they fell to a 1-0 defeat that could have been a lot more. Understandably, the players looked more off the pace and weary as the game wore on. Immediately after the match, Beattie resigned after falling out with the SFA. He felt that he was managing a team with his hands tied behind his back, and saw no way of improving for the next game given his minuscule squad provided him with only two players to change their fortunes, one of whom was a goalkeeper.

The dreaded selection committee was back for the clash against Uruguay. This would be the most glaring example of

Scotland's unpreparedness for the tournament, and the SFA's stolid determination to stay set in their old ways – and not spend a penny more than they needed to. Rather than buying some more lightweight kits better suited to the climate, the Scottish team were again sent out in the bulky rugby tops they'd worn against Austria. Furthermore, now without a manager, there was no one to run down how the Uruguayans played and who their biggest threats were. The players that day were like lambs to the slaughter.

On 19 June, in Basel, the World Cup holders massacred Scotland 7-0. With that, Scotland's tournament was over. Two games played. Eight conceded. None scored. The Uruguay match in particular was an embarrassment played out before the eyes of the world, and left the SFA reeling.

Scotland and the World Cup have never been easy bedfellows. But their Swiss shambles in 1954 made them reassess their approach to international football to ensure such a humiliating feat would never be repeated.

1954: The One with All the Goals

Saturday, 26 June 1954
Stade Olympique de la Pontaise
Lausanne, Switzerland

The World Cup's return to Europe in 1954 brought with it a gigantic opportunity for FIFA to secure the tournament's future: live television coverage. For the first time, audiences across the developed world would have a chance to see what all the fuss was about, and hopefully the competition's popularity would grow even more. The TV offerings were a fair bit different to how they are now – some broadcasters elected to only show the second half of games, believing seeing the full-time result was the most important thing – but this new platform gave the World Cup a greater reach than ever before.

From FIFA's point of view, the opening matches of the 1954 tournament couldn't have been any better. Goals were the order of the day as teams plundered record-breaking numbers in the group stage. There was that Uruguayan demolition of Scotland, a 4-4 draw between England and Belgium, a thrilling 7-2 win for West Germany over Turkey, and Hungary, who scored a frankly ridiculous 17 goals in their two group matches.

It transpired that that was just the starter. On 26 June, the knockout stages began. In one of the quarter-finals, England were defeated 4-2 by Uruguay in Basel. That was the most boring game of the two played that day. The other match, which kicked off at the same time in Lausanne, was a clash between Austria and hosts Switzerland, and would produce a feast of goals the likes of which the World Cup had never seen before.

When the quarter-final match-ups were decided, it's fair to say that Austria vs Switzerland was, outside of those two nations, the least talked-about of the fixtures. Fans were excited to see reigning champs Uruguay take on football forefathers England. There was curiosity as to how West Germany, the first of the newly divided German nations to compete at a World Cup, might fare against Yugoslavia. And then there was the salivating prospect of free-scoring Hungary taking on 1950's runners-up Brazil.

This was perhaps a little unfair on Austria. Their *Wunderteam* of the 1930s had been denied what was a very real chance of winning the World Cup in 1938 when, after the country's annexation, their national side was forcibly absorbed into the Nazi German team. Now they were trying to rebuild around some excellent footballers. They'd won both of their group games – the 1-0 against Scotland and a 5-0 battering of Czechoslovakia – and only came second in their group to Uruguay on goal difference.

Switzerland, too, had shown quality. With home advantage on their side, they'd produced one of the shocks of the tournament by defeating Italy 2-1 in their opening match. After losing their next fixture against England, they contested a play-off against the Italians to decide who would claim second place in the group and advance in the competition (another quirk of FIFA's peculiar format in 1954). They won that 4-1.

The signs were there that these two sides could produce a top game of football after all. But in truth, their ability perhaps played second fiddle to one other factor on the day of the fixture: the weather.

As the Scots had already found out, the temperatures in Switzerland that summer were sweltering, and the match between Austria and Switzerland saw the very worst of it. At the 5pm kick-off, the temperature was recorded as a blistering 40°C. The sides were about to play football in a furnace.

It didn't take long for the heat to start playing its part. Austria's team at the time was renowned for its watertight defence, and hadn't conceded a goal in seven matches prior to the Switzerland clash. In the Lausanne heat, it took only 19 minutes for them to find themselves 3-0 down, with goalkeeper Kurt Schmied looking disoriented and dizzy between the sticks.

The temperature soon started to take its toll on Switzerland, too. Defender Roger Bocquet – who it later emerged was suffering from both sunstroke and a brain tumour – began acting strangely, running around aimlessly. The Swiss keeper that day, Eugène Parlier, remembered, 'He even passed by in front of me without noticing me and carried on behind the goal.'

In spite of their now bizarrely fractured defence, the Swiss continued to push forward. It was a disastrous tactic. Their three-goal lead lasted for only six minutes. By the 25th minute, Austria had got one back through indomitable forward Theodor Wagner. A minute later, it was 3-2. And a minute after that, 3-3. Between the 16th and 27th minutes, six goals had been scored.

The first-half action was far from over. The Austrians marauded forward relentlessly, and with ten minutes to go before half-time they'd managed to make it 5-3. Then Switzerland got one back, before Austria were awarded a penalty by the brilliantly named Scottish ref Charlie Faultless. The spot-kick, however, was not faultless; striker Robert Körner missed. The half-time whistle brought a respite to what had been 45 minutes of pure, unfiltered chaos with the score at 5-4.

Both sets of players were in bad shape by this point. Many received oxygen on the side of the pitch, while according to his team-mates, Bocquet was so confused that he thought they were still winning 3-0. In the Austrian camp, Schmied collapsed during the interval and, in the days before substitutions, was encouraged on by a coach who stood beside his goal for the entirety of the second half, shouting instructions to him.

By contrast, the second period was less eventful, yet not without its drama. Wagner made it 6-4 to Austria not long after the game was restarted, his third goal of the match. Swiss forward Josef Hügi, who had opened the scoring, also claimed a hat-trick as he made it 6-5. Switzerland threw absolutely everything at their opponents in the hope of grabbing an equaliser. They started shooting from distance, aiming to catch the delirious Schmied off-guard in the Austrian goal. Their efforts finally subsided when Austria scored a seventh 15 minutes from time.

This had been a game like no other. Austria were the 7-5 victors of an epic, sun-drenched contest. But they were scarred. Schmied was hospitalised straight after full time, and a mish-mash side of second-string players and weary survivors from the quarter-final was crushed 6-1 in the semis by West Germany.

The game is remembered by the nations involved as *Hitzeschlacht von Lausanne*, which roughly translates to 'the heat battle of Lausanne'. It remains to this day the highest-scoring match in the history of the World Cup.

1954: The Battle of Bern

Sunday, 27 June 1954
Wankdorf Stadium
Bern, Switzerland

While those quarter-finals in 1954 boasted some fascinating ties, none caught the eye more than Hungary vs Brazil. Hungary were the team capable of producing the most attractive football on the planet at the time, while Brazil were determined to exorcise the demon that was their home humiliation in 1950. The fixture had all the hallmarks of a potential classic.

It was. But not for the reasons anyone expected.

Brazil were in a transitional state in 1954. The *Maracanazo* had prompted them to ring the changes, and they went to the World Cup in Switzerland with a new coach and a squad largely packed with fresh, younger talent. This was not the domineering Brazil side that scored goals for fun four years earlier, but they were still a force to be reckoned with. They easily swept aside Mexico 5-0 in their opening match, before a 1-1 draw against Yugoslavia was enough to see them top their group on goal difference.

In the early 1950s, Hungary were *the* team. With superstars like Sándor Kocsis and Ferenc Puskás, the Hungarians were feared across the globe. Manager Gusztáv Sebes had what he termed a socialist approach to football; every player should share responsibility and be able to play in any position. This ethos and their ultra-attacking 4-2-4 formation would form the blueprint for the Netherlands' 'Total Football' years later. And it really worked. They were reigning Olympic champions and had gone a whopping 32 matches unbeaten prior to the 1954 World Cup. That run included a game dubbed the 'Match of the Century' the year before, when the magnificent Magyars humbled England 6-3 at Wembley.

They had begun their World Cup campaign in the same ruthless fashion that everyone had come to expect. In the groups, a 9-0 destruction of South Korea was followed by a momentous 8-3 victory over West Germany. Hungary were on a mission.

This match promised to be a spectacle. Even English referee Arthur Ellis, who officiated, was excited. 'I thought it was going to be the greatest game I'd ever see,' he remembered. 'I was on top of the world.'

Hungary and Brazil were treated to what were essentially the opposite conditions of the Austria Switzerland clash the day before. Rain battered down in Bern, making the pitch muddy and slippery. The Magyars adapted to the weather much quicker than Brazil, and found themselves 2-0 up inside seven minutes. Amid some questionable Brazilian defending, Nándor Hidegkuti had hammered home a rebound after his initial shot was saved, while Kocsis flew in with a pinpoint header for Hungary's second. The early signs indicated that Brazil were about to be on the wrong end of another Hungarian attacking masterclass.

Hungary, though, were without Puskás, who missed the game through injury, and were not quite as clinical as their usual selves. Brazil's leaky defence managed to plug the gaps, and ten minutes later they were awarded a penalty when striker Índio was clattered into in the box. Brazil had plenty of attacking talent on the pitch, but it was right-back Djalma Santos who stepped up. He sent the keeper the wrong way, and Brazil were back in the game. The first half drew to a close with the score 2-1.

It didn't take long for Hungary to restore their two-goal cushion in the second half. On the hour Brazil's Pinheiro, under pressure from Kocsis in the box, stumbled and bizarrely placed his hand on the ball to prevent himself from falling. Ellis saw it clearly and for the second time in the game awarded a penalty. Again it was a defender who stepped up, Hungary's Mihály Lantos making no mistake in dispatching the spot-kick.

Up until this point the match had certainly been played with passion, and had delivered plenty of excitement. But shortly after Hungary made it 3-1, the battle truly commenced.

A couple of late fouls from both sides left opposing players in crumpled heaps on the floor. One such challenge caused Djalma

Santos to fall to the ground, needing medical assistance. This sparked a frenzied pitch invasion, as Brazilian photographers and journalists flooded on to the field to get the best shot of their injured hero. The Swiss police were forced to intervene, and some Brazilian players became embroiled in the melee.

When the chaos died down, Brazil were quick to take the game to Hungary and Julinho unleashed a sublime effort from the edge of the box, making it 3-2. After this, the contest really descended into brutality. Brazil, no strangers to footballing combat after their antics in Bordeaux in 1938, were unforgiving in their pursuit of an equaliser. When Hungary quelled their many attacks they resorted to the dark arts to try and unsettle them. Índio, in an incident that went unseen by Ellis, kicked Hungary forward Zoltán Czibor at full force. Soon afterwards, Nílton Santos harshly fouled József Bozsik, who was riled by the challenge. The two engaged in a full-on fist fight with Ellis left with no choice but to dismiss both players.

Brazil's efforts became frantic. They flooded men forward and, when dispossessed, would maniacally hurtle back in numbers to defend their goal. The many fouls continued, too, and Brazil were reduced to nine men when Humberto kicked out at Gyula Lóránt. Ultimately, the South Americans couldn't muster anything to get themselves level, and the game was put to bed when Kocsis headed another goal two minutes before full-time to make it 4-2 to Hungary.

The referee's whistle, however, did not bring an end to the bad blood between the two sides. As Hungary celebrated passing through to the semi-finals, there was another pitch invasion. Brazilian officials and fans again clashed with the Swiss authorities. Some of the players became involved, while others retreated down the tunnel towards the dressing rooms. But there would only be more violence there. Chairs and bottles flew as the two sides – joined by journalists, photographers, fans, officials and even the coaching staff – brawled. Gusztáv Sebes described the scenes inside the tunnel as a 'small war' incited by what had been a 'brutal, savage match'. He would need stitches after being struck by a broken bottle.

In all, an eye-watering 42 free kicks were awarded that day, along with the two penalties and three sending-offs. Years later, Ellis commented, 'In today's climate so many players would have been sent off the game would have been abandoned.' Peculiarly, though, no sanctions or punishments were handed down by FIFA, leaving it down to the respective national associations to discipline their players. Brazil flew back across the Atlantic, while Hungary made it all the way to the final.

1954: The Miracle of Bern
Sunday, 4 July 1954
Wankdorf Stadium
Bern, Switzerland

After that ferocious encounter with Brazil, Hungary had another testing challenge on their hands in the shape of reigning champions Uruguay. Again they passed the test, needing two extra-time goals from Sándor Kocsis to eventually win the semi-final 4-2. If anything, the gruelling Brazil clash had only served to make Hungary even more feared. Here was a team that could not only play their opponents off the park; they could dig down and fight when they needed to. They were the living embodiment of both style and substance, and they had very much earned their 'Golden Team' nickname.

Waiting for them in the final were West Germany, who were something of a question mark. Postwar, they weren't allowed to join FIFA until the end of 1950, meaning they'd missed out on the World Cup in Brazil. Ahead of the 1954 tournament they'd been blessed with what was in truth quite an easy qualifying group, consisting of a poor Norway side and the short-lived national team of the tiny Saar Protectorate (an area traditionally part of Germany but partitioned and ruled by France after the war). As such, they made it to Switzerland with relative ease.

Not much was expected of them at the actual tournament. At the time, the West German league was semi-professional, and players were required to hold a part-time job in another profession outside of football. In their opening match, they produced an excellent performance and defeated Turkey 4-1. But a much sterner test was to come in their second game, against the Hungarians.

Veteran coach Sepp Herberger – a controversial figure who had managed the Nazi German team between 1936 and 1942 and was re-appointed as the West Germany boss in 1950 – had a risky plan for the Hungary match. He felt a loss against the Magyars was an inevitability, given their strength and his own side's relative inexperience. He also rightly predicted that the amateurish South

Korea team would be swept aside by Turkey (the Koreans were battered 7-0). Given the tournament's unique format, that would mean a loss to Hungary would set up a winner-takes-all play-off against the Turks to decide who would advance to the knockout stages. With this in mind, Herberger rested two-thirds of his first-choice starting 11 against the world's best team. The result wasn't pretty; Hungary massacred the Germans 8-3, with Kocsis plundering four.

The game was not without incident for Hungary, however, as captain fantastic Puskás found himself on the end of a brutal tackle and sustained an ankle fracture that would keep him on the sidelines until the final. For their part, West Germany's plan went swimmingly, as three days later a fresh, well-rested side galloped past Turkey and into the quarter-finals with a 7-2 win.

There they met Yugoslavia, who were favourites for the match. The Yugoslavians had claimed the silver medal at the Olympics two years prior and had a very experienced team. But the Germans inched past them with a 2-0 victory. Then came Austria in the semis, fatigued from their battle with Switzerland in the torrid conditions in Lausanne. They were dispatched in impressive fashion, West Germany running out 6-1 winners.

Still, no one really gave them much of a chance in the final. There was a consensus even in German media that simply avoiding the kind of mauling the Hungarians had inflicted in the group stage would be a good result. As it transpired though, there were a lot more than just footballing factors at play in the days before the match.

West Germany had decamped to the sleepy lakeside town of Spiez and existed in a protected bubble away from prying eyes. A strong sense of team kinship was built up, later dubbed 'the spirit of Spiez'. Hungary, meanwhile, stayed in a busy town centre hotel. A summer fair that went on into the early hours of the morning disrupted the team's sleep the night before the final. And in a marvellously sneaky move that would make Marcelo Bielsa blush, Herberger instructed his assistant manager Albert Sing to check in to the Hungarians' hotel to keep an eye on their match preparations.

More than any of this, it was the weather that would have the biggest impact on the final. Sunday, 4 July 1954 had been a pleasantly warm, sunny day in Bern, until an hour before kick-off when the city was battered with heavy, driving rain. West Germany's talisman and captain, Fritz Walter, was renowned for playing at his best in wet conditions, so much so that such heavy rain was known as 'Fritz Walter weather' in Germany.

Most importantly, Herberger had a special weapon up his sleeve in the form of Adi Dassler, Bavarian shoemaker and founder of Adidas who had accompanied the West German team to Switzerland as part of the technical staff. Dassler had recently devised a new innovation: adjustable screw-in studs that allowed the size of the studs on players' boots to be altered depending on the conditions they were playing in. Ahead of kick-off, Dassler was instructed to add his new studs on to the West German team's boots, to give them greater grip and balance on the muddy pitch.

If this was supposed to give them an advantage as the first televised World Cup Final kicked off, it was not apparent in the opening stages of the match. Puskás, back in the Hungary team despite concerns over his fitness, fired his side ahead within six minutes with a close-range finish. A couple of minutes later it was two, Zoltán Czibor exploiting a dreadful error between defender Werner Kohlmeyer and keeper Toni Turek to tap into an open net. Yet another Hungarian masterclass appeared to be on the cards.

West Germany, though, were resilient. It was only another two minutes before they had managed to nick a goal back, Max Morlock bundling in a hopeful cross-cum-shot. In the 18th minute they equalised, Helmut Rahn poking the ball home after Hungary goalkeeper Gyula Grosics flapped ineffectively at a corner.

That crazy opening 20 minutes was followed by a Hungarian onslaught. In the West German goal Turek, with a point to prove after his earlier mistake, made a string of sensational saves to keep the opposition at bay. West Germany held on until half-time, but it felt only a matter of time before their resistance would crack.

During the interval, the rain continued to hammer the pitch. By the time the teams returned to the field it was a quagmire. The West Germans, with Dassler's new studs, were better able to keep their footing than their Hungarian counterparts. Still the Magyars assaulted Turek's goal relentlessly, albeit losing their balance more frequently. Stunning saves, goal-line clearances, last-ditch slide tackles and shots clattering against the woodwork meant the scores remained level.

Then the miracle happened. With 84 minutes gone, a rare foray forward saw Hans Schäfer ping a hopeful cross into the penalty area, which was cleared only as far as Rahn on the edge of the box. He took the ball down with his right, shifted on to his left and drove a deadly accurate shot into the bottom corner for 3-2.

The West German commentator Herbert Zimmerman was busy uttering words that would be carved into footballing folklore in his home country, his astounded reaction a perfect encapsulation of just how shocking this result was. 'Three-two to Germany,' he screamed. 'Call me mad! Call me crazy!'

Those celebrations were nearly cut short two minutes later when Puskás looked to have levelled. Welsh linesman Sandy Griffiths saved Herberger's men when he ruled the goal offside. West Germany held out. Just four years after their team had been established they were world champions, and had ended Hungary's four-year unbeaten run in the process.

There were seismic reactions to the result in both nations. Hungary, despite finishing as runners-up, had been dazzling. Sandor Kocsis bagged the tournament's Golden Boot after hitting the back of the net 11 times, while the 27 goals the team scored in just five games remains to this day the most scored by one team in a single World Cup. Alas, that was not enough for their fans back home. Goalkeeper Grosics was made a scapegoat and even temporarily put under house arrest for treason. Protests erupted across Budapest against both the team and the country's communist regime, which some believe sowed the seeds for the Hungarian Revolution two years later. By the next World Cup in 1958, the 'Golden Team' had largely been disbanded.

For West Germany, this win was monumental. A nation gripped by shame following the Second World War was reinvigorated. As legendary player and manager Franz Beckenbauer remembered, 'Suddenly Germany was somebody again. For anybody who grew up in the misery of the postwar years, Bern was an extraordinary inspiration. The entire country regained its self-esteem.'

For this reason, many Germans rank the Miracle of Bern as the nation's greatest sporting achievement, more so than later World Cup wins at home and abroad. The victory was akin to a medicine, healing many of the wounds that still gaped after the war. The win coincided with an economic boom in West Germany, forever entwining it with the nation's postwar recovery. As news outlet *Der Spiegel* put it decades later, 'In one 90-minute match against Hungary, modern-day Germany was born.'

Who ever said football was just a game?

1958: Northern Ireland a Sensation in Sweden

Tuesday, 17 June 1958
Malmö Stadion
Malmö, Sweden

The World Cup remained in Europe in 1958; the last time two consecutive tournaments were held on the same continent. Sweden were the hosts as the competition saw a huge growth in interest since the televised 1954 finals. In all, 55 teams entered the qualification stages for Sweden – 18 more than had ever taken part before.

The increased participation prompted FIFA to rejig the qualification format. European nations by far represented the greatest percentage of this number. Sweden and West Germany had already qualified as hosts and defending champions respectively, but that still left 27 European nations vying for a spot at the 16-team final tournament. FIFA decreed that nine places would be delegated to Europe, with the winners of each of nine mini groups of three qualifying for the World Cup.

Crucially, this meant that the British Home Championship would no longer also be used as a qualification group for the United Kingdom teams. England, Scotland, Wales and Northern Ireland were all drawn in different groups, which meant all four home nations could theoretically make it to the World Cup. Or none.

Of the home nations, it was Northern Ireland who arguably had the biggest mountain to climb to qualify. They were drawn in a group with two-time world champions Italy, who to that point had qualified for every World Cup they had entered. Completing the group were a novice Portugal side, very much in their infancy as a national team.

The Green and White Army's campaign to make it to Sweden got off to a terrible start with a draw against Portugal followed by a damaging 1-0 loss to Italy in Rome. However, after beating Portugal in their next game – the Portuguese, in turn, got a shock victory over Italy – Northern Ireland knew that a win against the faltering Italians in their final match would secure them top spot in the group and a place at the World Cup for the first time.

They had an agonisingly long wait for that fixture. Originally scheduled for December 1957, seven months after their last match, the winner-takes-all clash with Italy in Belfast hit a snag when the Hungarian referee assigned to officiate became stranded in London as heavy fog grounded flights across the Irish Sea. The football associations representing the two sides couldn't agree on a replacement, so on the day of the game, with thousands of spectators already in the stands at Windsor Park, an announcement over the tannoy declared that the game that day would instead be a friendly, with the actual qualifier delayed by six weeks.

When the big game finally did arrive, in January 1958, plenty of bad blood had been built up between Italy and Northern Ireland. The so-called friendly – a 2-2 draw later dubbed the 'Battle of Belfast' – had descended into chaos, with supporters in the stands voicing their contempt at the decision to delay the qualifying match. The Italian players were vicious in their tackling in the game and by the final whistle, a full-scale riot broke out, with fans spilling on to the pitch. The rematch ended up being one of the finest moments in Northern Irish football as the side triumphed 2-1. The Green and White Army were going to the World Cup.

Northern Ireland – despite being at the time the smallest country by population to ever make it to a World Cup finals – did possess some genuinely brilliant footballers. But their behind-the-scenes setup was less fantastic. Their own FA nearly prevented them from going to the tournament when they found out it would involve playing football on a Sunday, only to eventually be convinced by some more forward-thinking committee members. The team, based in a small coastal town near Halmstad, immersed themselves in the local community, but found the language barrier a problem. Without a translator, their solution was to welcome a football-mad 12-year-old Swedish boy with a good grasp of English into the fold. He would become something of a mascot for the side, and even sat on the bench alongside coaching staff during matches in case his communication skills were needed.

This affectionately basic approach to the World Cup was in sharp contrast to the methods of the teams in Northern Ireland's group. They were drawn alongside an up-and-coming Czechoslovakia side, an Argentina team with a point to prove having not played in a World Cup since 1934, and reigning champions West Germany.

FIFA had done away with the silly rule from 1954 that saw teams only play twice in the group stages, meaning the Northern Irish had the chance to test their mettle against all three of these considerable footballing powers. In their opening match, against Czechoslovakia, they produced another shock with a 1-0 win. Manager Peter Doherty set up his defence with a rigid, nigh-on unbreakable shape that held firm, and goalkeeper Harry Gregg, who just four months prior had survived the Munich air disaster with his club Manchester United, produced a dazzling array of saves to keep a barrage of Czechoslovakian attacks at bay. After taking the lead in their second game against Argentina, the South Americans fought back to win 3-1. That left Northern Ireland needing something against world champions West Germany to stand any chance of making it out of their group.

Gregg was stunning again as the resilient Northern Irish held the Germans in a 2-2 draw. Legendary forward Peter McParland actually put his side ahead twice, but a relentless attacking onslaught from West Germany saw them equalise both times. Czechoslovakia beat Argentina in the group's other game, leaving them level on points with Doherty's men. FIFA still resorted to a play-off in this situation, so a repeat of the group's opening fixture was arranged, to be played in Malmö two days later.

Any psychological boost Northern Ireland might have had from already defeating Czechoslovakia was limited by the fashion in which the eastern Europeans had dispatched Argentina. In a display of devastating attacking prowess, they had claimed a crushing 6-1 victory. This was a quality team growing into the tournament. The Northern Irish would also be without the magnificent Gregg, who'd been injured in the West Germany clash. Getting through to the knockout stages was going to take a gargantuan effort.

Czechoslovakia dominated the opening stages and put themselves 1-0 up in the 18th minute, Zednek Zikán nodding the ball past stand-in keeper Norman Uprichard. Things went from bad to worse for Gregg's replacement. Shortly after conceding, he landed awkwardly on his ankle, leaving him crumpled on the ground. With no substitutions in 1958, Northern Ireland resorted to some rather makeshift treatment to get their keeper on his feet again. Doherty ordered one of his trainers on to the pitch armed with two bottles of whiskey, which he proceeded to pour over Uprichard's injured ankle as the most Irish anaesthetic there ever was. But not before he took a nip himself.

Northern Ireland started to grow into the game as the first half wore on. McParland equalised a minute before half-time, momentum they carried into the second period as both teams exchanged attack after attack in an absorbing encounter. Uprichard was again in the wars, smashing and ultimately breaking his hand on his goalpost while making a diving save. Heroically, he continued to play on as the scores remained level. The match was going to extra time.

Ten minutes into the first period, McParland found the net for the fifth time in the tournament, volleying into the roof of the net from close range. The few Northern Irish fans who had made it to Sweden were joined in backing the team by swathes of local supporters who had taken the underdogs to their hearts. Uprichard, battered and bruised, would not see his goal breached again as his side held on. They'd made it to the quarter-finals.

Unfortunately the end of the road came in that next match, as France and their swashbuckling striker Just Fontaine ran out comfortable 4-0 winners. Northern Ireland were exhausted after the gruelling 120 minutes they'd played against Czechoslovakia just two days prior. Regardless, they exited the World Cup with their heads held high. Gregg took home the award for goalkeeper of the tournament and the team received a hero's welcome upon their return to Belfast. The play-off in Malmö was *their* final.

1958: Wales's Finest World Cup Hour (and a Half)
Tuesday, 17 June 1958
Råsunda Stadium
Solna, Sweden

As well as Northern Ireland, England and Scotland also topped their qualification groups for the 1958 World Cup, meaning three out of the four home nations would be represented in Sweden. Wales, however, were less successful. After a promising start, with a 1-0 win over the quality Czechoslovakia side that battled with Northern Ireland at the tournament proper, damaging losses in the return fixture and in East Germany put paid to Wales's hopes of topping their group. But as fate would have it, they would still end up at the tournament in Sweden, benefitting from a truly bizarre set of circumstances.

Their unlikely route to the World Cup began over in Turkey, who had been drawn in the Asian and African qualifying section to fight for the single place that was allocated to the two continents. The Turkish were angry that they hadn't been included in the European section, so decided to pull out of the qualifiers entirely. That left the opponents they'd been drawn against, Israel, with a bye into the next round.

Next up for Israel were Indonesia. Political upheaval in Indonesia led them to request that the two-legged fixture be played at a neutral venue – which FIFA rejected. So they withdrew too. Israel were through to the final round without playing a minute of football, where Sudan stood between them and a place at the World Cup finals.

That in itself was a problem. Israel was not exactly a popular nation in Muslim countries such as Sudan. The prospect of the two visiting each other was a potentially deadly one, but the Israeli FA were headstrong that they wanted the matches to go ahead. Sudan, not wanting to acknowledge Israel, decided they were going to pull out. The one place allocated to Asia and Africa was Israel's, and they hadn't even kicked a ball.

FIFA decided to intervene. They couldn't have a team qualifying without playing a match, so decided that Israel should face off against one of the second-placed sides from South America, Europe and North and Central America, the winner over two legs claiming a place at the World Cup. Belgium were the lucky beneficiaries of a random draw to decide who would get a second chance to make it to Sweden. For the fourth time, Israel's prospective opponents decided to withdraw. When lots were drawn a second time, Wales were the chosen team. Not looking a gift horse in the mouth, the Welsh packed their bags and headed to Israel.

Wales, with Juventus superstar John Charles up front, were a much better team than the Israelis, and ran out comfortable 2-0 winners in the first leg. The second fixture was to be in Cardiff three weeks later. This posed a problem for Wales manager Jimmy Murphy, who was also assistant coach at Manchester United. United were due to play Red Star Belgrade in the European Cup on the same date. Murphy chose to honour his duties for the national team; a decision that potentially saved his life. Twenty-three people lost their lives as a result of the Munich air disaster on the way back from United's match in Belgrade. But Murphy was back home, watching his Wales side defeat Israel 2-0 again to book their place in Sweden. To this day, it is the only instance of a team who were eliminated during initial qualifying still making it to the World Cup.

Their group consisted of the hosts, Mexico, and 1954 runners-up Hungary. They were to play the Magyars first. Many players had fled Hungary following the Hungarian Revolution of 1956, meaning they were not the indomitable Golden Team of the early '50s. But a handful remained, and they were still very much a distinguished side. The Welsh FA were not overly confident about their side's chances; they booked the team on to the first available flight home after the group stages.

This was in no small part down to the fact that it looked as though the talismanic John Charles wouldn't be taking part in Wales's World Cup campaign. The Italian FA, their team having failed to qualify at the hands of Northern Ireland, decided to play that year's Coppa Italia over the summer instead, and Juventus wanted their star striker to remain in Turin. There were only four days to go before the Hungary clash when Juve finally allowed Charles to travel to Sweden. It was just as well for Wales – he scored the equaliser in an impressive 1-1 draw.

Mexico were next up, a team Murphy described as 'only good for riding horses, not playing football'. As it turned out, Wales weren't very good at football that day either. They only just managed another 1-1 draw against their amateurish opponents. A battling 0-0 draw in their final group game against eventual runners-up Sweden gave Wales enough points to warrant a play-off against Hungary.

That match, in Solna just two days after the Sweden game, was to prove Wales's finest hour at the World Cup. Hungary, having learned about just how dangerous Charles was in their opening fixture, had a clear game plan for their second meeting: kick him out of the game. And at half-time, it looked as though it was working. Hungary led 1-0 thanks to a goal from prolific goalscorer Lajos Tichy.

Murphy's tactics had been reserved throughout the tournament to that point. He had put everything into ensuring his team didn't lose, rather than going all out to win matches. Now he had 45 minutes to keep his country in the World Cup. Loosening the shackles, a more attacking Wales found an equaliser ten minutes into the second half. A clipped ball over the Hungarian defence was met by Ivor Allchurch just inside the 18-yard box, who blasted a stunning volley into the top corner. Gyula Grosics, the Hungary keeper and one of few survivors of their Golden Team, was visibly incensed by his side's sloppy defending.

If that had upset Grosics, then Wales's second was the stuff of nightmares. In the 76th minute the experienced stopper rolled the ball out to a defender on the edge of his own box. Inexplicably off balance, the defender completely missed the ball under pressure from onrushing Wales winger Terry Medwin. The Welshman was icy cool as he nicked the ball away from the defender and slotted calmly past Grosics to make it 2-1. Hungary lost their heads; Ferenc Sipos was dismissed three minutes later for a brutal challenge that left Wales forward Ron Hewitt needing hospital treatment for a nerve injury in his leg. The ten Magyars couldn't find a way back into the game, and Wales headed into the quarter-finals. England and Scotland, meanwhile, crashed out in the groups.

Those early flights that the blazers at the Welsh FA had booked wouldn't be needed. Even in spite of Hungary's declining fortunes, this result was a seismic shock, not least because Wales had completely outplayed them in the second half. Their adventure in Scandinavia was halted when they came up against a certain 17-year-old Brazilian named Pelé in their next match. The Welsh – without Charles who didn't pass fit for the game after the Hungarians had brutalised him – fell to a respectable 1-0 loss against a Brazil team that were soon to be crowned world champions, with Pelé grabbing the winner for his first World Cup goal.

1958: Just Fontaine's Lucky 13

Saturday, 28 June 1958
Ullevi
Gothenburg, Sweden

There's no greater individual achievement for a striker than finishing as the top scorer at a World Cup. The opportunity to become one of the very few individuals with a prized Golden Boot on the mantelpiece only comes around once every four years (or even less if you're Scottish). Pelé, Johan Cruyff and Diego Maradona are just a handful of the truly legendary players who never quite took their chance to join the list of illustrious names on the honour roll. France striker Just Fontaine, on the other hand, grabbed his with both hands.

Fontaine, like so many of France's greatest players, had mixed heritage. He was born in 1933 in what was then French Morocco to a Spanish mother and a French father. He didn't even kick a ball in France until he was 19, when Nice signed him from Moroccan club USM Casablanca. Despite this, he settled quickly. In 1953 he earned a debut for the national team and bagged a hat-trick against minnows Luxembourg. But his impressive start to life in France didn't earn him a solid place in *Les Bleus'* line-up. He wasn't taken to the World Cup in 1954 and wouldn't score another international goal until a friendly in 1958.

Still, Fontaine's form in club football ensured he wasn't overlooked for the tournament in Sweden. He had moved to Stade de Reims in 1956, then the superpower of French football, and honed his ability as the ultimate 18-yard-box predator. In the season leading up to the World Cup he scored 34 goals in just 26 league games as Reims claimed a French league and cup double.

And yet in spite of all those goals, while there was no doubting that Fontaine would be going to the World Cup, it was expected he would be there as a squad player rather than a starter. France manager Albert Batteux was a notoriously stubborn coach who favoured players who he felt fitted his system best. When it came to strikers, his first choice was Fontaine's club team-mate René Bliard. Bliard was an accomplished striker himself, but possessed nowhere near the prolific ability of Fontaine; he'd scored a modest 15 goals in comparison to Fontaine's 34 that season. In the end, it was fate that forced Fontaine into the France team for the World Cup, with Bliard picking up an injury in a warm-up match that ruled him out of the tournament. After only playing five matches for the national side in as many years, Fontaine was straight into the starting 11 for France's World Cup opener in Sweden, against Paraguay.

Paraguay boasted a decent team themselves, having qualified ahead of Uruguay, and they showed that in a battling first-half display that saw the teams level at 2-2. Fontaine had marked his maiden 45 minutes at a World Cup by scoring both of France's goals – both clinical one-on-one efforts that showed his ruthless ability in the box.

For a short while, it looked as though the adept but unfancied Paraguayans might render Fontaine's strikes consolations, with the South Americans taking the lead just after half-time. Ultimately, France's prodigious attacking prowess proved too much. Fontaine, playing up top with the dazzling creative force that was attacking midfielder Raymond Kopa just behind him, completed his hat-trick while helping France to an eventually convincing 7-3 victory.

He plundered another two goals in the next group game – a 3-2 loss to Yugoslavia – before netting the winner in a closely contested 2-1 victory over Scotland. France were through to the quarters, and Fontaine had six goals to his name already.

Next up were Northern Ireland, exhausted after their gruelling encounter with Czechoslovakia two days earlier. It was a comfortable game for France who ran out 4-0 winners, Fontaine adding another two to his collection. His second in particular was the definitive example of a striker's goal. Collecting possession on the edge of the 18-yard box, he took three perfect touches: one to take the ball further into the penalty area, one to savagely dummy a defender and send him careering in the opposite direction, and one to swivel and strike the ball into the bottom corner in a single balletic movement. Fontaine was truly a master of his art.

Lying between him and the chance to play in the World Cup Final were Brazil, complete with their sparkling array of stars that included Garrincha, Vavá and Pelé. Fontaine nabbed another goal, but the teenager stole the show with a hat-trick as Brazil advanced to the final with a 5-2 victory.

Fontaine had one more opportunity to add to his goal count with the third place play-off against unseated champions West Germany, who had fallen to a shock defeat at the hands of hosts Sweden in their own semi-final.

Ullevi, a newly built stadium in Gothenburg, was the scene of Fontaine's finest World Cup hour. France controlled an exciting game from start to finish with a 6-3 win, and their Moroccan import scored four of the goals to take his final tally to 13.

Remarkably, Fontaine's ridiculous goalscoring feats didn't even earn him a spot in the team of the tournament. This was perhaps in part due to the poached nature of the majority of his goals. Yet he was always there, in the right place at the right time, to coolly deliver the ball into the back of the net. Nor did he get his hands on a Golden Boot straight away, as the trophy wasn't formally awarded until 1982. He was finally presented with one in 1998, 40 years after his heroics in Sweden.

Injuries ultimately brought a premature end to Fontaine's career. In the years following the World Cup, he suffered two broken legs and played only six more times for France (plundering another nine goals in the process). He retired from international football at the age of 27, with the frankly obscene record of 30 goals in 21 appearances. But that one World Cup he played in was enough to secure his place in history – no one since has come near to beating his seemingly impossible record of 13 goals in a single tournament.

1958: The Arrival of Pelé

Sunday, 29 June 1958
Råsunda Stadium
Solna, Sweden

Edson Arantes do Nascimento – Pelé to his friends and the rest of the world – arrived at the 1958 World Cup in Sweden as an unknown outside of his home country. The 17-year-old had been tipped for greatness back in Brazil, and understandably so, given that at the age of 16 he'd finished as top scorer in the league for São Paulo club Santos. But his fledgling career had yet to garner any attention outside of South America. After just four games in Sweden, he made sure that everyone across the footballing world knew his name.

Pelé had grown up in poverty 200 miles west of São Paulo, the son of former Fluminense footballer Dondinho. Unable to afford a football, in his early years he famously honed his skills using a grapefruit, and predominantly played indoor football for a local youth team. By the age of 16, he'd shown enough ability to be signed by Santos, one of the biggest clubs in the São Paulo region. And he had sparkled, instantly becoming the most prolific scorer in the Campeonato Paulista (the São Paulo state league, this being before Brazil had a unified national league).

In 1957, at 16, he became Brazil's youngest-ever goalscorer when he netted on his international debut against Argentina. Four more goals would come in his next four games for the *Seleção*, and the teenager was comfortably part of the national team setup when the 1958 World Cup came around.

However, Brazil coach Vicente Feola faced a problem when it came to selecting his squad. On the eve of the tournament in Sweden, Pelé was still recovering from a knee injury he'd picked up playing for Santos and wasn't even in full training. Furthermore, Pelé had performed poorly in psychological analysis the Brazilian FA had conducted on the players ahead of the World Cup. He'd been described as immature, with a damning, later laughably inaccurate assessment that he 'did not possess the sense of responsibility for a team game'. Ultimately, Feola decided the chance to unleash his 17-year-old football genius was worth the gamble of naming a potentially unfit player with a dubiously defined attitude problem, and Pelé was on the plane to Scandinavia.

There was no chance of him passing fit for Brazil's opener, against Austria. They didn't need him and cruised to a 3-0 win. He was back in training by the time of Brazil's next group match, against England, but again he wasn't selected as Brazil were lacklustre in a drab 0-0 draw. Their final group fixture, against the Soviet Union, would be a must-win if they were to make certain their advancement into the knockout stages.

Feola still wasn't sure about playing Pelé. The player himself assured him he was fit and ready. The story goes that his team-mates banded together and essentially demanded that Feola start Pelé, feeling that they stood the best chance of winning if he was on the pitch. True or not, the teenage talent was into the starting 11 for the pivotal USSR game.

Brazil played their best football of the tournament so far, epitomised by an opening three minutes that esteemed football writer Brian Glanville described as 'genius'. The Brazilians, playing a stunning brand of Samba football, steamrollered the Soviets with a relentless period of attacking play. Pelé and Garrincha both hit the post, before legendary striker Vavá made it 1-0. They controlled the match from then on, only the heroics of acclaimed Soviet goalkeeper Lev Yashin preventing it from becoming a rout. Vavá eventually struck a second time, and Brazil secured their spot at the top of their group.

In the quarters, they faced that plucky Wales side who had defied the odds to even make it to the World Cup, let alone the knockout stages. Brazil were heavy favourites, but at half-time the match remained goalless. The Welsh were superb, suffocating Brazil's many attacks. But they could only hold on for so long.

Naturally, it was Pelé – with his first World Cup goal – who broke the deadlock. Facing away from the goal, he controlled the ball with his chest inside the box, flicked it into the air while performing a 180-degree spin, and rolled it past a helpless Jack Kelsey in the Wales net, who gawped unbelievingly at the teenager's skill. It was a big moment. Pitchside photographers invaded the field to capture an image of this new star, who was bundled into the net in celebration by his team-mates. Wales couldn't respond, and Brazil moved into the semis.

There, France were swept aside in dominant fashion. Brazil took the lead through Vavá inside two minutes, and found themselves 2-1 up at the break. Then Pelé switched it on. He rifled in a lethal hat-trick in the second half to take the score to 5-1, before France added a late consolation. The enigmatic teenager had fired the Samba boys into the World Cup Final.

In the space of three games, Pelé had gone from relative unknown to global footballing superstar. His performances had attracted the eyes of the world. Journalists swarmed at Brazil's training camp to fight for an interview with him, while local Swedish girls begged him for autographs at every possible opportunity.

It was the hosts that they'd be facing in the final. Sweden were unfancied pre-tournament but had impressed with some clinical performances of their own. Still, Brazil were expected to triumph with relative ease. But the players were nervous. The *Maracanazo* eight years earlier still loomed large in the minds of Brazilians, and they were given added cause for concern ahead of the match. Both Sweden and Brazil played in yellow, and when the Scandinavians won the toss to wear their home kits, Brazil were initially told they'd have to play in white. They hadn't worn white since that humiliating defeat at the hands of Uruguay on home soil, so fearing that the colour was bad luck, the players point blank refused to wear it this time around. Instead, an official was sent out to purchase some blue shirts.

Even without the white ghost of the *Maracanazo* draped around their shoulders, Brazil started the match uneasily. Some haphazard defending allowed Swedish captain Nils Liedholm to fire his side into an unlikely lead on the four-minute mark. If anything, his goal served to jolt the *Seleção* into action. Five minutes later, Vavá put them level, before adding a second to give Brazil a 2-1 lead going into half-time.

The second half was going to be pivotal. Sweden were still in the game and had been pushing for an equaliser towards the end of the first period. Up stepped Pelé, the boy supposedly unsuited to team sports, to make certain that the Jules Rimet Trophy would be heading back to Brazil. In the 55th minute he produced one of the greatest goals ever scored in a World Cup Final. You'll have seen it before. Brazil's wonderkid nonchalantly flicks the ball over the head of a dumbstruck Swedish defender before volleying it home ruthlessly.

At 3-1, the Brazilians were able to enter full cruise control and the second half belonged to Pelé. His effortless, mesmerising play even earned him appreciation from the home fans, who applauded every time he got the ball. Mário Zagallo added a fourth for Brazil before Pelé made it five with a superb header, with Sweden nicking a goal in between to make the scoreline look less one-sided than it actually was. Brazil swaggered past the Swedes by five goals to two, and the World Cup was finally theirs.

Captain Hilderaldo Bellini got his hands on the trophy and made a bit of World Cup history of his own. When photographers clamoured for a better view of the cup, he raised it above his head, thus starting the tradition followed to this day. It was a day of healing for Brazil. They'd never forget the *Maracanazo*, but now they could move on.

As for Pelé, life would never be the same again. In its match report, the *Daily Herald* described him as a 'wriggling shadow of black lightning' that left a trail of 'mesmerised, head-shaking Swedish defenders in his wake'. He finished the World Cup with a wheelbarrow full of records that still stand now: youngest World Cup goalscorer; youngest player to score a World Cup hat-trick; youngest player to score in a World Cup Final; the list goes on. Wealthy, gigantic European clubs courted his signature. Not to mention he was now just about the most famous footballer on the planet. And his World Cup exploits were far from over.

1962: The Battle of Santiago

Saturday, 2 June 1962
Estadio Nacional
Santiago, Chile

When the World Cup returned to South America after a 12-year absence, excitement on the continent was palpable. They'd felt hard done by that the previous two tournaments had been in Europe – so much so that South American teams threatened to boycott the 1962 edition if it wasn't held there. The nations in the running to host were Argentina, by far the favourites given their high-quality stadia and advanced infrastructure, and Chile, who at first just seemed to be throwing a bid together for the sake of it.

It wouldn't be FIFA though if there wasn't some kind of controversy surrounding the selection of a host nation. After realising the potential economic benefits of hosting the World Cup, the Chilean football federation started to take their bid a lot more seriously. They sent delegates around the globe on a schmoozing mission to sweet talk the heads of various football associations. In 1956, it was announced that they had won hosting duties, and plans to send the world's best to Chile were put in place.

While South American fans were fervently eager to witness football's greatest spectacle once again, it became apparent from the beginning that what they were seeing was more akin to warfare than a game of soccer. The opening group matches had produced four red cards, a litany of serious injuries and very little football worth writing home about. A toxic atmosphere shrouded the tournament. Many nations had called for Chile to be stripped of the World Cup after a disastrous earthquake had destroyed four of the eight proposed venues in 1960, the claims angering Chilean fans. This ill feeling spilled on to the pitch, with many teams approaching matches armed with a siege mentality from the get-go. As the *Daily Express* put it, the tournament showed 'every sign of developing into a violent bloodbath'.

And all of this came before the most violent game the World Cup has ever seen, far eclipsing the antics in Bordeaux in 1938 and Bern in 1954. The offending match was in the second round of group games, between the host nation and Italy in the Chilean capital: the Battle of Santiago.

Of all the bad blood and toxicity that surrounded the tournament in Chile, there was no greater animosity than that between Chile and Italy. It was the Italians who were most critical of Chile hosting the tournament, feeling that taking the World Cup to such a poverty-stricken country was a backward step; an opinion that only intensified after the earthquake destroyed half of the intended venues. Italian media pulled no punches in telling the world exactly what they thought of Chile. As well as describing the nation as a 'backwater' and a 'dump', Italian journalist Corrado Pizzinelli wrote, 'Chile is a small, proud and poor country … Entire neighbourhoods are given over to open prostitution. This country and its people are proudly miserable and backwards.' Suffice to say, he wasn't a fan.

The Chilean media, meanwhile, reported heavily on these comments. As well as branding the Italians as fascists and drug addicts, journalists used them to stir up anti-Italian sentiment ahead of the fixture between the two nations. The Chile fans had been intensely passionate in their opening match, a 3-1 win over Switzerland, and the media was calling on them to double their efforts to make the situation as hostile as possible for Italy.

The scene was set for a horror show. The countries had no footballing rivalry whatsoever – they'd never actually played each other before – but the lead-up to the game had ensured that their first encounter would be an unforgettably brutal one. The man charged with officiating the madness was Ken Aston, a teacher from Colchester.

The first foul of the match was committed after just 12 seconds, and they didn't stop until the final whistle. A major flashpoint came in the eighth minute when Italian midfielder Giorgio Ferrini kicked Chile's Honorino Landa, who happened to be nowhere near the ball. This wasn't the first time such an incident had occurred in the match. But it was the first time Aston saw it happen. He didn't hesitate in dismissing Ferrini.

Ferrini, however, had other ideas. He resolutely refused to leave the field. A lengthy melee ensued, with players trading blows. Chile's talented winger Leonel Sánchez – the son of a professional boxer – landed a haymaker on Italy captain Humberto Maschio's nose, breaking it. Eventually, armed police had to be called on to the pitch to escort Ferrini off before play could resume.

The game continued in the same fashion it had started. Aston found himself helpless as Chilean players openly spat at and poked their Italian counterparts, who responded by kicking out at their opponents whenever they got the chance. After Sánchez was subject to a petulant series of unpunished fouls by Italy defender Mario David, he again demonstrated his pugilistic prowess by flooring David with a lethal left hook. Then it was David's turn to exact his own form of retribution. A few minutes later, he launched a flying kick that Bruce Lee would be proud of into Sánchez's head. This time, Aston was quick to react, sending the Italian off and reducing them to nine men. It wasn't even half-time.

When he came under fire after the match for not sending Sánchez for an early bath, Aston claimed he had seen neither of the punches the Chilean threw. This came as cold comfort to the Italians, as it was Sánchez who assisted Chile's opening goal, in the 73rd minute, from a free kick. They added a second 15 minutes later to earn a 2-0 win, but this was a day when football had very much taken a back seat in favour of the slugfest the two sides played out.

The second half had seen constant scuffles that required the police to enter the field of play three more times before the final whistle. When the game did end, the aftermath was almost as volatile. Italians in Chile were banned from visiting bars and shops, while the squad's training base had a 24-hour armed guard to prevent Chilean fans hurling missiles at the players. Back in Italy, the army were dispatched to the Chilean embassy to prevent any agitated fans taking vengeance there, and the media poured scorn on Aston, who they described as 'an unmentionable English vermin'.

In terms of football, Chile were the winners over the Italians both on the day and in the tournament as a whole. Ironically, Italy actually needed Chile to win against West Germany in their final group game to stand any chance of making it to the knockout stages. They didn't, and Italy were heading home. Chile made it to the semis, losing to eventual winners Brazil, before defeating Yugoslavia in the third place play-off.

While Chile's bronze finish was an impressive result for such a small nation, the lasting memory of their World Cup campaign would be that brutal afternoon in Santiago. Presenting the match highlights, the BBC's David Coleman declared, 'The game you are about to see is the most stupid, appalling, disgusting and disgraceful exhibition of football, possibly in the history of the game.' Sixty years on, Coleman's comments are still true.

1962: Garrincha's Greatness and Another Brazilian Win

Sunday, 17 June 1962
Estadio Nacional
Santiago, Chile

Of all the things the 1962 World Cup was remembered for, world-class football was not one of them. The violent play and disgraceful behaviour grabbed headlines. A big rule change came regarding players no longer being able to play for more than one nation in a World Cup, after several switched allegiances for the 1962 tournament (including the bizarre affair that was Hungary great Ferenc Puskás representing Spain). But the football itself? That was largely forgotten in the mire of the other dramas and controversies. And that is more than a little unfair on the little Brazilian genius that was Garrincha, who sparkled like a diamond in the footballing battlefields of Chile.

He was an unlikely superstar. Garrincha was born with one leg six centimetres shorter than the other, knees bent in opposite directions and curvature of the spine. Such were his physical limitations, that a childhood doctor certified him as crippled. Despite this, Garrincha showed a natural footballing ability from an early age and became well known around his small hometown of Pau Grande, near Rio de Janeiro.

His talent with a ball at his feet came second, though, to his zealous lust for life. He showed little interest in making a career out of football through his teens, preferring to concentrate on partying and womanising. It wasn't until the ripe old age of 20 that he signed his first professional contract, for Rio giants Botafogo in 1953.

It didn't take long for him to cement his status as one of the best wingers in all of Brazil. He scored a hat-trick on his debut and possessed a mesmerising dribbling ability that routinely saw him leave swathes of defenders in his wake. At 24, he was already a star in his country ahead of the 1958 World Cup, and featured in four of Brazil's six games as they lifted the Jules Rimet Trophy in Sweden. He was even named in the team of the tournament, but the exploits of the emerging Pelé overshadowed his own brilliance.

And it was Pelé's name that was on everyone's lips as the tournament in Chile began in 1962. In Brazil's opening match, against Mexico, he didn't disappoint. Pelé assisted one and scored

61

one in a 2-0 win. It seemed he would steal the limelight in Chile as he had done four years earlier.

Fate carved a different path. In Brazil's second group game, a laborious goalless draw with Czechoslovakia, Pelé picked up an injury that would rule him out for the remainder of the tournament. Brazil's talisman was gone, but they very quickly found a new one in Garrincha.

They needed a result against Spain to guarantee a place in the knockout stages. Their World Cup defence looked in jeopardy as the Spanish took the lead in the first half. An equaliser came through Amarildo in the 72nd minute, but a win was the only way the Brazilians could be 100 per cent sure of their passage through to the quarter-finals. Step up the bent-legged angel. With the ball at his feet 40 yards from the Spanish goal, he teased and tormented two defenders, feinting and dummying before surging past both of them to deliver an inch-perfect cross on to the head of Amarildo. He couldn't miss. Brazil won 2-1.

This moment lit the blue touch paper for Garrincha in the tournament. From then on, he was unstoppable. Brazil faced England in the quarters. Garrincha roamed around the final third of the pitch like it was his own back yard. He popped up with a header from a corner to put Brazil 1-0 up. England equalised shortly after, but Garrincha was again at the centre of the action as his side took a 2-1 lead. His goalbound free kick was tipped away by England goalkeeper Ron Springett, only to fall into the path of Vavá, who slotted home.

Play was stopped for a time when a stray black dog invaded the pitch. Eventually, Jimmy Greaves managed to coax the dog into his arms, where it promptly urinated all over him. Garrincha was said to have found the whole episode so hilarious that he was initially struggling to carry on playing. England should be so lucky. He recovered his composure and scored his second of the game – a beautiful, curling effort from 25 yards out that nestled sweetly in the top corner – to clinch a 3-1 Brazil win.

In the semis they faced the hosts. In what was probably the best game of the tournament, Brazil ran out 4-2 victors. Garrincha was in imperious mood again, his trickery befuddling the Chilean defence. He grabbed another two goals and assisted a third. Chile, however, were less accommodating of his antics than England were. After a physical encounter that saw Garrincha persistently fouled throughout the game, six minutes before the final whistle he finally snapped and kneed Chile's defensive midfielder Eladio Rojas in the back. The referee sent him off. Brazil were in the final, but their superstar would not be.

However, a truly extraordinary set of circumstances managed to get Garrincha's ban overturned. The Chilean fans, far from angry that his dazzling solo display had sent their team out, had been captivated and bewitched by the little Brazilian's majesty on the pitch. He'd won a legion of fans in the country. Thousands of Chilean supporters – as well as the country's president Jorge Alessandri – petitioned FIFA to allow him to play in the final.

They got their wish. Garrincha was named in the starting 11 as Brazil again faced Czechoslovakia. When the two had met in the group stages for that 0-0 draw, Garrincha had been quiet. He was less so in the final as Brazil, after going 1-0 down, swept to a 3-1 victory with goals from Amarildo, Zito and Vavá. The *Seleção* had claimed a second World Cup crown in a row in front of the applauding Chile fans at the Estadio Nacional in Santiago.

As well as winning a second World Cup, Garrincha shared the Golden Boot and was named player of the tournament. And that wasn't all he won. That pitch-invading dog from the England match had been adopted by the Brazil squad as a lucky mascot, and after the tournament it was raffled among the players. Garrincha's number was chosen, and he took the mutt home with him to Pau Grande.

Unfortunately, Garrincha's star faded fast after the 1962 World Cup. His unique knees started to give up on him in the ensuing years, and despite making the squad for the 1966 tournament in England, he never quite recovered the marauding, magnificent quality that inspired Brazil to their second world title. In later years his love of excess got the better of him, and he died of cirrhosis of the liver, aged 49, having fathered at least 14 children.

It's best to remember Garrincha for his excellence on the pitch. In 50 appearances in the famous gold and green shirt he tasted defeat only once, in his last international against Hungary. Pelé remembered, 'He could do things with the ball that no other player could.' But it was England's Johnny Haynes who delivered the best epitaph for Garrincha, following their clash in 1962, 'How do you set about stopping the unstoppable?'

1966: Pickles the Dog Spares the FA's Blushes

Sunday, 27 March 1966
David Corbett's hedge
London, England

By 1966, interest in the World Cup was higher than it had ever been. It had solidly established itself as the biggest tournament in football, and countries were falling over themselves to host. When England was chosen to put on the 1966 edition, it was a symbolic full circle moment for FIFA. The forefathers of football – who had once resolutely dismissed the mere notion of a tournament to decide the world's best team – were now fully on board.

This came as welcome news to English fans, who were thrilled by the prospect of seeing the best footballers from around the globe in the flesh. As the competition approached, anticipation grew. The FA, keen to drum up as much publicity as possible for the tournament, held special events with the Jules Rimet Trophy on display. In March of 1966, four months before the World Cup was to start, they granted permission for the trophy to be exhibited at, rather randomly, a postage stamp show in Westminster.

It was a huge attraction, and visitors flocked in great numbers to see the cup up close. Two uniformed police officers, working in shifts, were to guard the trophy around the clock. So it came as a surprise when on Sunday, 20 March – only a day after the display had opened – the guards returned from completing a sweep of the exhibition hall to find the World Cup was gone.

As the exhibition was closed on Sundays, it had been decided that when the public weren't around, the guards needn't be standing watch 24/7. Instead they would conduct hourly checks. Because surely, they reasoned, no one would be able to steal the World Cup when the exhibition wasn't even open.

Alas, the not-so impenetrable fortress that was Westminster Central Hall, with doors held shut by a single wooden bar, was not the safest of shelters for one of sport's most precious trinkets. The thieves managed to unscrew the wooden bar that held the doors shut from the outside, snuck in, removed the padlock from the glass case in which the cup was kept, and disappeared into the midday sun with the Jules Rimet Trophy for company.

To say the whole palaver was an embarrassment for the FA is an understatement. Senior figures from football federations the world over voiced their anger that the cup had, in these most bizarre and avoidable of circumstances, vanished into thin air. Senior Brazilian official Abrain Tebet went as far to suggest, 'Even Brazilian thieves love football and would never commit this sacrilege! It would never have happened in Brazil.'

Meanwhile, London's finest were on the job to recover the cup. FA chairman Joe Mears had received a ransom note the day after the theft, and promptly turned it over to the police. A meet-up was arranged with the supposed master behind the crime, a man who only referred to himself as 'Jackson', in Battersea Park.

Detective Inspector Len Buggy, pretending to be Mears' assistant, met him there armed with a suitcase full of scrap paper disguised as cash. 'Jackson' failed to spot that his ransom wasn't quite as valuable as it might have appeared, agreed to lead Buggy to the trophy, and willingly stepped into the detective's car.

Now at this point, you'd be forgiven for thinking that's the end of the story. But in a farcical scene that wouldn't have looked out of place in a *Police Academy* movie, 'Jackson' noticed an unmarked van full of coppers following him and Buggy a little too closely for comfort. He asked the policeman to pull over so he could get out and retrieve the cup. Of course, he scarpered, legging it through the gardens of south-east London in a bid to get away.

Buggy did manage to catch up with him and arrest him after what one can only imagine was a Benny Hill-style chase. 'Jackson' was revealed to be Edward Betchley, a used car dealer and small-time crook with a previous conviction for selling stolen corned beef. Not only that, it transpired he wasn't even the culprit. Or at least that's what he said, claiming that he'd been paid to act as a go-between by a man he didn't know, and didn't have a clue where the trophy was.

With the cup still missing and the police now devoid of ideas, it looked like it might be lost for good. Until Thames docker David Corbett decided to take his dog Pickles, a collie cross, for a walk in south London. Before he had chance to attach a lead to Pickles' collar, the mutt made a beeline for a hedge at the bottom of the front garden. Corbett noticed him pawing at a tightly wrapped package and picked it up to investigate.

Sure enough, what Pickles had discovered was the Jules Rimet Trophy. It had been discarded in a bush, someone involved in the theft clearly having decided that the whole debacle was more trouble than it was worth. Corbett hastily delivered it to a local police station, where he was initially suspected of being involved in the crime. When he was cleared, attention turned to his heroic pooch.

Pickles became a celebrity overnight. He won a year's supply of dog food, was invited to the celebrations after England won the cup, and even appeared in a film. Meanwhile, the trophy was returned to the FA, who made sure it didn't leave their headquarters again until the tournament kicked off.

For his honesty in returning the trophy, Corbett pocketed over £6,000 in reward money – four times the amount England players received for actually winning the tournament. Poor old Pickles met an untimely end in 1967 when he choked himself on his lead while chasing a cat. Betchley went to prison on a short sentence for his part in the crime, but was never convicted of the actual theft due to a lack of evidence. For decades it remained unsolved, until in 2018 a *Daily Mirror* investigation revealed the culprits to be a pair of London gangster brothers who nicked the cup simply to prove that they could.

And the Jules Rimet Trophy itself? That was given permanently to Brazil after their third title win in 1970. Apparently, Tebet's assertion that Brazilian criminals held the cup in too high regard to steal it wasn't so accurate: the cup was pilfered from the Brazilian Football Confederation in 1983. Unfortunately, no one has been able to emulate Pickles' feat, and the original World Cup has never been recovered.

1966: North Koreans Become the Toast of Teesside

Tuesday, 19 July 1966
Ayresome Park
Middlesbrough, England

When the World Cup finally arrived in England in July 1966, a cloud of controversy was looming – and not just because the FA had managed to panic everyone by misplacing the trophy. Protesting at the fact that only one qualification berth was granted to the entirety of Africa, Asia and Oceania, all African nations promptly decided to boycott the competition. South Africa – who'd been lumped into Asian qualifying as African teams refused to play them – were disqualified due to political pressures stemming from Apartheid. And South Korea withdrew, citing logistical issues. This left North Korea and Australia as the only two teams left to fight for the spot.

The North Koreans made light work of their amateur Australian counterparts over two legs, with a 9-2 win on aggregate. Their qualification in itself was contentious. The Korean War was fresh in the memory, and the British government questioned whether such a secretive country should be allowed to participate. It was mooted that the North Koreans might be refused visas, until FIFA intervened and assured the FA in no uncertain terms that if a team that had legitimately qualified were refused entry, then the tournament would be moved. North Korea were on their way to England.

To say they were an unknown quantity is an understatement. Their first official international had only been played two years prior, a goalless draw against Burma. It was widely accepted that they'd simply be making up the numbers, especially after being drawn in a tough group with Chile, the Soviet Union, and two-time champions Italy.

This prediction seemed as though it would ring true after North Korea were dispatched 3-0 by the USSR in their opening match. In their next fixture, against the Chile side who had claimed third place at the previous World Cup, the Asians earned an unlikely 1-1 draw thanks to an 88th-minute equaliser.

Despite this impressive result, no one gave them a chance in their final group game, against Italy. The Italians needed at least a draw to pass into the knockout stages, having beaten Chile 2-0 before losing by a goal to the Russians. Their team featured a raft of stars who had helped the Milan clubs win three of the last four European Cups. And they had a point to prove. Italy hadn't made it out of the group stage at a World Cup since they'd last won it in 1938.

It was the Italians who made the strongest start when the tie kicked off at Middlesbrough's Ayresome Park on a sunny Tuesday evening. Twice they came close to taking the lead in the opening stages. Perhaps what they hadn't banked on were the locals, who had taken the North Koreans to their hearts. The Boro fans had formed an affinity with the Asian underdogs after their plucky draw against Chile, and that day against Italy you'd have been forgiven for thinking the match was being played in Pyongyang rather than the north-east of England.

Unfancied though they were, the Koreans did not simply dig in and defend. They surged forward at every opportunity, the crowd cheering them on as they did so. Italy found themselves in an unexpected furnace and the task at hand got even harder when, on the half-hour mark, captain and esteemed midfielder Giacomo Bulgarelli injured his knee while sliding into a particularly enthusiastic tackle. He couldn't carry on, and in the days before substitutes, the *Azzurri* were forced to continue with ten men.

Twelve minutes later the unthinkable happened. A failed Italian clearance landed at the feet of midfielder Pak Doo-ik, who was calm in delivering a low, driven shot from the edge of the box past the flailing Enrico Albertosi in the Italy net. Ayresome Park erupted, prompting the BBC's commentator to exclaim, 'They don't cheer like this for Middlesbrough!'

Predictably, the second half saw Italy throwing the kitchen sink at North Korea to try and salvage their World Cup campaign. No matter what they did, they couldn't grind their way past the resolute defensive wall that stood in their way. The North Koreans didn't just set out to defend their lead, either. Every time a chance to counter presented itself, they rushed forward in numbers to try and put the game beyond Italy's reach.

Ultimately, they didn't need a second goal. Ten-man Italy never found a way through their tireless defence. North Korea had pulled off one of the most seismic shocks in World Cup history. The debutants – and lowest ranked team in the tournament – had knocked out the two-time champions.

Reaction in all quarters was frenzied disbelief. The *Daily Express* wrote, 'Pak Doo-ik last night detonated one of the great explosions in soccer. He scored the goal that hurled the Italians out of the World Cup.' Fans inside Ayresome Park celebrated their adopted team's win like Middlesbrough had won the European Cup. Back in Italy, the media was in meltdown over this fresh football humiliation. Their fans weren't too happy either, and turned up in numbers at the airport in Genoa to pelt the players with rotten tomatoes upon their return.

As for North Korea, they had an anxious wait to see if they'd made it through to the knockout stages. Providing Chile didn't heat the USSR the following night, they'd be in the quarters. In the end the Soviets won to complete a clean sweep of the group, meaning the North Koreans were through. Their wondrous upset earned them a quarter-final with Portugal, and one of the World Cup's greatest ever strikers.

1966: Eusébio and a Glittering Portuguese Comeback

Saturday, 23 July 1966
Goodison Park
Liverpool, England

When you think of the World Cup, there are certain players who instantly spring to mind. Diego Maradona and his spellbinding trickery; Pelé, with his three World Cup wins and unstoppable goalscoring ability; Johan Cruyff demonstrating the embodiment of Total Football in 1974. Undoubtedly, there's another name to add to that illustrious list of players: Eusébio, a footballing great who sometimes gets overlooked when remembering the magnificent stars of the 20th century.

The 24-year-old from Portuguese Mozambique arrived at the 1966 tournament in England with his stock already high, having featured in three European Cup finals (winning one) with Benfica. A relentless attacker, he had a reputation as the kind of player who could receive the ball anywhere in the opposition half and somehow make a goal out of it. His Benfica and Portugal team-mate Jaime Graça told of how 'he was so good that a bad pass to him would be reported in the press as a good pass the next day', because he'd still be able to get it under control and score.

Despite Eusébio's prowess, people weren't sure what to make of Portugal going into the World Cup. They had a squad packed full of the Benfica stars who'd been making their mark on the European stage, but none of them had ever been tested at this level before – 1966 was Portugal's World Cup debut. What's more, they'd been drawn in a tough group with a quality Hungary side and the all-conquering Brazil, who had won the previous two tournaments.

Any doubts people may have had about Portugal's ability were misplaced. They romped through their group, winning every game.

The highlight was a 3-1 victory over reigning champions Brazil when Eusébio scored twice to ensure the World Cup holders didn't even progress beyond the group stage. Portugal were delighting the English fans with their exciting brand of attacking football, with Eusébio the focal point. So when they lined up against fellow tournament debutants North Korea in a quarter-final no one saw coming, the smart money was on the Iberian stars making light work of their Korean counterparts.

North Korea had put their shaky start behind them to shock the world with that stunning win over Italy. Their energetic style had of course won many admirers, particularly in Middlesbrough. And they were not a team you could afford to underestimate.

When the quarter-final kicked off, it seemed that Portugal had done exactly that. North Korea found themselves unexpectedly leading within a minute. Pak Seung Zin's rocket of a shot from the edge of the box found the top corner, putting them 1-0 up. Portugal rallied to create some good chances of their own, but it was clear that the North Koreans were more than capable of giving them a game. Their intense work rate made it difficult for Portugal to keep hold of the ball, and when they attacked they did so in numbers, surging forward with pace and directness.

A second goal for North Korea arrived in the 22nd minute, leaving the Portuguese defenders looking rattled and nervy. BBC commentator David Coleman told viewers, 'Portugal really are in the most desperate trouble,' and that was before the brief Korean onslaught continued.

Supporters inside Everton's Goodison Park chanted 'we want three!' and North Korea obliged two minutes later. Portugal's defensive disorganisation was plain to see, and with 24 minutes played, their opponents found themselves 3-0 up and firmly in dreamland.

Portugal coach Otto Gloria exclaimed after the match, 'We do not like defence. Attack is our best defence.' Age-old cliché aside, this was an astute summation of how his team operated. Despite looking quite noticeably shaken, Portugal weren't done yet. And the fans in attendance knew better than most not to write off a team so early on in a match – a great deal of them would have been present at Wembley two months earlier when Everton came from two goals down to beat Sheffield Wednesday 3-2 in the 1966 FA Cup Final.

Gloria's commitment to attacking football soon started to bear fruit, and only one man was going to be the catalyst. Two minutes after the restart Eusébio quickly gave Portugal a glimmer of hope, ghosting sleekly into the box to get on the end of a neat through ball and hammer it into the top corner. On the verge of half-time he made it 3-2, putting the ball in that very same corner from a penalty awarded for a clumsy challenge on José Torres. The momentum was now very much with the Portuguese.

Only once before had a team overturned a 3-0 deficit to win a World Cup match (Austria's thrilling 7-5 win over Switzerland in the 1954 tournament), but as Portugal took to the field in the second half it became immediately apparent that it was going to be a long 45 minutes for the North Koreans. The opening stages were characterised by constant Portuguese attacks, and in the 56th minute Eusébio scored his best goal of the game to complete his hat-trick and draw his team level. An instinctive first-time finish from an awkward angle that yet again found his favoured spot in the top corner to keeper Li Chan Myong's right, it was a gleaming example of just how naturally goalscoring came to the striker.

Despite just scoring a wonderful World Cup hat-trick to resurrect his team's chances, Eusébio's celebrations were understated. Perhaps he knew he wasn't done yet – after all, it was still only 3-3. Shortly after that equaliser we were denied what would have been one of *the* great World Cup goals. Picking up the ball inside his own half, Portugal's talisman set out on an exhilarating run down the left wing. A defender tried to foul him as he reached the edge of the box, but Eusébio's movement was too slick. He preceded to audaciously nutmeg the next defender and advance towards goal. Another attempted foul. Finally, at the third time of asking, North Korea felled him as defender Lim Zoong Sun swept both legs from under him with a cynical slide tackle. Penalty to Portugal.

Not one to mess with a winning formula, Eusébio put the ball high to the goalkeeper's right for the fourth time in the game. Portugal had completed a remarkable comeback against a defiant, resilient North Korean side. They stayed firmly in control for the remaining half an hour, with Jose Augusto adding a fifth late on to make it 5-3.

Both teams were raucously applauded at the final whistle, with the immense effort the Koreans had put in appreciated alongside

Portugal's stylish attacking play. A young fan evaded the stewards to break on to the pitch and chase Eusébio for an autograph; the match-winner duly obliged. One can only wonder what that scribble might be worth now.

There was no doubting that those at Goodison that day had witnessed a true great underlining every ounce of his brilliance. The match report in *The Times* the following day summed everything up, 'Eusébio; one word, one name is enough to explain Portugal's climb from the trough of adversity to tomorrow night's semi-final against England.'

That semi-final was the end of the road for Portugal as England defeated them 2-1 (with Eusébio grabbing Portugal's goal, naturally). He'd score again in the third-place play-off, comfortably claiming the Golden Boot with nine goals. Another 20 years would pass before Portugal would make their next finals appearance, with Eusébio long retired. But his sole campaign was more than enough to earn his status as a true World Cup legend.

1966: Argentina, England and the Birth of a Rivalry

Saturday, 23 July 1966
Wembley Stadium
London, England

While Eusébio was leading Portugal into the semis in the north-west, a game with fewer goals but plenty of fire was going on in the capital. England were facing off against Argentina in a match that would become infamous for sparking the bitter footballing rivalry that the two nations share today.

The hosts had kicked off their tournament with a typically anti-climactic goalless draw against Uruguay. They followed it up with comfortable 2-0 wins against Mexico and France to top their group and secure their spot in the knockout stages. Argentina had a tougher time of it, producing some battling performances to finish second in Group 2 behind West Germany, earning themselves a quarter-final against England at Wembley.

Argentina's heritage in the sport was intrinsically linked to Britain, thanks to a large population of English and Scottish expats in Buenos Aires. One of these, a Glaswegian schoolteacher named Alexander Watson Hutton, was credited with being the man who brought football to Argentina, first teaching his pupils at a school in the city the beautiful game in the late 19th century. And British influence loomed large over Argentina's first international, against Uruguay in 1902. Most of their team had roots in the UK, producing a comically eye-catching team sheet featuring names such as Carlos Buchanan, Ernesto Brown and Argentina's first captain, Juan José Moore.

Ahead of the 1966 meeting, England and Argentina had already faced off in five good-natured fixtures, including in the group stages at the previous World Cup (a 3-1 England win). Their sixth clash that Saturday in London changed the dynamic of their rivalry for ever.

From the off the match was a feisty encounter beset by fouls. Much coverage in the English media painted the Argentinians as the primary aggressors, and in the 1960s their style of play was certainly typified by a brutality that would never fly in the modern game. But England's players were by no means innocent, and come the final whistle their foul count outnumbered Argentina's by 33 to 19. The problem was that West German referee Rudolf Kreitlein only seemed interested in cautioning the South Americans.

As for the football, it was England who had the edge. Argentina defended astutely but spent most of the first period pinned back in their own half. And while England's fouls were greater in number, the Argentinians' were greater in severity. Antonio Rattín was given a warning after a particularly nasty kick on Geoff Hurst, the Argentinian captain being one of many names Kreitlein pencilled into his notebook.

The 35th minute saw the moment that ignited a mutual footballing hatred between the two nations that remains to this day. The Argentines had the ball on the edge of their own box, looking to begin a rare advance towards the England goal. But their play was brought to a halt by a fracas near the centre circle. It seemed that Rattín had been sent off.

What for, exactly, wasn't 100 per cent clear. The official reason given was dissent, with Kreitlein taking exception at Rattín's angry gesticulations suggesting to the ref that he should be penalising more of England's players. Indeed, after the match, the German official explained he'd dismissed Rattín for 'violence of the tongue', despite the fact that Kreitlein spoke no Spanish.

Rattín and his team were incensed, leading to a lengthy on-pitch melee. The captain refused to leave the field for a full 11 minutes as he, the rest of his team-mates, and several officials crowded around the referee. Rattín pleaded for an interpreter, while commentators both English and Argentinian were flummoxed as to why he'd been sent off. But the South Americans did themselves no favours, aggressively waving at Kreitlein and hurling insults.

Eventually Rattín gave in and moodily trudged off the pitch. He didn't get far though. With a toddler-like pettiness, he sat cross legged on the pitchside red carpet intended for The Queen. After a while, two police officers were deployed to escort him down the tunnel, with Rattín angrily crumpling a British flag pennant on his way.

With the infuriated skipper finally gone, England made the most of their numerical advantage, winning 1-0 thanks to a Hurst header 12 minutes from time. But the fire was far from over. The game had continued in a volatile atmosphere, typified by the bitterness after the final whistle. The chaos that ensued led *The Observer*'s Hugh McIlvanney to describe the fixture as 'not so much a football match as an international incident'. In the tamest of the post-match exchanges, England right-back George Cohen was prevented from swapping shirts with his Argentine counterpart by Alf Ramsey, with the England manager reportedly declaring, 'George, you are not changing shirts with that animal.'

Ramsey doubled down on his 'animal' comment after the game, which was probably fair when taking into account the Argentines' conduct. José Pastoriza reportedly threw a punch at the referee as he left the pitch, while forward Ermindo Onega spat in the face of FIFA vice-president Harry Cavan. Someone urinated in the tunnel, where the incensed Argentine players then threw a chair into the England dressing room. The post-match warfare came to a close with the Argentina squad attacking England's team bus as it left the stadium.

The bad blood built up that day never dissipated, with more volatile encounters between the two nations to come in later years. But the impact stretched far beyond England and Argentina's football teams. The South American press in general slated the 1966 World Cup, citing Rattín's sending off as a prime example of biased officiating that they felt was rife throughout the tournament. A senior member of Argentina's FA went as far to suggest that the South American nations may split from FIFA, such was their anger.

This ultimately proved to be a lot of hollow talk, but a whole continent felt it had been slighted. Bolivia's biggest newspaper reported the day after England's win in the final, 'They hatched a football conspiracy against Latin America. We may be animals and savages but we would never consider what the cultured and civilised English have done.'

The match even changed the way football was refereed. Ken Aston, the man who had overseen the Battle of Santiago four years earlier, had since been appointed to a senior position on the FIFA Referees' Committee. He'd noted the confusion that reigned as a result of the sheer number of names Kreitlein had scrawled into his book, and decided to introduce a colour-coded system that would make it clear to everyone watching when a player had been cautioned or dismissed: yellow and red cards respectively.

Argentina went home as heroes, with fans gathering in their thousands to welcome their plane as it landed. They were even thanked by the president for representing the country so well; an interesting take on relieving themselves in the Wembley tunnel and trying to overturn a coach full of the opposition players. For England, the match was an unpleasant encounter that they'd never forget, but more than anything a stepping stone on the way to their greatest ever triumph.

1966: The Wembley Final

Saturday, 30 July 1966
Wembley Stadium
London, England

After their bruising battle with Argentina, England faced Eusébio's Portugal in the semis. It proved a defining 90 minutes for Bobby Charlton, who turned in one of his greatest England performances by scoring both goals in a 2-1 win. The hosts were into the final at Wembley, where West Germany were waiting.

The Germans had looked worryingly lethal throughout the tournament, and unlike England they had hit the ground running from their very first game. In a 5-0 rout of Switzerland, a 20-year-old midfielder called Franz Beckenbauer grabbed the spotlight with his spectacular link-up play and two goals. They topped their group before comfortably dispatching Uruguay – who England had only managed a goalless draw against in the groups – 4-0 in the quarter-finals. They'd earned their spot in the final after beating the Soviet Union 2-1, with Beckenbauer scoring the winner.

The match-up was a tantalising one. England had grown into the tournament and after their rather flat start had looked organised and clinical as they advanced through the knockouts. Alf Ramsey had tweaked his system throughout the group stages before settling on a balanced 4-4-2 diamond, a contrast to West Germany's decidedly more gung-ho 4-2-4 setup. With two very different strategies in play, journalists anticipated an exciting encounter ahead of the match. It didn't disappoint.

England – wearing those now iconic plain red shirts after having lost the toss of a coin to determine who would wear their home strip – lined up at Wembley in front of a raucous home crowd of nearly 97,000. Far from the dread that now goes hand in hand with the Three Lions having to face the Germans, confidence would have been high in the England camp. Before their 1966 encounter, in seven previous fixtures between the two nations England had drawn one and won six.

While the pre-match omens were good, the home side's optimism was surely supplanted by worry when, in the 12th minute, West Germany took an unexpected lead. After some very open early exchanges, left-back Ray Wilson struggled to clear a searching long ball into the box and headed it to the feet of forward Helmut Haller. He arrowed it calmly to goalkeeper Gordon Banks's bottom right and *Die Mannschaft* were 1-0 up.

It took just six minutes for England to respond. Captain Bobby Moore was fouled while surging into the Germany half and elected to take the free kick quickly. His speedy thinking was matched by West Ham team-mate Geoff Hurst. Hurst had only played his first match of the tournament in that combative quarter-final against Argentina, coming in for the injured Jimmy Greaves. He scored the winner and Ramsey kept him in the starting 11 for the semis and final ahead of prolific superstar Greaves. It was an effective gamble, with Hurst given the freedom of London as he drifted into the box unmarked to head the ball home precisely past West German keeper Hans Tilkowski. After a pulsating first 18 minutes, the teams were level again.

The remainder of the first half was similarly exciting. England were the slightly more dominant force, with both Charlton and then Hurst going close, and forcing midfielder Wolfgang Overath to chaotically scythe a goalbound effort off the line after Tilkowski found himself in no man's land.

The German was a thorn in England's side at the other end of the pitch too, bludgeoning a 20-yard effort towards goal that was only repelled by a magnificent save from Banks just before the interval.

Wembley had some time to breathe again before the hectic to and fro of the match continued. Early in the second half, Bobby Charlton went to ground in the box and half-heartedly appealed for a penalty, but Swiss referee Gottfried Dienst waved the play on. As the clock ticked on, England were the side in ascendancy, Alan Ball in particular terrorising the West German defence with cross after cross, while also seeming to magically teleport back up the pitch to help quash the German counter-attacks.

But for all their pressure, England couldn't put the ball in the net. Until they won a corner in the 78th minute, that is. Ball, from the right-hand side, produced an uncharacteristically poor delivery, his high ball easily headed away to Geoff Hurst on the edge of the box. With two defenders blocking his path to goal, he produced a soft, speculative shot that looked to be heading straight into Tilkowski's arms. Crucially, centre-back Willi Schulz tried to get in the way of it and badly misjudged his clearance, slipping as he made contact with the ball to send it looping up into the air six yards from goal. Martin Peters pounced, volleying it coolly to give England a 2-1 lead.

The Three Lions had a little over ten minutes to hold on to become world champions but they faced a German onslaught that saw them throw the kitchen sink at England in the closing stages. It paid off in the 89th minute, stunning the Wembley crowd, who had spent the last five minutes maniacally howling for the final whistle, into dismayed silence. Like England's second, the goal came after a frenzied passage of ricochets and deflections. A German free kick fired towards goal deflected off George Cohen and landed at the feet of Sigfried Held. His shot hit team-mate Karl-Heinz Schnellinger in the chest, confusing the England defence before finally arriving at Wolfgang Weber, who fired it into an open goal. The final was heading for extra time.

The teams had 30 minutes to put their name on the trophy. In the days before penalty shoot-outs, if the scores remained level, they'd have to come back on the following Tuesday night and do it all again in a replay. Remarkably, had they still been drawing at the end of that encounter, it had been agreed by FIFA before the tournament that the World Cup winners would be decided by a lottery. Ultimately it didn't come to that, thanks to some Hurst heroics and a certain Soviet official.

Extra time continued in the same vein as the second half. England were largely on the front foot, Ball and Charlton both unleashing shots early on that forced good saves from Tilkowski. The Germans, despite having one more day of rest before the final than the English, looked noticeably more fatigued. But still they looked capable of creating something on the counter attack. Then, in the 101st minute, one of the most controversial decisions in World Cup history gave England the lead.

A pinpoint pass from Nobby Stiles down the right flank released Ball, who crossed with his first touch. It's often forgotten in the hullabaloo that ensued after the goal was awarded, but Hurst controlled the ball with sensational composure on the turn before firing a shot high above Tilkowski. It hit the underside of the bar, bounced down on to the goal line and was quickly headed over for what would have been a corner by Weber.

Confusion reigned. Liverpool striker Roger Hunt, who was actually nearer to the ball than Weber when it bounced down off the crossbar, made no attempt to tap in the rebound and instead raised his arms aloft in celebration, so certain was he that it went in. Naturally, West Germany's players protested that it hadn't. Dienst was too far from the action to make a call, so went over to linesman Tofiq Bahramov for his opinion.

The so-called 'Russian linesman' – who was in fact not Russian at all but from Soviet Azerbaijan – took little time in indicating that he considered Hurst's effort a goal, nodding emphatically to Dienst. The Germans were outraged, but that didn't matter to England, who were now 3-2 up.

In later years, with advanced computerised simulations able to recreate the goal, it's been largely accepted that the entire ball almost certainly didn't cross the goal line when it bounced down. But Bahramov, writing in his memoirs, remained convinced that it had crossed the line before then, reasoning that he gave his decision so confidently because he had seen the net move at the top of the goal when Hurst first fired his shot. His contentious call certainly didn't affect his career. He went on to officiate at the 1970 World Cup, and is a legend in his home town, the Azeri capital Baku, where the national team's stadium is named after him, along with a statue of the official outside.

With England now leading, West Germany again threw everything they could at nabbing another equaliser. As a minute remained, every outfield German player pressed into the England half, firing cross after cross into the box as quickly as they could. When the last of these ended up at the feet of Moore deep inside his own half, the England captain launched a long effort upfield towards Hurst in acres of space.

Members of the crowd spilled on to the pitch in celebration, thinking the final whistle had already gone and prompting BBC commentator Kenneth Wolstenholme to quip the immortal line, 'Some people are on the pitch, they think it's all over. It is now!' It *was* over. Hurst had advanced towards the German net and scored by far the best goal of the afternoon with a clinical, barnstorming finish into the top corner. England had won the World Cup.

Looking back at the footage now, Hurst's celebrations are markedly understated. He'd just scored the goal that guaranteed England would be world champions, as well as becoming the first – and to date only – man to bag a hat-trick in a World Cup Final. Perhaps that's partly explained by the fact that he never actually intended to score at all. Hurst revealed years later that his thumping third goal was actually an epic mishit, as he'd intended to fire the ball as far into the crowd as possible to waste time while the clock ticked down.

You know the rest. The famous photo of Bobby Moore held aloft; The Queen presenting the Jules Rimet Trophy; the jubilant on-pitch celebrations. It's easy to forget amid all this pomp just how astonishing the match itself was. An attacking, end-to-end display from start to finish, there were a mind-boggling 87 attempts on goal. The spectacular game remains to this day the most watched event in British television history.

1970: Bobby Moore and the Bogotá Bracelet

Monday, 18 May 1970
Fuego Verde Jewellery Shop
Bogotá, Colombia

The 1970 World Cup in Mexico marked a new era for the tournament. It was the first time the competition would be broadcast in colour, as well as the first edition to be held outside of the footballing heartland of Europe and South America. England would be travelling there as world champions, and arguably no player in the squad taken to Mexico by Alf Ramsey was as lauded and iconic as captain Bobby Moore.

The classy defender had remained a mainstay in Ramsey's side since the 1966 triumph, and in the ensuing years had become an instantly recognisable figure both at home and abroad. He'd barely missed an England game in that time and would be pivotal to the Three Lions' efforts to defend their World Cup crown.

Confidence was high that they could go all the way again. Aside from the heroes of four years prior, the squad featured exciting younger talent like Peter Osgood, Colin Bell and Francis Lee. The English public's appetite for the team was enormous. Ahead of the tournament, the squad released the track 'Back Home' – beginning the long tradition of England World Cup songs – and the record went straight to number one. Perhaps less memorably, the success of the single spawned an entire 12-track album, *The World Beaters Sing the World Beaters*, which comprised a catalogue of covers of popular tunes, including Moore and Lee's haunting rendition of 'Sugar, Sugar' by The Archies, and a frankly regrettable take on The Beatles' 'Ob-La-Di, Ob-La-Da'.

With their pop careers well and truly launched, Ramsey's squad jetted off to South America before the tournament to acclimatise to the hot weather. There, they were to play two warm-up games against Colombia and Ecuador before flying to Mexico for their first group game against Romania.

When the players arrived at the opulent Hotel Tequendama in the Colombian capital Bogotá two days before their first friendly, they found their rooms weren't yet ready. In the hotel's grand foyer, there was a jeweller's shop named Fuego Verde. As the players milled around waiting for their keys, the story goes that Bobby Charlton spied a ring that he wanted to buy as a gift for his wife in the shop window. Moore joined him in the store, where the two men browsed briefly before leaving empty-handed, Charlton having decided the asking price for the ring was too extortionate.

As the pair left, a commotion broke out. A shop assistant came running from the store, insisting that an expensive bracelet was missing, and that Moore must have taken it. Police, hotel staff and the rest of the England contingent gathered in the lobby to try and sort out the messy situation. The players were resolute that they had taken nothing and offered to be searched. After being questioned by police, they were told they were free to go without charge. It was far from a nice welcome to Colombia, but the matter was now over. Or so they thought.

In contrast to what was happening off the pitch, England's friendly matches couldn't have gone more smoothly. They cruised to an easy 4-0 win over Colombia before flying to Quito and dispatching Ecuador 2-0, with Moore and Charlton featuring in both matches. With the World Cup on the horizon and their mini tour over, the team were finally heading to Mexico. But not before a short stopover in Bogotá while they waited for their connecting flight.

Shortly after their return to the city, Moore was arrested out of the blue by Colombian police for the theft of the bracelet. Apparently while the team were in Ecuador, a sketchy new witness had emerged from the shadows and implicated him in the crime. While his team-mates boarded a plane to the World Cup, Moore was left behind in Colombia, being repetitively interviewed by police long into the night.

Worse for the England captain, they eventually decided to charge him, meaning he'd be sent to a notoriously rough Colombian prison to await trial. An unlikely saviour for Moore came in the form of Colombian FA president Alfonso Senior Quevedo. Recognising that the defender's life would be in danger if he was sent to the jail, he pleaded that Moore be allowed to stay at his own home under house arrest.

The request was granted, but with no date set for the end of Moore's detention, Ramsey had to start making preparations to tackle the World Cup without his captain. News of the incident spread globally, making front-page headlines. Even British Prime Minister Harold Wilson intervened, giving direct instructions to the British Embassy in Colombia to do everything in their power to ensure Moore's release. The scandal was fast becoming a major diplomatic incident.

As the investigation roared on, Colombian journalists were critical of their own police, with leading national newspaper *El Tiempo* writing, 'We should have more faith in his [Moore's] statements than those of the witnesses who contradict themselves.' They were right about the unreliable witnesses. On the second day of Moore's detention, the shop assistant who first accused him claimed she had seen him take the bracelet and put it in his tracksuit pocket. An impressive feat, Moore pointed out, being as the tracksuit he was wearing didn't have any pockets.

The credibility of his accusers' story fell further apart when it emerged that the new witness was a known criminal who had accepted money from the jewellery shop owner in exchange for helping with the case. After four days of detention, it was announced that Moore was free to go.

It seems at least that the West Ham man didn't let his morale be too affected by the whole affair. He reportedly joined in with the birthday celebrations of one of the guards assigned to watch him one evening, drinking and partying late into the night. It was a party atmosphere when he finally arrived in Mexico to join up with his team-mates too, with the squad applauding him and giving him a guard of honour as he arrived at their base in Guadalajara, three days before their opening match.

Despite his far from ideal preparations, Moore played the full 90 minutes as England kept a clean sheet and defeated Romania 1-0. He'd be in the headlines again during the tournament for the right reasons. And as for the bracelet? No one ever found any concrete evidence that it existed in the first place.

1970: The Save (and Tackle) of the Century
Sunday, 7 June 1970
Estadio Jalisco
Guadalajara, Mexico

With England looking to put the Bobby Moore fiasco behind them and having won their opening game, full focus was now on football. Their second match was a tantalising one, against two-time champions and free-scoring dynamos Brazil.

The *Seleção* had regrouped in the years following their disappointing group stage exit in 1966. A new era of players, led by 25-year-old captain and legendary right-back Carlos Alberto, was making waves, and they went to Mexico as one of the favourites to win the tournament. This came after a dominant display in qualifying that saw them maintain a 100 per cent record and average nearly four goals a game.

They were equally rampant in their opening match at the tournament proper, routing Czechoslovakia 4-1. The new generation melded together with some of the stars of old to show that this Brazil team was an entirely different beast to anything the World Cup had ever seen before. After going a goal down, attacking midfielder Rivelino marked his World Cup debut by equalising with a free kick so thunderous it might have registered on the Richter scale. They then took the lead through Pelé, who at 29 was one of the old men in the young team. Jairzinho, a fleet-footed winger who had truly come into his own since Garrincha's decline allowed him to move to his favoured right-wing position, notched the other two. His second was nothing short of breathtaking; a mazy, unstoppable run in which he seemingly went past half of the Czechoslovakian team before finishing clinically. This was attacking prowess on a meteoric scale.

It was going to take a monumental defensive effort from England to keep the Brazilians at bay. But among their line-up in the searing midday Guadalajara sun that day were Gordon Banks and Bobby Moore, two men who were going to stop at nothing to keep England in the game.

The match developed predictably, enthralling to watch though it was, with England defending meticulously and looking to create something on the counter, while Brazil surged forward at every opportunity in an attempt to steamroller the opposition. Banks was forced into several fine saves to keep the score at 0-0. But none was finer than one in particular he made in the first half to deny Pelé.

One of Brazil's many attacks saw Jairzinho released down the right wing. He charged to the byline and clipped a threatening ball into the box. Banks had drifted to the post nearest to where the cross came from, attempting to block off any attempt Jairzinho may have made to cut inside and shoot. So when the winger instead elected to fire the ball high towards Pelé at the far post, Banks found himself marooned, having surrendered an open goal to the world's greatest striker.

It was an inevitability that Pelé would score. He leaped majestically to meet the ball and direct a perfect, powerful header towards the gaping net. He remembered years later, 'When you are a footballer, you know straight away how well you have hit the ball. I hit that header exactly as I had hoped. Exactly where I wanted it to go. And I was ready to celebrate.' So was the Brazilian commentator, who emphatically screamed 'Gol!' as Pelé's header flew towards giving Brazil a 1-0 lead. Except it never quite got there.

Banks hurled himself across his goal line at Usain Bolt-esque speed towards his other post, where the ball was about to bounce soundly into the net, and produced an inexplicably acrobatic diving save to somehow flick the ball out for a corner.

No one could believe it; not least Pelé. 'Banks appeared in my sight, like a kind of blue phantom,' the Brazilian said. 'He came from nowhere and he did something I didn't feel possible. He pushed my header, somehow, up and over. I couldn't believe what I saw. I can't believe how he moved so far, so fast.'

It was the moment that came to define Banks's career, earning him plaudits for the rest of his life, and fairly came to be labelled the 'Save of the Century' shortly after the game. His captain Moore, however, was less praising. 'You're getting old, Banksy,' he quipped sarcastically in the immediate aftermath. 'You used to hold on to them.'

England survived the ensuing corner and made it to half-time with the scores still level. But the overwhelming Brazilian pressure eventually paid dividends, with Jairzinho scoring on the hour mark to put them 1-0 up. At this, the Three Lions' game plan morphed into a much more attacking display of fast, direct football. Alf Ramsey rang the changes and England pushed forward more and more in search of a valuable equaliser, in turn leaving themselves increasingly vulnerable to a potentially devastating Brazilian counter.

After one such attack, Brazil managed to clear to Jairzinho on the right wing, and he smelled blood. With England out of shape, he charged towards Banks's goal, carrying the ball from inside his own half. Enter Bobby Moore. Bracelet incident long behind him, the England captain stayed with Jairzinho every step of the way, running backwards. But with every yard the Brazilian ate up, England looked evermore in peril, while Moore continued to retreat without attempting to dispossess him.

Jairzinho looked certain to put the game beyond reach. But then, as he shaped up to shoot just inside the England box, Moore stretched out a perfectly timed leg to nick the ball away, then bounced to his feet to calmly dribble the ball out of danger. It was a moment of sheer defensive genius that gave England a fighting chance of getting something out of the game.

They might have, too. Jeff Astle, a second-half substitute, squandered a glorious opportunity to equalise following a terrible mix-up in the Brazilian defence. Ultimately, despite Banks and Moore's heroics, it wasn't to be for England, and Brazil hung on for a 1-0 win.

It had been a true clash of titans between two giants of the game. There was only one goal, but it was a tremendous advert for the World Cup. Pelé and Moore embraced warmly after the final whistle, with the latter reportedly telling the Brazilian that he'd see him in the final.

England did win their next group match against Czechoslovakia to ensure their progression to the quarters, but Moore's promise went unfulfilled. There, they met West Germany in another pulsating match that saw the Germans get some revenge for their loss in 1966. Banks, alongside Moore as England's most important player, was famously struck down ahead of the game with a mysterious case of food poisoning. Stand-in keeper Peter Bonetti had a shocker as England threw away a two-goal lead to lose 3-2 after extra time. It proved to be all those 1966 legends' last dance on the biggest stage, with the Three Lions failing to qualify for the World Cup again until 1982.

1970: The Game of the Century
Wednesday, 17 June 1970
Estadio Azteca
Mexico City, Mexico

West Germany's unexpected turnaround against England set up a semi-final three days later against Italy, and the styles of play the two sides operated with couldn't have been more different. The Germans had blitzed through the group stages, winning every game and scoring ten goals in the process. *Der Bomber* himself, unstoppable Bayern Munich striker Gerd Müller, had plundered seven of them, including back-to-back hat-tricks against Bulgaria and Peru and the winner against England.

Italy, meanwhile, played with the defensive rigour that has become synonymous with Italian football. And it worked. The *Azzurri* hadn't made it past the group stages since they'd last won the World Cup in 1938, but in 1970 they ground out two goalless draws and a 1-0 win against Sweden to top their group and make it through to the quarters. There, they'd loosened the goalscoring shackles a bit to dispatch hosts Mexico 4-1. Their greatest strengths were keeping things watertight at the back, though, and they'd need to be at the top level to squeeze past Müller, Beckenbauer and Co into the final.

The match that unfolded between the two European giants in front of 102,000 spectators in the Mexican capital was nothing short of explosive. It was so packed with drama that the encounter was very shortly afterwards dubbed the 'Game of the Century', and there's even a plaque outside of the Azteca commemorating the fixture. But, as Franz Beckenbauer pointed out years later, amid all the hullabaloo that has seen the game pass into football folklore, 'people forget how ordinary the first 90 minutes were'.

He wasn't wrong, because to say the match was a slow burner is an understatement. Italy grabbed the lead early on, Roberto Boninsegna driving a powerful shot from 20 yards past Sepp Maier in the German goal in the eighth minute. From then on the Italians did what the Italians do best, and defended with all the resilience they could muster in the face of an evermore dangerous West Germany determined to equalise.

Wolfgang Overath, Uwe Seeler, Beckenbauer and Müller all came close to nabbing a leveller, but the ball just wouldn't go in. Italy keeper Enrico Albertosi came closest to making it 1-1, kicking the ball from his hands directly at Jürgen Grabowski. It rolled tantalisingly towards the open net, and Müller sprinted after it to make sure, but Albertosi managed to rush back and hack it away on the goal line. Then, in age-old German tradition, the very last seconds of normal time brought them some salvation.

It came from an unlikely source. Italy had found themselves pinned further and further back as the second half had worn on. With 92 minutes gone, Grabowski delivered a beautiful cross from the left wing into the centre of the box, where defender Karl-Heinz Schnellinger – who played his club football in Italy for AC Milan – surged in to volley it home from close range. The German TV commentator screamed, 'Schnellinger, of all people!' It was his first and only goal for *Die Mannschaft*, 12 years after he'd made his debut. The match was heading for extra time, a 30-minute period in which it established itself as one of *the* great games in football history.

The sweltering afternoon heat had by this point taken its toll, and players on both sides looked battle-weary. Beckenbauer had dislocated his shoulder, but with West Germany's substitutions all used up, he was forced to play on with his arm in a sling. It was his team who started extra time the stronger, Müller twice going close to giving them the lead before, in the 94th minute, he squeezed the scrappiest of goals into the Italy net when they failed to clear a simple corner.

A full Italian collapse looked to be on the cards. Grabowski nearly made it 3-1 shortly after as the Germans continued to apply the pressure, looking to put the game beyond reach. Then, in the 98th minute, they decided to return Italy's favour and gift them an equaliser. An innocuous chipped free kick from Gianni Rivera floated harmlessly into the German box towards number ten Sigfried Held. He turned out to be the last person they wanted defending it, cushioning the ball down perfectly with his chest towards the feet of Italy's Tarcisio Burgnich, who levelled things up at 2-2. It would have been hailed as a sensational assist had Held managed to do it at the other end.

At this, Italy found their feet and the game developed into a pulsating end-to-end spectacle. Just before the extra time interval, the Italians countered following a spell of German pressure. Gigi Riva received the ball on the edge of the opposition box and expertly turned Schnellinger before hitting a trickling cross-goal shot into Maier's far-left corner to give his side a 3-2 lead.

Things didn't calm down after the players had a breather. Italy returned to the backs-against-the-wall defensive strategy that they'd employed when 1-0 up earlier in the match, while West Germany searched for a chance to make it 3-3. Albertosi, who apparently that day was on a one-man mission to help the Germans out, inexplicably threw the ball from close range into the back of one of his defenders, off whom it bounced into the path of Müller. The beleaguered Italian goalkeeper realised his mistake and zipped out of his box to promptly foul *Der Bomber*, and West Germany nearly scored from the resulting free kick.

Five minutes into the second period, Germany's renewed attacking vigour paid off again. Müller struck another goal, a diving header from a short-corner routine. His tenth of the tournament, it ensured he finished three clear at the top of the goalscoring charts and claimed the Golden Boot. But most importantly, West Germany were level once more.

They had next to no time to enjoy it. Italy kicked off quickly, keen to re-establish their lead. Still in the days before penalty shoot-outs, someone had to win in extra time to avoid the match being decided by a coin toss. The *Azzurri* weren't going to let their destiny be taken out of their hands. Straight from the restart, they flooded players forward. Their stoic captain Giacinto Facchetti fired a long ball from the halfway line to Boninsegna down the left flank. He carried it further forward and arrowed towards goal, making as if to shoot, before slicing the ball back across the box towards the penalty spot, where Rivera arrived just in time to wrong-foot Maier and tap the ball coolly in. The Germans didn't touch the ball between Italy kicking off and scoring. Meanwhile, viewers across the world missed Rivera's strike as it happened – the TV coverage was still showing replays of the West Germany goal.

There was delirium in the stands as the fans reacted to yet another plot twist in this most rollercoaster of games. But that mayhem didn't infect the Italian players on the pitch. They were calm and assured as they steeled themselves for a final nine minutes and successfully defended their lead to win 4-3. They were going to the World Cup Final.

1970: Brazil's Greatest Team and Pelé's Swansong

Sunday, 21 June 1970
Estadio Azteca
Mexico City, Mexico

Italy's opponents in the final were the all-conquering Brazil side that had battled with England in the groups. After beating Peru 4-2 in the quarters, their semi was notably less stressful than Italy's, overcoming Uruguay 3-1 after falling behind early on. Despite that, it was a match they had controlled with ease. Jairzinho was still sparkling and the Brazilians played in such a way that they carried a goal threat in practically every position on the pitch.

And then there was Pelé. After 1966, he'd vowed to never play at a World Cup again after getting injured following a series of brutal fouls. But he was back for one last dance in Mexico, and pulled the strings as both a goalscorer and creator in Brazil's run to the final. It was in that Uruguay game that he pulled off one of the most outrageous pieces of skill ever seen on a football pitch, whipping out a mesmerising dummy when through on goal to dumbfound the Uruguayan goalkeeper and leave himself an open net. Which he then missed. But that's how good this Brazil side was. They could miss those opportunities and still run out comfortable winners. Unsurprisingly, they were strong favourites to lift the Jules Rimet Trophy for a third time.

A crowd of 107,000 – the record attendance at a one-off World Cup Final – crammed into the Estadio Azteca in Mexico City to watch a sublime 90 minutes of football that saw Brazil put forward a very convincing argument that they were the greatest team to ever play the game.

The match began in much the fashion everyone had expected. That is, the Brazilians attacked relentlessly, while Italy set up with a deep defensive line to try and keep the South American magicians at bay. They managed to do that for 18 minutes, before Pelé decided enough was enough and leaped majestically into the air, rose high above Italy defender Burgnich, and headed home a Rivelino cross. His celebration produced the most enduring image of his career, held aloft by Jairzinho with his fist raised defiantly above his head.

The Italians had to come out and play, but Brazil remained firmly in the driving seat. The team in the golden shirts displayed that day all the wonderful virtues of a sport so often referred to as 'the beautiful game'. But their audacious skill actually gave Italy cause for hope when, in the 37th minute, and with his team in comfortable possession, Clodoaldo attempted a nonchalant flicked back-heel pass inside his own half and failed to see Boninsegna charging him down. The Italy forward intercepted with his chest and, while never in full control of the ball, barrelled towards the Brazil goal, managing to evade several tackles in the process. Goalkeeper Félix rushed off his line to meet him but still Boninsegna couldn't be stopped, and he rolled the ball into an empty net from the edge of the 18-yard box. Italy, despite not really being in the game, were level.

They made it to half-time. Brazil manager Mário Zagallo, who'd won the World Cup twice as a player already, made no changes at the interval, and seemingly told his players to do more of the same, as the Brazilian blitzkrieg continued as soon as the referee started the second half. Pelé came agonisingly close to restoring their lead when he slid in to get on the end of an inviting Carlos Alberto ball across the face of goal, but it was just out of his reach and he could only poke it wide. Shortly afterwards, Rivelino hit the bar from a free kick. Italy were creaking.

Then, as the clock ticked past 66 minutes, they cracked. Midfielder Gérson launched a powerful shot from outside the box, and Albertosi in the Italy net could only flail at it helplessly as he watched it land sweetly in the corner of the goal.

This was the straw that broke the camel's back and the floodgates opened. Five minutes later, Pelé again evaded Burgnich to get on the end of a long ball from Gérson, directing a perfect cushioned header to Jairzinho, who bundled it in from close range to make it 3-1. In doing so, he completed a feat as-yet unmatched, by scoring a goal in every match of a World Cup.

By this point, Italy were undoubtedly beaten. They were only two goals down in a World Cup Final, where anything can happen, but Brazil's dominance was such that the primary objective became preventing the South Americans from inflicting a cricket score on them. The weariness of their classic with West Germany in the semis showed, and Brazil were largely allowed to walk around with the ball, easily crushing the precious few attacks that the Italians managed to mount.

In the 86th minute came the crowning moment, a strike so sublime it stands as the best team goal in the World Cup's long and colourful history. And it typified everything that the 1970 Brazil team stood for.

With the game long since over as a contest, Brazil's attacking intensity had dropped with the realisation that they were about to win a record third World Cup. But there was still time for them to produce something spectacular. A rare Italian venture forward was halted by Brazil's number nine, Tostão, who tracked back to steal the ball away. He laid the ball off to a defender, starting off a historic nine-pass move on the way to a legendary goal. After a series of short, sharp passes in their own half, the ball found its way to Clodoaldo near the halfway line. More than making up for his earlier blunder that led to the Italy goal, he embarked on a stunning dribble, taking four Italian players out of the game before shifting the ball over to Rivelino, in acres of space on the left wing. Rivelino fed the ball further down the left flank to Jairzinho, who left another Italian defender for dead before clipping it across to Pelé, 25 yards from goal and with three *Azzurri* blocking his path. Enter Tostão again. From beginning the move in his own half, he'd run back up the pitch to arrive just at the right time to point out to Pelé that Carlos Alberto was onrushing into the box at speed down the right.

He didn't need telling twice. In fact, he didn't even need to look up. With his eyes fixed on the ball, Pelé played a beautifully weighted pass in front of his captain. Alberto rifled the ball low to Albertosi's right with his first touch. The World Cup was already theirs, but Brazil had a fourth. And it was a thing of majesty.

Pundits gushed. *The Observer*'s Hugh McIlvanney in his match report said the goal exhibited 'the qualities that make football the most graceful and electric and moving of team sports', and said it prompted 'undiluted joy'. The goalscorer himself was shy to take the plaudits, for ever crediting his team-mates and his coach Zagallo. Those inside the Azteca had witnessed something special. Italy were a brilliant team; Brazil were on a different planet.

For their endeavours, they got to keep the Jules Rimet Trophy permanently. The man himself had decreed way back in 1930 that whichever team first won the World Cup three times should be allowed to keep the original trophy, so it went back to Brazil. No one could argue that they didn't deserve it.

The 1970 tournament had been a memorable and groundbreaking one, not least for the exciting goalscoring exploits of so many of the teams involved. It stands to this day as the World Cup with the most goals per game. But it was also Pelé's last time out on the biggest stage. He retired from the *Seleção* the following year, at just 30. He went out on the highest of highs, winning the Golden Ball for player of the tournament in 1970 after his stunning performance in Mexico, and to this day is the only player to have three World Cup winner's medals. As Burgnich, who'd had a torrid time when tasked with man-marking him in the final, later said, 'I told myself before the game, "He's made of skin and bones just like everyone else." But I was wrong.'

1974: Haiti's Five Minutes of Fame

Saturday, 15 June 1974
Olympiastadion
Munich, West Germany

The 1970 World Cup was a barnstorming success. New technologies and the allure of colour TV had brought the tournament to larger audiences than ever before, and millions across the globe were now hooked on this sensational footballing festival which happened every four years. So, naturally, FIFA decided to make some changes to their winning formula just in time for the 1974 competition in West Germany.

The straightforward format of 16 teams split into groups of four followed by a knockout stage, which had been used since 1954, was abandoned. Instead, FIFA devised a plot to generate more revenue by creating more games. The 1974 tournament would still feature 16 teams, but the top two from each group would enter a second group stage of four where they'd play another round robin, with the winners of each contesting the final, and the runners-up going into the third-place play-off. This brought the total number of games up from 32 to 38.

FIFA also rang another more enduring change. Fortunately, a World Cup game had never been decided by the dumb luck of a coin toss, the system which had been in place for many years should any match remain level after extra time. But the spectre of this lottery had loomed large in previous tournaments, not least during that magnificent 1970 semi-final when Italy and West Germany battled to avoid their fates being taken out of their own hands. For 1974, FIFA had a new plan in place: the penalty shoot-out. It had been used with much success in various club tournaments in the years prior, and football's governing body decided to adopt it in its marquee competition as a decider for any knockout games that remained level after 120 minutes.

That wasn't all. The qualification process had been changed four years earlier to open up more berths for continents previously sparsely represented at the World Cup finals. A spot was guaranteed for the winner of the 1973 CONCACAF Championship in North and Central America, of which the small Central American nation Haiti were the surprising beneficiaries. Mexico, a much more established footballing country enjoying a boom in the sport after hosting in 1970, were the nailed-on favourites to make it to West Germany. But while the Mexicans fell to some frustrating draws in qualification against lowly Guatemala and Honduras, Haiti – who were also tournament hosts – didn't falter. They did enough to finish top and earn a place at the World Cup for the first (and so far only) time.

Now, the World Cup throughout its history is littered with these amazing stories of tiny teams that qualify against all the odds and make it to football's crowning event. Yet very rarely do they ever do anything particularly special at the tournament proper. But for five minutes, this little Caribbean nation believed that they could.

Their opening match saw them pitted against previous runners-up Italy. The *Azzurri* had largely the same team that had made it all the way to the final in Mexico, but with one notable difference between the sticks. Enrico Albertosi had in the intervening years been displaced as the Italian number one by Juventus's notoriously unflappable shot stopper Dino Zoff.

At 32, Zoff had started making his name with the national team relatively late in his career. But once he was first choice for his country, he didn't let the opportunity pass him by. He didn't concede a single goal in qualification. In fact, his clean sheet record stretched beyond that, all the way back to a friendly against Yugoslavia back in 1972, and included some high-profile shut-outs against England, West Germany and Brazil. So the Italians went to the 1974 tournament with a defensive line so watertight it could have plugged the hole in the *Titanic*.

The World Cup has a habit of throwing up the unexpected, though. It had been thought that Italy would rout the Haitians, a team of amateur players from halfway across the world. But the first half in Munich remained goalless. The fans inside the Olympiastadion adopted the Caribbean side as their own, cheering every time they touched the ball. Which, by all accounts, wasn't much; Italy dominated the opening 45 minutes, flooding men forwards in an effort to break the deadlock. But Haiti's goalkeeper, Henri Françillon, produced a string of spectacular saves to deny them, in a performance described by *The Observer* as 'supernatural brilliance'.

Then, at the start of the second half, Haiti did something amazing. It looked like it was going to be more of the same, with the Italians surging forward again from the kick-off. But a headed clearance found its way to midfielder Philippe Vorbe, who arrowed a beautiful long pass in front of forward Emmanuel Sanon. Sanon, a 22-year-old who'd bagged five goals in qualifying, wasn't short of confidence. Ahead of the match, he'd prophesied that he would score, stating, 'The Italian defence is too slow for me.'

The kid from Port-au-Prince was bang on the money. He zipped past Italy's Luciano Spinosi with ease, though the defender did try his best to drag him back. Then came the seemingly unbeatable Zoff, who rushed out to close down the shooting angle. Sanon was quick of mind, too. He dropped a shoulder and flummoxed the legendary keeper, leaving him in a heap and giving himself an open net, which he duly tapped the ball into. Haiti 1 Italy 0.

A crescendo erupted in Munich and on the streets of the Haitian capital, where the match was being shown on a big screen. Sanon for ever wrote his name into the footballing heritage of the nation with that goal, in the process ending Zoff and Italy's amazing defensive streak. For five minutes, tiny Haiti led against the might of the two-time world champions, before Gianni Rivera grabbed an equaliser.

This captivating match was ultimately not the mammoth upset it briefly promised to be, with Italy going on to win 3-1. But it was justification for Haiti as a footballing country. Global stars like Gerd Müller, Jairzinho and Rivelino hadn't managed to score against Italy. But they had.

It was a high point that the Haitians couldn't match in their remaining World Cup fixtures. They were routed by eventual third-place finishers Poland 7-0 in their next match, before losing 4-1 to Argentina in their final game, with Sanon grabbing another goal. He and Françillon earned big moves to Europe following the tournament, and the striker is to this day Haiti's all-time top goalscorer.

For Italy's part, they attempted to publicly shrug off their five minutes of panic against the Caribbeans. Zoff claimed he was happy that he'd conceded, because now people could stop asking him about his record. But despite their turnaround in that match, all was not well in the Italy camp. Divisions between younger players and more established stalwarts festered, and after a 1-1 draw with Argentina, they joined Haiti in crashing out of the World Cup, after a 2-1 loss to Poland. The returned home to a mob of angry supporters waiting in Rome with blunt instruments. Haiti were welcomed back as heroes, having firmly put their football team on the world map.

1974: The Cruyff Turn?
Wednesday, 19 June 1974
Westfalenstadion
Dortmund, West Germany

It's a clip seasoned football fans have seen countless times. A moment so magical it came to define the sensational Netherlands team of 1974's entire 'Total Football' style of play. A slice of spellbinding skill that followed its inventor, Johan Cruyff – one of the finest players to ever grace the game – around for his whole life. But it seems that the Cruyff Turn might have been born in Preston.

The fabled Netherlands team of the 1970s are often billed as the greatest international side to never win a major tournament, but Dutch football had been simmering away quietly and ineffectively in the years following the Second World War. The national side hadn't qualified for a World Cup since 1938, and the big clubs failed to make a mark on the European stage. Then, in the late 1960s, revolutionary coach Rinus Michels came up with his own reworking of the 'Total Football' tactical system for his Ajax side, in which all outfield players should be adept at playing in any position on the pitch.

It allowed for fluid, seamless attacking play that rarely left a team vulnerable to conceding on the counter attack. And it was devastating. Feyenoord, playing a similar style, became the first Dutch club to win the European Cup in 1970, before the Ajax team Michels moulded won the next three. Heading into the 1974 World Cup, with their squad full of Feyenoord and Ajax's continent-conquering stars, there could be no doubt that the best football on the planet was being played in the Netherlands.

At the centre of it all was that man Johan Cruyff. A stunningly gifted centre-forward who roamed around the pitch freely as though it was his back garden, he'd been pivotal in helping Michels' take on 'Total Football' become so effective, with otherworldly technical ability and prophetic vision to anticipate what would happen in the game around him. After taking his talents to Barcelona in 1973, Cruyff continued to impress, claiming a second Ballon d'Or as the world's best player at the end of that year. It didn't matter that they hadn't made a World Cup in 36 years; this Dutch side was going to be hard to beat.

As if the opposition didn't have enough to worry about with the galaxy of superstars in the Dutch ranks, Cruyff's old compadre Michels was appointed as the team's manager in the months prior to the tournament. Their opening game was a comfortable 2-0 win over Uruguay. Next up were Sweden in Dortmund. And this was the match in which Cruyff chose to unveil the ingenious trickery that bears his name.

In the 23rd minute the wiry, almost languid figure of Cruyff received a powerful long pass from Arie Haan near the left-hand corner flag. He caressed it out of the air and it glued to his foot, naturally. But there was nowhere for him to go. Swedish right-back Jan Olsson was blocking his path towards goal, pressing into the Dutchman's back. Cruyff took a couple of close touches, clearly giving himself the time he needed to devise a brutal plan. Still facing away from goal, and with Olsson lying in wait, Cruyff dropped his shoulder and turned 180 degrees on his heel in one swift, balletic movement, dragging the ball with him as he went. The Swede was left for dead, the first victim of the Cruyff Turn.

The Netherlands didn't score from the subsequent cross that Cruyff, now in yards of space, was able to deliver. They didn't even win the game; Sweden held on for a goalless draw. But what the *Oranje*'s talisman had produced left everyone watching awestruck. It was so simple, so beautiful and so audacious. Olsson's reaction to Cruyff's perfect pirouette was the same as that of fans around the world. 'My team-mates after the game, we looked at each other, they started to laugh and I did the same,' he later remembered. 'What more could we do?'

So what, exactly, has this got to do with the Lancashire town most famous for Preston North End, a brutalist bus station and Freddie Flintoff? Well, it turns out there's plenty of evidence to suggest that Johan Cruyff, one of football's great pioneers, nicked it from a bloke who was born there. And worse still, that bloke was playing at the very same World Cup.

Adrian Alston was an apprentice striker at his hometown club in the north-west of England when he was approached to play in Australia's rather fledgling football league in 1968. He settled quickly down under and was persuaded to switch his allegiance to the Socceroos a year later. He played a pivotal part in their qualifying campaign for 1974, and helped the nation to its maiden World Cup as their top scorer.

In their tournament opener against East Germany in Hamburg, five days before Cruyff debuted his own version, Alston, like the Dutch captain, found himself stranded in the far-left corner of the pitch facing away from goal, a defender breathing down his neck. And sure enough, he produced that exact same mesmerising swivel to leave his marker in the dust.

Unfortunately for Alston, the East Germans were far less forgiving of such ludicrous skill than the Scandinavians. The defender marking him, Konrad Weise, was able to stretch out a trailing leg before the adopted Aussie could fully make his escape, hauling him down in a cynical foul. He never quite got the chance to complete the spin that might have seen his name forever etched into footballing folklore.

In the years following, Alston revealed that he chatted to a team-mate of Cruyff's about the turn. 'Later on, his room-mate told me that he was watching it on TV and said, "I think I can do that!"' And so he did. And in fairness, he did it better. Alston at least got some credit from West Germany manager Helmut Schön, who in his press conference ahead of Australia's next clash, a 3-0 loss against the hosts, said, 'We have nothing to fear from Australia … apart from Adrian Alston.'

The Socceroos earned a goalless draw in their final group game, against Chile, to ensure Alston and his team-mates went home with a point to show from their first World Cup. As for the Netherlands, there was a lot more to come.

1974: Zaire and the Worst Free Kick Ever

Saturday, 22 June 1974
Parkstadion
Gelsenkirchen, West Germany

Africa had been sparsely represented at the World Cup since the tournament's inception. Egypt in 1934 and Morocco in 1970 had been the only nations to make it to the finals, and none from below the Sahara Desert. With FIFA's more global approach to qualification, there was a continent-wide scramble to earn the sole spot for the 1974 edition in West Germany. Just in time for a new African footballing force, this time from outside the regular heartlands of North Africa, to arrive on the sport's biggest stage.

Zaire (now DR Congo) had precisely zero history in the World Cup. In their entire existence as a football team, under various guises as the nation flitted from Belgian rule to an unstable series of independent states, they'd never even entered qualification. But that was about to change at the behest of their autocratic president.

Mobutu Sese Seko inserted himself as leader of DR Congo following a military coup in 1965. A noted egomaniac (his full, self-composed title translated roughly to English as 'the all-conquering warrior, who goes from triumph to triumph, leaving fire in his wake'), Mobutu developed a cult of personality. Key to this, he felt, was establishing a strong, authentically African national identity, so in 1971 he changed the country's official name to Zaire, which had been used centuries earlier. He also ordered the Zairian people to abandon their more modern Francophone names in favour of traditional, tribal monikers.

And like Mussolini before him, he saw the power of sport as a political tool. From 1966 onwards, Mobutu began ploughing money into football. All of a sudden, a country with very little footballing heritage found itself with astronomical resources at its disposal to develop the sport. And it was a popular strategy. Mobutu compelled players of Congolese descent playing professionally overseas to return to their country, buying out their contracts and selling them this new vision for football in Zaire, which included healthy wages and cushy government jobs when they retired. The team went on months-long training camps to develop their skills, a string of European coaches were hired, and major world clubs visited the capital city of Kinshasa to play them, including Pelé's Santos.

This new era really came to fruition in 1968, when they claimed their first Africa Cup of Nations title in Ethiopia. On the streets back home, football fever overwhelmed the nation, and the team were greeted as heroes upon their return. Just the kind of patriotic unity Mobutu was after. As economic woes gripped Zaire in the years following, the brilliance of its football team created a respite. It kept people happy, so Mobutu kept funding it.

In 1971, Yugoslavian manager Blagoje Vidinić was hired to get the team to the World Cup. He'd just taken Morocco there in 1970, and managed to repeat the feat with Zaire. In qualifying, the Leopards were unstoppable. They cruised into the final round, a three-team group stage, and won all four matches to claim their place in West Germany. Then, three months before the tournament began, they romped to another AFCON title. Mobutu had succeeded in making Zaire the best team in Africa.

Off the pitch, things weren't so rosy. By the time the 1974 World Cup rolled around, Mobutu had fully established a dictatorship in Zaire. What's more, he'd gone back on the earlier promises made to his players. The big salaries had never materialised, and by 1974, many players had side jobs to supplement their irregular income from football. When wealthy European clubs came knocking, Mobutu blocked his players from leaving. But there was one saving grace on the horizon: the World Cup. FIFA awarded a bonus of $750,000 to teams that qualified, to be shared among players and staff. So the Zaire squad waited it out, excited to play in football's biggest tournament and earn their share of the spoils.

In spite of their troubles, the players travelled to West Germany with high hopes. They were told by a Zaire government official upon arrival that he was dividing the FIFA money up equally, and he'd have it ready by the time they'd played their first game, against Scotland. Zaire lost 2-0 in Dortmund but put in an impressive performance to go toe to toe with the Scots. It was considered a success against a superb side featuring stars like Peter Lorimer, Kenny Dalglish and Billy Bremner. Post-match, and with their spirits high, they went back to their hotel, expecting a visit from the government official with their money. But he never came.

The players' anxieties grew as the days passed before their next game, against Yugoslavia. Worry that they may have been swindled was rife, and the situation boiled over late on the night before the match. The Leopards' star centre-back, Bwanga Tshimen, remembered how one of his team-mates went around the players' hotel rooms to wake them up, 'He insisted that we meet and kept saying that the money had to show up.' Striker Mayanga Maku described the scenes as 'total chaos', as the players argued about whether to storm into the minister's suite and demand their money.

Eventually they decided to go back to bed, reasoning that the tournament was far from over, and they should try to concentrate on the football. But they awoke the morning of the game to disturbing news: the official had left the hotel early to go to the airport. They never saw him – or the FIFA money – again.

The team were devastated, and it showed in their performance against Yugoslavia. Gone was the Zaire side that had looked adept and professional against Scotland, replaced by a squad of crushed players that ultimately lost by a humbling 9-0 scoreline. It was humiliating. But soon, the players' sadness turned to anger and resentment over the broken promises their government had made to them.

It wasn't going to get any easier for Zaire in their final group match, against reigning champions Brazil in Gelsenkirchen. The South Americans cruised to a 3-0 victory without really getting out of second gear. And it was in that match that Zaire left a misleading, unfortunate imprint on the World Cup that they'd forever be remembered for.

Towards the end of the game, Brazil were awarded a free kick 30 yards from the opposition goal. As a trio of Brazilians gathered around the ball, the ref blew his whistle for it to be taken. At that, Zaire's right-back Mwepu Ilunga sprinted out of the defensive wall to hoof the ball at full pelt upfield.

It flabbergasted everyone. Brazil's players stood still, confused. John Motson, in his commentary of the game, screamed, 'What on earth did he do that for?' The referee approached Ilunga and gave him a yellow card. In the years that followed, the narrative was predictably reductive; 'African innocence', as Motson called it. A bunch of amateurs who didn't know the rules of the game properly. Ilunga's free kick has travelled around the world, shown countless times on World Cup blooper reels of the tournament's funniest moments. But the explanation was far from comical.

This was a player who'd just become an African champion and had helped his side through a barnstorming qualifying campaign. He knew full well the rules of the game. Ilunga, so incensed at the team's treatment by Zaire's government, had intended to get sent off, to try and humiliate Mobutu further – because if the dictator was intent on sharing the glory of any victories, then he'd have to shoulder the shame for any embarrassments. Years later, when Mobutu was long since deposed, Ilunga spoke out about the incident. 'I did that deliberately,' he said. 'I was aware of football regulations. I didn't have a reason to continue getting injured while those who benefit financially were sitting on the terraces watching.'

It's sad that a genuinely brilliant team of players is remembered for such a misunderstood flashpoint, driven by a devastating financial blow. They went home after conceding 14 goals, losing three games, and not scoring once. To add insult to injury, upon their return to Kinshasa, the players were collected from the airport by a bus that whisked them straight to the presidential palace, where Mobutu called them mercenaries, informed them that none of them would ever be permitted to play abroad, and withdrew all of his support for the national team. DR Congo, in any guise, haven't made it to a World Cup since.

1974: East Beats West

Saturday, 22 June 1974
Volksparkstadion
Hamburg, West Germany

On the same day that Zaire made their unfortunate contribution to World Cup history, another team of tournament debutants were making their own waves in a politically charged game in Hamburg that had the eyes of the world upon it.

By 1974, a divided Germany was old news. The Cold War was raging on, with the capitalist West and communist East split down a very real border through the European nation. In footballing terms it was host nation West Germany who were very much in the ascendancy. They'd won the competition back in 1954 and hadn't failed to qualify since being admitted to FIFA. They'd just won the European Championship in 1972, and their squad for their home World Cup boasted some of the planet's best players, with a now very experienced Franz Beckenbauer pulling the strings at the back and Gerd Müller still banging in the goals up top.

It was a different story in the East. They first entered World Cup qualification four years later than their neighbours in 1958, but they were far from successful, never realistically coming close to making the finals. But that changed in 1974 when they earned their spot just across the border following a superb qualifying campaign that saw them win five of their six games. For the first time, East Germany would be at the World Cup.

And wouldn't you just know it, they were drawn in the same group as their old pals from the West. The sides had never met in a full international before, despite numerous attempts from the West Germans to set up a friendly. The East had always declined, and as the Cold War grew ever more hostile the chances dwindled. But at a World Cup, they had no choice. The date with destiny was set for 22 June, the final first group stage match.

East Germany's World Cup bow came against Australia, in that match when Adrian Alston performed his own Cruyff turn. They won 2-0 and followed that up with a 1-1 draw against Chile, just over the wall in West Berlin. Going into the final game against their neighbours, the East Germans had a chance to win the group, if they could just beat their brothers from the West.

That would be no easy feat. West Germany had won both of their matches to that point, scoring four goals and looking fully in control for the entirety. Their team of stars was in stark contrast to East Germany's industrious side who, despite having won an Olympic bronze two years earlier and boasting some talented players in their ranks, weren't even fully professional, with members of the team required to hold a separate job outside of football.

From the moment the teams were drawn together, much was made about the political significance of the match. Opposing ideologies were to go head to head in an arena that had absolutely nothing to do with politics. But the symbolism was enormous. Interest in the game was massive, both in Germany and around the globe. People recognised that this was a moment that stretched beyond sport. On the football pitch at least, Germany was going to be reunified for 90 minutes.

For the players' part they felt little political pressure, which was by far dwarfed by the great excitement they had for the game. 'We were looking forward to comparing ourselves to the West,' East German midfielder Hans-Jürgen Kreische remembered. 'It was something we repeatedly strived for, but the authorities always prevented it.'

It was widely expected that West Germany would win, and this included in their own camp. They had all the stars and were the home team, after all. But there was an acknowledgement in the press that the East would surely make it tough for them. While the players mightn't have felt it beforehand, the palpable political edge to the match was undeniable, with armed police guarding the stadium and a military helicopter hovering nearby. It was bound to have an effect.

As the sides lined up against each other, there was an evident mutual respect between the players. West German captain Beckenbauer and his opposite number Bernd Bransch greeted each other with warm smiles before kick-off, and the Hamburg crowd's rapturous, unending chants of 'Deutschland! Deutschland!' as the teams emerged felt like a statement as well as support for the home side.

From the ref's whistle, tension became the new order of the day. It became clear that both sides were desperate simply not to lose, with the goalkeepers rarely bothered in a fraught first half. The play was cautious but the East Germans had held their own against their more illustrious western opponents, who were in the ascendancy but couldn't break through the East's rigorous defensive line.

The game remained the same for much of the second half. West Germany pressed more but seemed happy not to commit too many players forward. After all, a 0–0 draw would suit them fine and see them top the group. Then the 77th minute came around and everything changed.

Substitute Erich Hamann galloped down the right wing after receiving the ball from his own keeper, who'd just prevented another tame West Germany attack. The West had plenty of players back to cover the counter, including Beckenbauer. But Hamann, who only ever played three times for his national team, unlocked some space beyond the West's defence with a pinpoint long ball into the path of onrushing striker Jürgen Sparwasser, a mechanical engineering student. The forward chested it past a slipping Beckenbauer, coaxed Sepp Maier off his goal line and fired the ball high into the roof of the net to give his team an unlikely lead.

At this, West Germany finally came out to play but they found in front of them a determined, organised defence that proved impenetrable. The East, in their neighbours' back yard, completed a stunning 1-0 win and topped the group.

The result was seismic. Politicians in the East were quick to milk the win for everything they could. But the players themselves were less ecstatic. They were delighted to have proven themselves, but reluctant to become pawns in the regime's propaganda machine. What's more, they'd thoroughly enjoyed the experience of playing the West, and didn't want to be disrespectful by over-celebrating. In the tunnel post-match, the players swapped shirts and chatted. 'We got on very well,' Kreische later reminisced. 'We spoke the same language after all.'

The West German players, on the other hand, were devastated. They felt embarrassed, especially for their manager Helmut Schön, who was originally from Dresden in the East. It was widely reported that the side drank heavily through the night following their defeat. Ultimately the match proved to be the only official fixture between the two nations, meaning the giants from the West never got chance to avenge what was a humbling result.

Yet, red-faced though they may have been, the loss against the East proved pivotal. A re-focused, re-shaped West Germany went into what was actually an easier second group, winning three from three against Yugoslavia, Sweden and Poland to make it to the final. Meanwhile, East Germany had the brutal task of facing Brazil, Argentina and the Netherlands, and finished bottom. As Beckenbauer later said, 'The goal from Sparwasser woke us up. Otherwise we would never have become world champions.'

1974: German Efficiency Trumps Total Football
Sunday, 7 July 1974
Olympiastadion
Munich, West Germany

West Germany were safely into their home final. And you'd be forgiven for thinking that surely a second World Cup was merely a formality in front of a raucous German crowd in Munich. But going into that match, West Germany found themselves as outsiders: the smart money was on the Netherlands.

Since that frustrating goalless draw against Sweden, when not even Cruyff's magic could unlock the Scandinavians' defence, the Dutch had gone on a blistering run, playing some of the most attractive football the World Cup had ever seen. They'd battered Bulgaria 4-1 ahead of the second group stage, where they really unleashed their majestic abilities against some of the best sides in the world. Argentina were dispatched 4-0, before a comfortable 2–0 win against the East Germans. Next to fall were reigning champions Brazil in another 2-0. In that second group stage, the *Oranje* struck eight goals without reply. They were on fire.

Away from the pitch, too, West Germany were up against it. The 'Total Football' of the Dutch had very much won the hearts of spectators the world over. After spending a month swaggering around Germany with their long hair, frolicking with supermodels in hotel swimming pools, and swashbuckling about each pitch they played on like they owned it, they were already the people's champions. They just needed to get through one more match before claiming their rightful prize.

There was also the small matter of the Netherlands team's strong personal desire to embarrass the host nation. The Dutch–German rivalry is today well established as one of the most intense, ferocious beefs in international football. But in 1974, it was a much more one-sided affair. Anti-German sentiment in the Netherlands still loomed large in the national psyche following German occupation in the Second World War. For them, this match stretched beyond football. 'I didn't give a damn about the score,' midfielder Wim van Hanegem said of his feelings before the game. 'One-nil was enough, as long as we could humiliate them. I hate them.'

Suffice to say, people expected a combative performance from the Dutch. But the Germans were far from fazed. Remember, this was a team with a barrage of their own superstars, and reigning European champions at that. Their playing style may have lacked the lustre of the Netherlands' approach, but it was far from dreary. How could it be with the likes of Beckenbauer and Müller in their ranks? The scene was set for a fantastic game.

Any anxieties harboured in either camp weren't helped by a delay to the kick-off, caused by the ground staff at the Olympiastadion forgetting to return the corner flags after removing them for the pre-match closing ceremony. When it did finally start, the 75,000-strong crowd didn't have to wait long for some drama.

The Netherlands kicked off and passed it around themselves in their usual casual fashion, creeping forwards. Not to worry for West Germany; it was early days and they sat back in numbers to keep the Dutch out. Except, with less than a minute played, Johan Cruyff produced more of the magic that had made the world fall in love with him. In an incisive, jinking run, he dashed past a cluster of German defenders and found his way into the box, where Uli Hoeness scythed him down. Penalty to the Netherlands. West Germany had yet to touch the ball.

The sensational Johan Neeskens, whose own magnificent performances in 1974 often get forgotten amid the Cruyff fanfare, dispatched the spot-kick calmly. The *Oranje* had the lead after just 90 seconds – the fastest goal ever scored in a World Cup Final.

It was a dream start. But perhaps it came too soon for the Netherlands, who arguably shot themselves in the foot in the period that immediately followed. At 1-0, arrogance slipped into their game as they tried to make fools of the West Germans. They passed the ball around nonchalantly without creating any real threats to the German goal. This was not the rotating, relaxed style of pressing leading to goalscoring chances that the Dutch had been so masterful at earlier in the tournament. This was pure overconfidence, born of a desire to exert complete superiority over West Germany, and not try too hard while doing it. Fatefully, that superiority they felt they had proved false.

The German players handled themselves superbly while on the back foot following Neeskens' goal, defending resolutely and waiting for their moment to play their way into the game. Beckenbauer started to find his feet, *Der Kaiser* again becoming the focal point of some tremendous passing play from deep.

In the 25th minute they found a way through. Veteran midfielder Wolfgang Overath found Bernd Hölzenbein on the left wing. He must have been taking notes earlier when watching Cruyff evade the German defence, because he unleashed a doppelgänger of a run to dribble beyond several Dutch defenders and deep into the box. As he readied to shoot, Wim Jansen slid in, appearing to fell Hölzenbein. English referee Jack Taylor pointed to the spot for a second time.

This decision is still a contentious one in the Netherlands today, but replays showed that Jansen did *just about* nick Hölzenbein's leg before he fell. It was a soft one but it gave West Germany the chance they needed. Paul Breitner and his fantastically big hair made no mistake to make it 1-1.

Unlike the Netherlands, they seized the initiative, and were on the front foot for the remainder of the half. Two minutes before half-time, it paid off through Müller, of course. The ultimate goal poacher collected a delivery from the right inside the Dutch box, but miscontrolled it only for the ball to spin out behind him. He swerved and swung an acrobatic leg at it, placing it low beyond Dutch keeper Jan Jongbloed. It proved a fairytale goal for *Der Bomber,* his 68th international strike on his 62nd and final appearance. He retired from the national team after the match.

Müller's last goal for his country won them the World Cup. Despite a more spirited fightback in the second half, the Netherlands' game was up. Cruyff lost his head at half-time, receiving a booking for arguing with the ref, and the Dutch couldn't break the home side down. Müller even put the ball in the net a second time only for it to be ruled out for offside. Replays suggest it probably should have stood.

For West Germany, their second World Cup win was one of team spirit and resilience. They'd gone close in 1966 and 1970 but never lifted the trophy, and had overcome a difficult beginning to their campaign in 1974 – not least the result against the East – to go all the way on home soil. The Dutch were devastated, and the nation mourned their wasted opportunity. The ultimate prize against their ultimate enemies had been within touching distance, only to evaporate in front of them. Unfortunately, that was a fate they'd have to get acclimatised to.

1978: Zico and the Welsh Referee

Saturday, 3 June 1978
Estadio José María Minella
Mar del Plata, Argentina

The World Cup headed to Argentina in 1978 mired by more controversy than ever before. Twelve years had passed since the South Americans were awarded hosting duties for the first time, and much had changed, not least in 1976, when the ruling president Isabel Perón – widow of iconic Argentine leader Juan Perón – was ousted in a coup that saw a military dictatorship established. The resulting political and economic instability in the country left many nations reluctant to travel, and comparisons were drawn with the 1934 tournament in Mussolini's Italy. FIFA ploughed ahead, and despite criticisms, no nations pulled out. Argentina would have their World Cup.

Amid all of this tension, it's surprising then that one of the biggest controversies at the tournament came courtesy of a referee from the Rhondda Valley in south Wales.

Clive Thomas had worked his way up the officiating pyramid in the Football League in England. He'd taken control of a couple of group games at the previous World Cup in 1974, and at 41 was in his refereeing prime ahead of the tournament in Argentina. A strong performance in his first assignment – a Group 3 clash between Brazil and Sweden on the opening weekend – would surely put his name in contention for bigger matches as the tournament progressed. As it happened, it ended up being the last World Cup game he'd ever oversee.

Brazil were no longer the silky, sensational champions of 1970. Aside from new talisman Zico, who Brazilian media had christened the 'white Pelé', the *Seleção* were a young, battling side renowned for their overly aggressive tactics. Sweden manager Georg Ericson stoked the fire ahead of the match by branding the Brazilians as 'dirty'. It seemed Thomas might have a feisty encounter on his hands.

The Welshman needn't have worried. The match was an uneventful one, with Sweden taking the lead late in the first half only for Brazil to equalise just before half-time. Thomas only had to dole out two yellow cards as the second half settled into the Swedes defending what could be a precious point and the Brazilians pushing forward relentlessly to grab a winner. An easy day at the office. That was, until, the very last second, when Thomas decided to produce one of the most bizarre decisions ever seen at a World Cup.

As the final moments ebbed away, Brazil's pressing had Sweden pinned back practically in their own box. The South Americans won a corner. And then another. And then a third. Right-back Nelinho ambled over to take the kick and placed the ball just outside the permitted arc. The linesman told him to move it. Nelinho obliged, again in no rush. He knew this was to be the last play of the game, and was willing to take his time if it helped him pick out a team-mate who could score the winner.

Thomas, meanwhile, was getting impatient. The Brazilians had the nerve to take the match a whole *six seconds* beyond the 90 minutes, even though he'd added no stoppage time. The audacity! But he had a plan to teach those unpunctual Brazilians a lesson.

Nelinho took the kick, whipping a lethal ball into the Swedish box. As soon as his boot struck the ball, Thomas blew his whistle for full time and turned on his heel to march towards the tunnel. Just in time for him to completely miss Zico aim a bullet header beyond the Swedish keeper and, so the player thought, win the game for Brazil.

The decision understandably enraged the Brazilian players and staff. Zico, upon realising his goal wouldn't stand, stood in the net in disbelief, hands raised to his head. Thomas marched on with a string of protesting Brazilians in tow, the Welshman defiantly gesturing with his hands as he did so that the goal did not count. The match had finished 1-1.

'I find it unbelievable, incredible,' said the incredulous Brazil manager Cláudio Coutinho afterwards. The denial of the goal didn't stop his side progressing to the second group stage, but it did prevent them from topping their group, an honour that instead went to Austria. This pitted Brazil against the hosts Argentina, who seemingly had some ominous forces at play helping them towards the final (more on that later). The *Seleção* ultimately came third, defeating Italy 2-1 in the play-off.

Thomas was not the kind to shirk from the spotlight. This was just the latest in a long line of contentious decisions he made throughout his career. 'There is a view that the best referees make themselves as inconspicuous as possible,' wrote Clive White in *The*

Times in 1981, after the Welshman had awarded a conspicuous last-minute penalty to Wolverhampton Wanderers against Tottenham Hotspur in that year's FA Cup semi-final. 'I am not sure that Mr Thomas shares that belief.'

The official remained headstrong in the aftermath that he'd made the right call. This was not an opinion shared by FIFA's refereeing committee, who told him in no uncertain terms that this was to be his last act on the World Cup stage. Thomas felt aggrieved, feeling the chance to oversee the biggest game in football had been taken from him. He wasn't bitter, though. 'He sounds like a dance band leader,' he said of his Italian colleague Sergio Gonella, who was awarded the final. 'And, to my mind, he referees like one.'

1978: Glorious Gemmill's Bittersweet Strike
Sunday, 11 June 1978
Estadio Ciudad de Mendoza
Mendoza, Argentina

With England's post-Ramsey period of decline in full swing, and Northern Ireland and Wales coming nowhere near qualifying, it fell to Scotland to be the sole British representatives at both the 1974 and 1978 World Cups. In West Germany they were incredibly unlucky, winning against Zaire and earning draws against Yugoslavia and holders Brazil, only to miss out on the second group stage on goal difference despite not losing a game. But there was yet another wave of optimism surrounding the team as they travelled to Argentina.

This was in no small part down to Scotland's hubristic, ever-assured manager Ally MacLeod. In his short period in charge before the World Cup, he'd guided the team to qualification, knocking out European champions Czechoslovakia in the process, and a British Home Championship title in 1977, including a famous win over England at Wembley. A legendary anecdote of conspicuous repute tells how MacLeod, when asked what he planned to do after the World Cup before the side left for South America, bluntly replied, 'Retain it.' True or not, MacLeod was an emphatically confident coach with a talented side at his disposal, featuring Kenny Dalglish, Joe Jordan and Graeme Souness, and 'Ally's Tartan Army' went to Argentina with a spring in their step.

MacLeod also had in his ranks the undeniably talented – though oft overlooked – Archie Gemmill. A diminutive midfielder, at 31 Gemmill was the second-oldest member of MacLeod's squad, and already had a hairline that even Phil Mitchell wouldn't want. A favourite of Brian Clough, he spent the best days of his career at Derby County and Nottingham Forest, collecting three league titles and a European Cup in the process. But this was to be his first World Cup, after missing out on the squad in 1974.

Things didn't change for him in Scotland's first match at the tournament, either. Gemmill was named on the bench for their opening clash again Peru, who boasted the mesmerising attacking talents of Teófilo Cubillas. The Scots had to find out how good he was the hard way, MacLeod having declined the opportunity to do his homework on the Peruvians at a World Cup warm-up game in favour of attending a family party. At 1-1, Scotland having led early on and missed a chance to retake the lead from the penalty spot, Cubillas turned it on to devastating effect. In the 71st minute he powerfully finished off a slick passing move to make it 2-1, then six minutes later he struck a second time from a nonchalant free kick. Gemmill made a late cameo but Scotland were already floored.

A spanner in MacLeod's plans, but no matter; they still had two games to make up for it. Next up were Iran, who were making their World Cup debut. No one knew much about the side from the Middle East but the omens didn't look good for them. They'd been flattened 3-0 by the Netherlands in their first game, and looked well off the pace of such a high level of football. MacLeod rang the changes in an ultimately near-sighted attempt to keep his squad fresh, giving Gemmill both his first World Cup start and the captain's armband.

It was a disaster for Scotland. Despite being gifted the lead late in the first half by a truly farcical Iran own goal that saw defender Andranik Eskandarian produce an accomplished finish to volley the ball into his own net, a languid Scotland floundered and were subjected to a humbling draw when Iran equalised on the hour. Ally's World Cup dream was very quickly falling apart.

Their final match, against the Netherlands, presented Scotland with a mountain to climb. Only a win by at least three clear goals against one of the best sides in the world would be enough to see them through to the next stage of the tournament.

From the off it looked as though MacLeod had set a rocket off underneath his Scotland side. For the first time in the tournament he finally opted to set up his midfield from the start with the brilliant Graeme Souness, who in his last start at club level had won the European Cup with Liverpool. The new-look team dominated the opening stages of the game. Souness planted a perfect cross on to the head of Bruce Rioch, who rattled the crossbar but almost certainly should have scored.

Shortly after that, Scotland did manage to put the ball in the net only to see it ruled out for offside. Another was chalked off seven minutes later, Dalglish adjudged to have fouled a Dutch defender in the build-up to him slotting it past keeper Jan Jongbloed. It remained 0-0 but Scotland had the Dutch reeling. It seemed only a matter of time before they'd break the deadlock.

Then, in true Scottish style, it was instead the Netherlands who struck first to go one up. The superb Rob Rensenbrink was bundled over in the box, got up and slotted a 34th-minute penalty past Alan Rough.

Remarkably, despite now needing four goals in less than an hour, Scotland's heads didn't go down. Dalglish managed to find an equaliser on the stroke of half-time, before Souness won a penalty just after the restart. Archie Gemmill stepped up to make it 2-1. But the wee man from Paisley had a much bigger moment up his sleeve.

Twenty minutes passed and Scotland remained in the ascendancy. Dalglish picked the ball up on the right wing near the Dutch box and tried to fashion an opening but was dispossessed comfortably by a sliding tackle. The ball ricocheted towards Gemmill, who with his first touch nicked it away from a stretching Wim Jansen. With his next five, he produced the finest moment Scotland ever had at a World Cup.

First, a magical dummy saw him knock it past hapless Netherlands captain Ruud Krol and advance to the edge of the 18-yard box. Another jink past left-back Jan Poortvliet – who was left flat on the deck by Gemmill's trickery – saw the Scot clean through on goal. He set himself before dinking a curling finish over Jongbloed for 3-1 to Scotland.

The Tartan Army in attendance were in raptures after a goal of pure majesty, grace and skill, bettered only for those qualities by some bloke called Diego when he danced past half of England's team eight years later in Mexico. It's been immortalised in the film *Trainspotting*, and rightfully holds its place alongside the very best moments in the history of Scotland's national team. More important than all of that, the Scots were only a goal away from achieving the impossible, knocking out the Netherlands and making it to the next round of the World Cup. And the way they were playing, you wouldn't have bet against them.

Or, given Scottish football's long-standing relationship with stoking fans' hopes only to squash them soon after, maybe you would have done. Supporters only had three minutes to enjoy being on the verge of making it beyond the World Cup's opening stages for the first time before Johnny Rep thundered a 30-yard screamer into the top-left corner to make it 3-2. Deflation, yet again.

Scoring another two goals was beyond Scotland, and the match finished 3-2. It was a defiant, spirited win, but a failure all the same. MacLeod was much derided in the press for his handling of the tournament, and managed the national side only once more before resigning. He'd promised far too much and delivered far too little.

As time has passed, though, nostalgia has been kind to MacLeod. He was the manager who oversaw one of Scotland's greatest ever wins, against a Netherlands side who would eventually make it to the final. Along with Gemmill, he'd helped give Scotland a slice of euphoria, fleeting though it was. The Tartan Army haven't felt that good since.

1978: Dodgy Dealings in Rosario
Wednesday, 21 June 1978
Estadio Gigante de Arroyito
Rosario, Argentina

As with Mussolini's tournament in 1934, the 1978 World Cup held in military junta-ruled Argentina sits uncomfortably in the annals of the competition's history. Despite some standout moments and iconic players like Teófilo Cubillas and Mario Kempes running riot, the competition remains shrouded in allegations of corruption and intimidation. And there's no game more representative of that than the host nation's second group stage clash with Peru.

The backdrop to Argentina's World Cup was an unpleasant one. Since that military coup in 1976, new dictator Jorge Rafael

Videla sought to tighten the stranglehold placed around the country. Opponents of his regime vanished with increasing frequency, becoming part of an ever-growing group in the nation known as *Los Desaparecidos*: The Disappeared. The atmosphere in Argentina on the eve of the World Cup was akin to that in Stalinist Russia.

Like Mussolini before him, Videla recognised how important a polished, successful tournament could be, with the eyes of the world on the country and his regime. Impoverished neighbourhoods near the stadiums being used were forcibly cleared, while the grounds themselves were subject to extensive redevelopment. The junta did everything to present the best possible version of Argentina that they could.

Part of that was ensuring that performances on the pitch went as smoothly as the infrastructure off it. Argentina were drawn in a tough first group that would see them face Hungary, France and Italy. After sneaking a 2-1 win against Hungary in their opener in Buenos Aires – a match played less than a mile from one of Videla's notorious torture camps for political prisoners – goalscorer Leopoldo Luque encountered a junta official. Smiling, the military man told Luque, 'This really could be the group of death as far as you're concerned.'

With the pressure on the players suitably applied, Argentina next played France and their young superstar Michel Platini. Another 2-1 win was enough to ensure the hosts would be in the next group phase. But it was a game that rang alarm bells. Swiss referee Jean Dubach waved away a very substantial French claim for a penalty in the first half, only to award Argentina a very dubious one shortly afterwards. An anonymous French player reportedly overheard the referee tell Argentina's captain Daniel Pasarella, who'd bundled over Didier Six for their penalty claim, 'Don't do that again please, or I might have to actually give it next time.'

Questions were raised about the condition of the Argentine squad, too. A cluster of French players and staff members claimed to have seen some of the Argentina team taking mysterious blue pills before the match. Rather than a pre-emptive homage to *The Matrix*, they were certain that these must have been amphetamines. None of Argentina's players ever tested positive for anything illegal during the course of the 1978 tournament. However, FIFA officials were astonished to find that one of the urine samples returned indicated that one of the players was pregnant.

Argentina were defeated 1-0 in their final group game by Italy. They already knew they were through though, their second-placed finish securing them a spot in the second group stage with Brazil, Poland and Peru. The group quickly settled into a two-team shoot-out between the hosts and Brazil for a spot in the final, both sides winning their opening clash before playing out a goalless draw with each other.

Brazil were up first in the final set of matches, beating Poland 3-1. This presented Argentina with the advantage of knowing exactly what they needed to do to make it to the final when they lined up against Peru that evening in Rosario. This in itself was strange, given that the final two games in the other group kicked off at the same time. The Argentine FA requested that their fixture be moved until after Brazil's, reasoning that it would allow any Argentinian fans attending the earlier game to make it home in time to watch their match on TV. A thinly veiled request, but outrageously FIFA obliged. Still the task, even though they knew exactly what it was, wasn't easy: they'd need to beat Cubillas and Co by four goals.

The match passed into infamy. Peru were playing only for pride, but were expected to make it tough for the Argentines. They'd won their first group, including holding the Netherlands to a goalless draw, and had shown the world their footballing chops. So it came as a great surprise when, having conceded only six goals throughout the tournament to that point, they shipped another six to hand Argentina a 6-0 victory and a spot in the World Cup Final.

It didn't take long for the rumours and conspiracies to swirl post-game. Naturally, it was members of the Brazilian contingent who were most critical, feeling they had been denied a place in the final by what they saw as clear and obvious corruption. Fingers were quickly pointed at Peru's goalkeeper, Ramón Quiroga, an Argentinian by birth. In an open letter, he defended the honour of himself and his team-mates, and the narrative both nations pushed was that Argentina had simply been too good for Peru to handle on the day.

'I played the match, and I can swear there was no arrangement,' said Cubillas. If there was no formal deal offered to the Peruvian players, then at the very least they were subject to some unusual pressure before the game. It later emerged that Videla himself had visited the Peru dressing room ahead of the match. Players present have been sketchy on the details of what he said, but it's known that he gave a lengthy speech about how vital the World Cup was to Latin America as a whole. He also read a letter from Peru's own dictator, Francisco Morales-Bermúdez, who emphasised the importance of good Argentinian-Peruvian relations. This was hardly the most inspiring team talk Peru's players could have received before their match.

Peru went home under a cloud despite an admirable performance at the tournament. 'They shouted at us that we had been bought,' remembered captain Héctor Chumpitaz of the supporters' reaction when they got home to Lima, a sad end to their World Cup campaign. FIFA investigated the corruption claims, but much to Brazil's vexation they could find no concrete evidence (although, in the months following the tournament, Argentina did send tens of thousands of tonnes of grain to cash-strapped Peru). Videla's boys would have their chance on the biggest stage of all.

1978: The Ticker Tape Final
Sunday, 25 June 1978
Estadio Monumental
Buenos Aires, Argentina

The hosts would face the Netherlands in the final. The Dutch had improved somewhat since their 3-2 loss to Scotland helped them through to the second group stage on goal difference. They trounced Austria 5-1 in their opening match of the second phase, outlining that they still possessed some of the quality that had seen them finish as runners-up four years earlier. They were without Johan Cruyff, who had unexpectedly retired from the national side in 1977, but with the likes of Johan Neeskens, Rob Rensenbrink and Johnny Rep in their ranks, they remained a team to be feared.

Also in the Dutch ranks was Arie Haan, a powerful Anderlecht midfielder who blasted his country into the final. In their second group match, a repeat of the 1974 final with West Germany, he smashed in a strike from 35 yards in a 2-2 draw. That turned out to just be his warm-up act, letting rip another thunderbolt from 40 yards to score the winner against Italy in their last group match to send the Netherlands into their second World Cup Final in a row.

The pre-game narrative was fascinating. Argentina, of course, arrived in the final surrounded by allegations of corruption. This sharply contrasted with the Netherlands, who of all the teams in the 1978 World Cup were most critical about the tournament going ahead under the stewardship of such a brutal regime.

If that wasn't enough to ensure an explosive encounter, the teams engaged in various spats before kick-off to really get the blood boiling. With River Plate's packed Estadio Monumental already feverish to cheer on the hosts, a forest's worth of white and blue ticker tape having been fired across the stadium prior to kick-off, Argentina decided to whip them up even more. With the Dutch ready and waiting to go the home side showed up five minutes late, building the tension further.

If the Argies hadn't already riled the Dutch up enough with their tardiness, they decided to take issue before kick-off with René van de Kerkhof's plaster cast. The Dutch winger arrived at the tournament with a broken hand, and had worn a heavy cast for protection in all of the Netherlands' previous games. Van de Kerkhof had this cleared with FIFA ahead of the World Cup, but Argentina captain Daniel Passarella decided to complain to Italian referee Sergio Gonella about the protective sleeve. He reasoned that it could be used as a weapon to injure one of his players.

This petty argument nearly saw the game called off entirely. Gonella, perhaps himself intimidated by the hostile Buenos Aires crowd, sided with Passarella. Van de Kerkhof was told he couldn't play with the cast as it was. In response, his captain, Ruud Krol, said that if that was the case, none of the Dutch team would be playing. The *Oranje* marched off.

With the Netherlands side stood at the side of the pitch, backed by manager Ernst Happel who felt Argentina's conduct was ridiculous, Gonella came up with a compromise. Van de Kerkhof was to wear a soft sling around the cast, making it supposedly less dangerous. Argentina's gamesmanship meant that the kick-off was now delayed by nearly 20 minutes. But finally, the teams were ready to play.

Unsurprisingly, the match that ensued was a hot-blooded affair, with the moments of genuine footballing quality dwarfed by a series of vicious fouls both teams unleashed on one another. The ticker tape that had been released before kick-off littered the pitch, making for a memorable image when, in the 38th minute,

Argentina's talisman Mario Kempes slotted the ball under Jan Jongbloed from 12 yards to make it 1-0. He ran towards the crowd, arms aloft, blue and white confetti strewn at his feet.

The second half saw the Netherlands take control in their pursuit of an equaliser. It came late on, substitute Dick Nanninga nodding in a header after 82 minutes to draw the teams level. It was a special moment for the forward, who missed the pivotal match with Italy after picking up a bizarre red card in the previous fixture against the Germans. Yellow-carded for an off-the-ball incident, Nanninga laughed heartily at the decision of the referee, who promptly produced a second yellow in response to Nanninga's derision. Bewildered and devastated, he was led off, but now could join the exclusive club of World Cup Final goalscorers.

He nearly became one of the select few to get his hands on a winner's medal, too. In the closing moments of the game, Rensenbrink latched on to a long ball in the box and guided it towards the Argentina goal. Van de Kerkhof remembered, 'That was our moment. We thought we had won the World Cup.' They hadn't – Rensenbrink's effort ricocheted agonisingly off the post and was cleared.

The final was heading for extra time. Apparently rejuvenated by their brush with defeat, the hosts wrestled control. Kempes was unplayable. In the 105th minute he danced past two Dutch defenders and into the box, firing a shot towards goal. Jongbloed managed to make the save but couldn't direct the ball to safety. Kempes managed to get it under control and poke into an empty net – a strike that won his country the World Cup and, as his sixth goal of the tournament, won the Golden Boot for himself.

Argentina added a third through Daniel Bertoni five minutes before time, sealing the nation's first World Cup win and consigning the Dutch to a second consecutive final defeat. It was a particularly painful one for Happel to swallow, the Austrian having also lost in the European Cup Final a month earlier as coach of Club Brugge. It marked the end of the barnstorming *Oranje* side of the '70s, as the Netherlands team entered a difficult era that saw them fail to qualify for the next two World Cups.

Meanwhile, the hosts' victory sparked wild celebrations across Argentina, and dictator Videla had his wish. The country was united and euphoric, brushing his own murderous regime under the carpet, if only for a short while. He beamed as he presented the trophy to Passarella, his sportswashing plan having succeeded.

For the players involved, it was bittersweet. They'd achieved the zenith of their careers but inadvertently helped Videla in the process. Midfielder Ricky Villa said years later, 'There is no doubt we were used politically.' It was a source of sadness to many, their achievement of winning the greatest prize in football overshadowed by feelings of anger towards the junta in power. Left-back Alberto Tarantini was a little more direct in expressing his distaste, making a point of shaking Videla's hand as he was given his medal with the hand he had just used to wash his genitals.

The junta eventually collapsed five years later, but Argentina would have to wait until 1986 for a win unsullied by the shadow of Videla's regime.

1982: El Salvador's Hungarian Humiliation
Tuesday, 15 June 1982
Nuevo Estadio
Elche, Spain

Despite the widespread criticism of the 1978 tournament, the World Cup entered the 1980s with a spring in its step. Its popularity had continued to grow, leading FIFA to expand the 1982 edition in Spain to 24 teams. This again gave more opportunity for smaller nations to play on football's biggest stage. Qualifying berths for North and Central America doubled from one to two, and war-torn El Salvador grabbed their chance.

It was seen as miraculous that Central America's smallest nation had even made it to the tournament. In 1979 the Salvadoran Civil War had broken out. The conflict, which lasted 12 years, had seen the country fall into a ruinous era of widespread murder, human rights violations and economic devastation. Hardly the greatest circumstances for a football team to thrive in. But somehow, El Salvador finished ahead of mighty Mexico in qualifying and booked their place in Spain.

The nation had actually qualified once before, in 1970, when they endured a terrible tournament that saw them lose all three games without scoring a goal. There was a determination among the players to ensure the 1982 campaign wasn't so disastrous. Supporting the national side seemed to be the one thing that could unite the people of El Salvador, midfielder Mauricio Alfaro remembering, 'When we played the qualifiers, we made the killings from both factions cease.'

Despite this added motivation, the task facing the team was monumental. In the build-up to the tournament, a FIFA official visiting their training camp noted that their preparations were actually well-coordinated and extremely professional. But the situation in the country prevented them undertaking their plans to maximum effect. Defender Francisco Jovel explained, 'If some of us arrived late, it was because we had to assist wounded people abandoned alongside the road.' The cash-strapped country struggled to provide funding for the team to travel to play warm-up matches, and professional sides elsewhere couldn't be convinced to visit El Salvador while such a bloody war was going on.

Ultimately, events conspired to make El Salvador's preparations for the World Cup extremely chaotic, leading to a campaign littered with controversy and cock-ups that scriptwriters on *Mike Bassett: England Manager* would have thought too far-fetched. Already travelling to Spain with both the youngest squad and youngest manager, government officials decided they couldn't spare enough money to pay for the full 22 players to go to Europe, so the team went two men light.

What's more, they only arrived after a gruelling journey across the Atlantic three days before their first match, against Hungary in Elche. Then they found that the 25 balls FIFA supplied to each team hadn't made it to Spain with them, so had to borrow a few from the Hungarians to train with. The players were also embarrassed to discover that, as was customary prior to World Cup games, they had no national team pendants or gifts to exchange with their opponents. Instead, 20-year-old goalkeeper Luis Guevara Mora took it upon himself to improvise something: he found a piece of wood and crudely carved 'EL SALVADOR' on it to give to Hungary.

It should be no surprise, then, that El Salvador's tactics for their opening clash were equally haywire. Inexperienced 36-year-old manager Pipo Rodríguez sent his team out against Hungary with next to no knowledge of their opponents' playing style and a plan to dazzle the Spanish spectators with an all-out attack game plan. It couldn't have gone worse.

Within four minutes Hungary were ahead, striker Tibor Nyilasi heading the Europeans in front. By the time 23 minutes had gone it was 3-0. Rodríguez decided a change was needed, and in the 27th minute he hauled off one of his midfielders for another forward, Luis Ramírez Zapata. Because clearly what El Salvador needed was more firepower.

To be fair to Rodríguez, the change did actually sway things slightly in his side's favour. They produced a string of promising attacks, prompting the 23,000-strong crowd in Elche to cheer them on each time they advanced forward. Maybe a comeback *was* on the cards. They hadn't scored yet, but a much-improved El Salvador had halted the early Hungarian rout to keep the score 3-0 at half-time.

Alas, the Salvadoran renaissance proved short-lived. Rodríguez sent his team back out for the second half with the same attacking vigour but Hungary were wise to them. Exploiting their opposition's freely marauding wing-backs, they made it 4-0 five minutes after the restart. Shortly after that it was five and Rodríguez finally realised the potential humiliation he had on his hands. Wanting to spare Mora any further scrutiny, he asked substitute keeper Eduardo Hernández to warm up. Hernández refused; he wanted no part in proceedings.

Then, in the 64th minute, came a brief glimmer of joy for El Salvador. Sub Zapata popped up on the edge of the six-yard box to give the country their first – and to date only – World Cup goal. It was in the main created by a stunning piece of skill from the Central Americans' standout performer Jorge 'Mágico' González, who baffled two Hungary defenders with his dribbling to find Silvio Aquino in the box, who in turn put it on a plate for Zapata. The substitute celebrated like a man who had just scored the winner in the World Cup Final, not struck a consolation goal to make it 5-1. He ran around aimlessly, screaming in jubilation.

It was a fleeting moment of respite before things got much, much worse. Five minutes after Zapata's strike, Hungary began an eight-minute romp that saw them score four goals, making it 9-1. László Kiss, who'd only been brought on in the 55th minute, wrote his name into the history books in that time, becoming the scorer of the fastest hat-trick in World Cup history, as well as being the first substitute to bag three goals.

Nyilasi, the man who'd started the scoring, completed El Salvador's humiliation shortly before full time. Hungary became the first and only side to reach double figures in a World Cup match, defeating the Central Americans 10-1 to equal the record for the largest margin of victory at the tournament.

The defeat sparked even more chaos in the El Salvador camp. A group of senior players overthrew manager Rodríguez, who never coached again, and wrestled control of the team's tactics for the remainder of their matches. There was no fairytale but they were much better under the players' stewardship, losing 1-0 and 2-0 to Belgium and reigning champions Argentina respectively.

These more respectable performances did nothing to recover the opinion of those involved in the World Cup campaign in the eyes of the Salvadoran supporters. Mora in particular moved to Spain and then the US, feeling uncomfortable back home in the years following the Hungary match. Remarkably, something good did come of the tournament for one man: González impressed enough to earn a move to Spain, where he enjoyed a fruitful ten-year spell, largely for Cádiz. Fans of the club still regularly vote him as the greatest player in their history.

In spite of their record-breaking win, Hungary crashed out in the group stages along with El Salvador. To commemorate the 25th anniversary of the match the teams played a friendly in 2007. There was no such humiliation this time around, with the spoils shared in a 2-2 draw.

1982: England's Return and Rapid Robson

Wednesday, 16 June 1982
San Mamés Stadium
Bilbao, Spain

Smaller footballing nations weren't the only ones to benefit from FIFA's expansion of the tournament to 24 teams. More berths were allocated to European teams too, meaning the top two sides from each five-team qualifying group would earn a spot at the finals. This ultimately helped England end their long spell out in the World Cup cold. Under Ron Greenwood, a tumultuous qualifying campaign that saw the team fall to a humbling loss to minnows Norway ultimately ended successfully, England leaving it to their final match to secure second place in their group and earn a place in Spain.

Despite a talented squad featuring stars like captain Kevin Keegan, Bryan Robson, Ray Wilkins and Trevor Brooking, expectations of the side ahead of the tournament were somewhat understated. Perhaps the 12 years away from football's centrepiece had limited ambitions. Even the squad's official World Cup song, 'This Time (We'll Get It Right)', was hardly a bombastic declaration of intent.

Optimism perhaps wasn't helped by England's draw for the tournament. A tricky group would see them take on rising stars France and a Czechoslovakia side that had just come third at 1980's Euros. Even with a supposedly easy fixture against Kuwait, the Middle East side making their tournament debut, it wasn't going to be easy to squeeze past the quality European teams they'd been drawn against.

If England's World Cup return wasn't to be another crushing disappointment, they'd need to hit the ground running. Their first game, against the French, arrived at a difficult time. Greenwood's squad was plagued by injuries, with both Brooking and Keegan – undeniably two of the team's most creative forces – ruled out of the early stages of the tournament. This against a dangerous French side with a fearsome midfield led by Michel Platini. It didn't look promising.

In a surprisingly benevolent move wholly uncharacteristic of England sides, they decided to soothe fans' nerves early on. From the kick-off in the Bilbao evening sun, the Three Lions decided that 12 years was far too long a time to wait for a World Cup goal. Within the blink of an eye, England had a throw-in deep in the French half, adjacent to the right-hand side of the 18-yard-box.

As Steve Coppell lined up to take the throw, the legendary John Motson on commentary for the BBC noted, 'Already the French are marking up man-to-man.' Motty didn't get many things wrong in his career, but he'd failed to see that as Coppell launched a long throw into the box, the French had given Bryan Robson a chasm of space and time at the back post. Towering centre-back Terry Butcher, who'd forayed forward for the occasion, nodded the ball into the path of a quite laughably unmarked Robson. The Manchester United midfielder contorted his body to sweep at left foot at the bouncing ball on the half volley, straight past a befuddled Jean-Luc Ettori in the French net. With 27 seconds on the clock, England were 1-0 up.

It was about as good a start as England could have hoped for on their return to the big time, setting off the thousands of fans who'd made the journey to Spain for the tournament into raptures. Robson's strike is still comfortably England's fastest goal in the World Cup and it set them on their way to a memorable 3-1 victory.

Next up were Czechoslovakia, who were swept aside in another straightforward win, this time 2-0. England were already guaranteed a spot in the second group stage before they'd even played their gimme against Kuwait, a game in which Greenwood rested a few regular starters to keep them fresh for the latter stages. His side won again, defeating the debutants 1-0. It was the first time England had managed a 100 per cent record in the groups, and up to and including the 2018 tournament in Russia it remains the only time they have managed it.

Unfortunately for England, the 1982 tournament is remembered only for what might have been. The expanded 24-

team competition saw a key format change from FIFA. The top two sides in each of the six four-team groups went through to another group stage, this time with four sets of three teams, before the winners of those advanced to a conventional semi-finals setup.

The Three Lions were unlucky to have been randomly allocated a series of opponents that would contain another group winner alongside themselves. They ended up in a group of death with reigning European champions West Germany and tournament hosts Spain, while France's second-placed finish earned them a much easier group, taking on Austria and Northern Ireland.

The challenge proved too much for England. They managed a hard-fought goalless draw against the Germans in their first game, and knew a win by two goals against Spain would seal a place in the semis. Brooking and Keegan both made brief World Cup cameos towards the end of that match, the latter spurning a simple header that would have put England ahead. It wasn't to be, and England went home after another 0-0 draw.

Greenwood retired after the World Cup, achieving the unique feat of managing the only England side other than the 1966 winners to go unbeaten at a major tournament. It was a cruel way to be eliminated. But at the very least, Robson's strike in the first seconds of the competition gave England fans a moment to remember – and cause to celebrate on the biggest stage for the first time in a generation.

1982: The Kuwaiti Prince and the Strangest Pitch Invasion Ever

Monday, 21 June 1982
Estadio José Zorrilla
Valladolid, Spain

Football fans are no strangers to frustration. Ask any seasoned match-goer and they'll tell you there's nothing more infuriating than watching their team when things are going against them. Whether it's a poor performance or a refereeing decision you don't agree with, sitting there powerless, quietly seething, is an unforgiving experience. But imagine if you *could* do something to try and change your team's fortunes. That's exactly what one spectator decided to do at a group game at the 1982 World Cup.

The match in question was France vs Kuwait. The Arab nation were competing in their first World Cup, and had earned an impressive result in the form of a 1-1 draw against Czechoslovakia in their opening match. They were managed by Carlos Alberto Parreira, the Brazilian who would go on to win the tournament coaching his country of birth in 1994, and there were hopes in the Gulf nation that they could be a surprise package. When their second game came around though, they faced a much sterner test in the form of that star-studded French side who'd fallen to England in their opener.

And so it showed. After half an hour of relentless attacking, France broke the deadlock thanks to a stunning curled free kick from Bernard Genghini. Michel Platini soon surged through a static Kuwait defence to add a second on the cusp of half-time, and a third goal was notched by *Les Bleus* just after the break. Less than 50 minutes played, and Kuwait found themselves deservedly 3-0 down.

Things were looking bleak for the Kuwaitis, and one can only imagine the frustration of a certain Sheikh Fahad Al-Ahmed Al-Jaber Al-Sabah (or Prince Fahid to his friends), Arab royalty and president of the Kuwait Football Association, as he watched his team crumbling from the stands. Not that any imagination was necessary; the TV coverage of the game seemed to conveniently cut to Prince Fahid every time France scored another goal. The Sheikh was visibly annoyed, the cameras at one point catching him slumped forward with his chin resting in his hand.

That was until a little glimmer of light in the form of a goal from Abdullah Al Buloushi in the 78th minute. Kuwait had got one back, and the manner in which they'd done so was excellent; a snappy set piece saw Al Buloushi wriggle through the French defence to slot in from a tight angle. If they could do it once, then maybe there was hope of an unlikely comeback? It can surely only be this thought racing through Prince Fahid's mind as he decided to take action into his own hands and seal his improbable place in World Cup history a few moments later.

His journey into the history books began with France winning possession of the ball just inside their own half and mounting a pacy attack. Their fluid, flowing play had caused problems for the Kuwaitis all afternoon, and they made light work of advancing towards goal. Fortunately for Kuwait, their defenders had learned their lesson, and they'd left plenty of men back to hopefully deal with France's firepower. However, it was their commitment to the age-old adage 'play to the whistle' that proved their downfall. Because just as Platini played a perfect through ball to Alain Giresse on the edge of the box, a loud whistle was heard, and the Kuwait players all stopped in their tracks. Meanwhile, Giresse fired the ball into the net from what they assumed, because of the referee's whistle, was an offside position.

The problem? The whistle hadn't come from the referee at all. It had come from the crowd.

What ensued was a unique form of pandemonium that the World Cup had never seen before. As the France players celebrated, the Kuwait team congregated at the side of the pitch adjacent to the halfway line. It didn't take long for the television cameras to find Fahid again. Except this time he wasn't slumped down, looking dejected. He stood gesturing peculiarly towards the pitch, and appeared to be beckoning the Kuwait team off in outrage at the injustice he felt his team had suffered. And the players seemed to obey their Sheikh's command as they grouped near the sideline.

More was to come. It seemed Fahid didn't just want his players off the pitch – he wanted the referee, Soviet official Myroslav Stupar, to come and speak to him. Stupar, not accustomed to having to go into the crowd to remonstrate with oil-rich Sheikhs, remained on the field. So the Sheikh decided to go to him.

Fahid descended the steps, through the bemused Spanish police, and headed out on to the pitch. He made a beeline straight to where the referee stood, surrounded by the Kuwait players. Some reports at the time suggested that he clapped slowly and sarcastically in the direction of the officials as he approached. The ref and Fahid subsequently had an animated discussion pitchside, Fahid apparently pleading his country's case that his players would have continued playing and stopped the goal had they not heard the whistle from the crowd.

What followed, no one expected. Following his chat with the ref, Fahid returned to his seat in the stands with a swarm of Spanish police in tow, while Stupar ran across the field to his linesman. After a quick talk, the referee (totally of his own volition, of course) ruled the France goal out and ordered the teams to play on. The French coaches were incensed, but Fahid didn't care. He'd just conducted a pitch invasion and managed to get a goal against his team overruled.

Ultimately, any hopes the Sheikh might have had about his team completing an epic comeback once he'd had France's latest goal chalked off were misplaced. An uneventful final ten minutes was punctuated with a French goal in the 90th minute, and the Gulf nation lost 4-1 – essentially, all Fahid had done was prevent it being five.

In the aftermath, FIFA slapped Fahid, one of the world's richest men, with a whopping $12,000 fine; a sum that must have given him many a sleepless night. (Not!). Stupar, meanwhile, never refereed another official international game again.

Fahid defended his actions by claiming it had been the Kuwait players who had threatened to leave the field, and that he had actually stormed the pitch in order to convince them to continue the match. News reports at the time weren't so sure, with most claiming that Fahid had told the referee he'd pull Kuwait out of the match if he didn't overrule the goal. Either way, the Sheikh made more of an impact on the World Cup than his country ever did – Kuwait crashed out of the tournament after that 1-0 loss to England in their following game and haven't qualified since. And Prince Fahid seemed to get over his disappointment pretty quickly after the match, stating, 'I have no quarrel with the result. France deserved to win.' Sure, Fahid. Sure.

1982: The Disgrace of Gijón

Friday, 25 June 1982
Estadio El Molinón
Gijón, Spain

Kuwait weren't the only ones to find themselves at the centre of controversy in Spain. In fact, Fahid's antics were far outstripped by two well-established European sides. West Germany and Austria had played at plenty of World Cups before and were respected footballing countries with a rich heritage in the sport. But that didn't stop them playing out a match at the end of the group stage that raised more than a few eyebrows for being really, *really* dodgy.

West Germany swaggered into the tournament on a high – they'd won the European Championship two years earlier in Italy, had superstar players like Karl-Heinz Rummenigge and Klaus

Fischer, and were fancied as one of the favourites to lift the World Cup after winning every one of their qualifying games. So when they were drawn to face tournament debutants Algeria in their opening group match, it's safe to say it was widely expected that the Germans would cruise past their North African opponents. Goalkeeper Harald Schumacher asserted that his side would score 'four to eight goals just to warm up', while manager Jupp Derwall said he'd have to 'jump on the first train back to Munich' if his team lost.

Surely, then, the result would be nothing other than a dominant display of West German attacking prowess?

Wrong. Algeria produced an almighty shock by claiming a well-deserved 2-1 win, leaving German World Cup hopes hanging in the balance. A 4-1 win over Chile in their second match meant West Germany had it all to play for in their final game, against neighbours Austria. And that's precisely where this story gets more than a little suspicious.

Algeria had already completed their three group games; they'd followed up their famous victory against the Germans with a loss to Austria, before beating Chile themselves. In the days of two points for a win, the group – going into that final West Germany vs Austria clash – had Austria and Algeria both on four points, going through to the second round in first and second place respectively, with West Germany set to lose out in third with two points. It was simple: the Germans *had* to win their final match.

That final match, however, came with an interesting caveat. Algeria had already played all of their games, so like in the case of Argentina's clash with Peru four years earlier, the Germans and the Austrians knew exactly what they needed to qualify. Namely, a win for West Germany by one or two goals would ensure both teams would pass through safely into the next round, sending World Cup novices Algeria – who had gained a lot of neutral fans thanks to their unexpected tournament heroics – home in the process.

Fortunately for Algeria and their newfound supporters, all they needed to progress was for Austria to not lose, or for West Germany to win by three or more. Given the two were fierce rivals with a complicated political history, the chances of the two teams coalescing in order to get through to the next round were deemed slim. Austria manager Georg Schmidt even came out before the game in Gijón and said, 'My players always find a special motivation against Germany.' And from the German perspective, it was thought they'd be keen to teach their opponents a footballing lesson; Austria had defeated West Germany by a 3-2 scoreline at the 1978 World Cup for a famous win, and many fans wanted revenge.

When kick-off came at 5.15pm in the Spanish evening sun, the West Germans burst out of the traps with pace and virility. Their attacking was furious and non-stop, and was soon rewarded when Hamburg centre forward Horst Hrubesch bundled the ball into the Austrian net from a dazzling cross in the tenth minute; 1-0, and the way they'd started, it looked as though Germany could grab a hatful.

Algerian hopes of a German rout that would see the North Africans go into the next round alongside them were dashed, though, by an ensuing 80 minutes of football that would see 25 June 1982 go down as one of the most shameful days in FIFA World Cup history.

Shortly after Hrubesch's goal, West German midfielder Wolfgang Dremmler took what would prove to be the final shot on target of the game. The teams then began a brazen display of settling for a result that would see them both through. Players would rarely attempt to tackle the opposition when they were in possession of the ball. The game trundled on in a lackadaisical manner. Attempts on goal were non-existent.

The game descended into a dismal and embarrassing nadir in the final 15 minutes. Prior to this, the two teams had at least had the decency to put some semblance of effort into making the match look like a real contest. However, by the time the 75th minute rolled around, this was dead in the water. West German players closed out the game at walking pace, leisurely kicking the ball to one another with all the effort of a hounded, slightly drunk dad who's been talked into having a kickaround with the kids at a barbecue. Unsurprisingly, the match finished 1-0. West Germany qualified for the next round as group winners with Austria going through as runners-up. Algeria, after a valiant tournament debut, were sent packing.

Reaction to the game was universally negative. It was reported that Algerians in the crowd were seen burning peseta notes as a statement to suggest corruption. Spanish fans in the stadium had been booing the teams from the 50th minute onwards, and chanted 'Algeria! Algeria!' as the game trudged to an end. ITV's commentator Hugh Johns said the final whistle was a 'relief'.

The best reactions, though, were reserved for TV commentators from the offending nations themselves. West Germany's Eberhard Stanjek at one stage refused to commentate on the game any longer, while the Austrian Robert Seeger went so far as to tell viewers to turn their televisions off.

The Guardian's match report branded the display as 'European cooperation taken to ridiculous limits', and the game very quickly became a headache for FIFA. There was genuine outrage that this could be allowed to happen, that two teams could so blatantly agree on the pitch to a result that would benefit both. Some even called for West Germany and Austria to be disqualified from the tournament, with Algeria reinstated. But as FIFA vice-president (and, suspiciously, German Football Association chief) Hermann Neuberger said at the time, 'FIFA cannot sanction a team if they did not fight properly.'

He was right. There weren't any rules against what Austria and West Germany had done. Sportsmanship went out of the window along with integrity and any desire to put on a show for fans. But laws? None were broken.

The two nations continued in the tournament. Austria fell at the next hurdle, crashing out in the second group phase, while Germany would go all the way to the final. And Algeria headed home with their heads held high, having shown just how good African teams could be on the world stage.

The match soon became known in the press as the 'Disgrace of Gijón', and would lead FIFA to change the format of the competition to ensure the final games of each group would always be played at the same time. Who'd have thought a boring 1-0 could so dramatically change the history of the World Cup?

1982: Northern Ireland Shock Hosts Spain

Friday, 25 June 1982
Estadio Luis Casanova
Valencia, Spain

Later that evening, another decisive group match was played, but this time there could be no suggestion of collusion between the teams involved. Northern Ireland, who along with Scotland qualified for the 1982 tournament out of a tough group containing Portugal and Sweden, were back at the World Cup for the first time since their heroics in 1958. The Green and White Army weren't given much of a chance after being drawn with hosts Spain and Yugoslavia, who had topped their qualifying group ahead of giants Italy. Honduras made up the quartet, seen as the best chance the Northern Irish would have to get some points on the board.

Except it didn't quite work out that way. After a solid goalless draw against the Yugoslavs in their opening match, Billy Bingham's side could only manage a 1-1 against the Central American minnows. This left them staring down the barrel ahead of their final game, against Spain and their raucous home crowd in Valencia.

With Yugoslavia having played and beaten Honduras the night before, and Spain in top spot, Northern Ireland knew they essentially needed to win – or play out a high-scoring draw – to make it through to the second group phase. Still, their experienced squad had hope. There was stoic captain Martin O'Neill, who'd won two European Cups with Nottingham Forest. The magnificent 37-year-old goalkeeper Pat Jennings was still pulling off remarkable saves for fun, while at the other end of the spectrum talented 17-year-old forward Norman Whiteside was taken to the World Cup despite only having played two competitive games for his club, Manchester United, and remains the youngest player to have appeared at a World Cup.

Then there was Gerry Armstrong, Northern Ireland's ultimate big-game player. The Watford striker had scored the goal that had sealed his country's place at the tournament in a 1-0 win over Israel in the final match of qualifying, and the strike that had earned them their point against Honduras. Against Spain, he would again be the man in the spotlight.

The match started in an unexpected fashion. Bingham had prepared his side for an energetic Spanish onslaught, believing that the hosts would want to advance into the next round by sealing top spot with an emphatic win. Spain had different ideas in the opening stages. After all, a draw was also enough for them to win their group, and they adopted a conservative early approach, moving the ball slowly and never committing too many men forward. This method was not appreciated by the 50,000-strong Valencian crowd, who jeered their side for not playing with more gusto. Northern

Ireland, meanwhile, were sticking to their game plan. Bingham had wanted his team to hold back in the first 20 minutes to gauge what kind of performance Spain might put in, and they were certainly doing that, approaching with caution themselves.

Midway through the first half, tempers started to simmer a bit more. Spain, who despite their languorous play to that point had created the only meaningful chances, committed to some very full-blooded tackles that BBC pundit Jimmy Hill described as 'ruthless and cynical' as the Northern Irish played their way into the match. Naturally, Bingham's boys weren't going to take this lightly and produced some tasty challenges of their own. By half-time the referee had shown three yellow cards and the match had seen a few challenges already that may well have warranted a red today. But most importantly, the score remained goalless.

This was a problem for Northern Ireland. As O'Neill put it in his pre-match interview, 'We would rather come off losing by two or three and having attacked them. That seems like a paradox but a goalless draw does us no good.' A high-scoring affair certainly didn't appear to be on the cards. The task was simple: just get the ball in the Spanish net.

They set to work on this immediately after the restart, leading to perhaps the finest moment in Northern Ireland's footballing history. It started and finished with Armstrong. With Spain on the attack, themselves looking to respond well after an underwhelming first half, the Watford man intercepted in his own half and bombed forward. He carried the ball half the length of the pitch before Miguel Alonso, who went on to have a rather gifted footballing son called Xabi, tried to fell him. Armstrong saw it coming and managed to shift the ball across to Billy Hamilton on the right wing, while Armstrong himself surged into the box, waiting for a return cross.

Hamilton sold a brilliant dummy to knock it clear of his man and move forward, and searched for Armstrong with a cross, who was hovering near the penalty spot. However, Spain had plenty of defenders back, and Armstrong was the only target for Hamilton to aim at. Unsurprisingly, his ball couldn't find the one white shirt in a sea of red.

It didn't find a red shirt, either. Instead, Luis Arconada, the legendary Real Sociedad goalkeeper in his blue kit, rushed out uncertainly to claim the ball. It turned out to be a rare mistake from Spain's ultra-reliable number one. He stretched to get a hand on Hamilton's cross, parrying it away from two waiting Spanish defenders in comfortable positions to clear it. The ball bounced towards Armstrong, who let rip with a lethal driven shot, firing his shot underneath a jumping Arconada and his country into a 1-0 lead.

Armstrong's celebrations were understated, walking slowly and hugging team-mates with his arms aloft. He later explained that on account of the eerie quiet in the stadium, he thought the goal had been disallowed. That wasn't the case. The home fans had been shocked into silence.

It still felt like Northern Ireland had a mountain to climb. Their goal had come in the 47th minute, meaning they still had basically an entire half to hold on. What's more, hosts Spain were now in danger of going out themselves – they'd be crashing out early if Northern Ireland won by two goals – so had even more reason to grind the Northern Irish down. *La Roja* set about it straight away, piling men forwards.

Then, on the hour, came disaster for Northern Ireland. Defender Mal Donaghy was sent off harshly after he and José Camacho had a brief skirmish near the touchline, ending with Donaghy petulantly but harmlessly pushing Camacho. Perhaps damning for the Belfast man was the fact it happened right under the nose of the Peruvian linesman, who seemed to instruct the referee to dismiss Donaghy. Bingham didn't even see what had happened and was seen frustratingly asking his player, 'What did you do?' as he trudged off.

Like so often happens when a team goes down to ten men, it actually served to galvanise Northern Ireland. It was all-out defence for the remainder of the match but Spain's attacks lacked the incisive quality needed, and when they did fashion an opening the evergreen Jennings repelled all comers. Northern Ireland held on for an historic 1-0 win, and were through to the next round – as group winners to boot. And so as not to be rude to their hosts, the scoreline meant that Spain also progressed as runners-up over Yugoslavia on goal difference. A happy coincidence, rather than any kind of Gijón-esque skulduggery.

For the players it was party time. They weren't expected to make it to the World Cup, let alone win their group, and the Northern Irish FA had already booked their flights home.

Bingham was quick to ensure the players didn't overdo it, but after some hasty calls to change their travel arrangements allowed them to enjoy a night of celebrations. Armstrong, however, was absent, at least at the beginning. He was selected for a drug test and was so dehydrated he'd lost over half a stone in the Valencian heat and couldn't urinate until he'd spent an hour drinking water. When he was finally reunited with his team-mates, it wasn't water he was drinking.

The tournament ended in the second round for Northern Ireland. A 2-2 draw with that Austrian side who'd embarrassed themselves was followed up by a disappointing 4-1 loss to France, who went through to the semis. It might have been a different story had O'Neill not had an early strike preposterously ruled out. Even so, the team were welcomed back as heroes, and Bingham's boys would return four years later in Mexico. But the Green and White Army haven't had a World Cup night as memorable as that one in Valencia in 1982 since.

1982: History and Harm in Seville

Thursday, 8 July 1982
Estadio Ramón Sánchez-Pizjuán
Seville, Spain

After two World Cups where the places in the final were decided by whoever had finished top in the second group stage, 1982 saw a welcome return of proper semi-finals for the first time in 12 years. The final four was an all-European affair. Italy and Poland had topped their respective groups in the second phase and met each other in Barcelona, where Italy claimed a comfortable 2-0 win. Later that same evening, West Germany and France met in Seville to decide who would face them. The match that ensued couldn't have been a greater advert for semi-finals if FIFA had scripted it themselves.

Despite both reaching the latter stage of the tournament, neither side had truly impressed on their way to getting there. West Germany's route to the semis was understandably overshadowed by that disgraceful encounter with Austria, while France had only managed second in their first group behind England, and cruised past Northern Ireland and the Austrians in by far the easiest of the second groups. Still, these were teams with undeniable talent in their ranks, and it felt inevitable that someone would eventually light the blue touch paper.

The pre-game narrative installed the Germans as favourites. They were European champions, after all. But their star man, Karl-Heinz Rummenigge, started on the bench, nursing a hamstring injury. A boost for the French, perhaps? It didn't seem that way from kick-off. West Germany dominated, spearheaded by the fantastic Cologne winger Pierre Littbarski, given that first name because his parents loved France so much when visiting there on holiday. Their son didn't share the same regard. He was at the centre of a number of early German attacks on the French goal, and clattered the crossbar with a free kick from 20 yards. In the 17th minute he went one better, drilling in a rebound from the edge of the box to put his team one up.

The French were undeterred, and ten minutes later they had the chance to equalise from the spot after Dominique Rocheteau was bundled over in the box. Michel Platini's worryingly long run-up proved no cause for concern as he sent keeper Toni Schumacher the wrong way and side-footed it into the corner.

Seemingly, this moment got Schumacher's blood boiling. The goalkeeper was renowned for his hot temper. After losses with his club, Cologne, he was known to punch sandbags until his knuckles bled. That version of him reared its head after France's equaliser, seizing every opportunity to unsettle his opponents. After collecting a pass in the box, he threw himself forward to clatter into Platini's legs. Then he pinned Didier Six to the ground by landing on him while claiming a cross. Everyone else on the pitch followed Schumacher's example, both sides exchanging petty fouls as tempers frayed. The half-time whistle brought a chance to cool down, the match still tied at 1-1.

The vitriol on the pitch by no means disrupted the quality of the game, though. There were too many stars on show for that to happen, and both teams attacked with purpose. In the 50th minute, Patrick Battiston was brought on, the defender tasked with playing out of position in midfield to replace the injured Bernard Genghini. Within 60 seconds he showed how versatile he was by marauding forward on a slaloming run before firing a shot wide. France were gaining the upper hand.

After Rocheteau had a goal disallowed for a dubious challenge in the build-up, *Les Bleus* had a golden chance to take the lead. Platini launched a long ball to Battiston, who'd magnificently sliced through the centre of the German defence with his run. Schumacher surged out to meet him and close the angles, and the Frenchman was only able to guide the ball wide of the post.

Tragically, that was not the end of the story. The shot-stopper had sprinted at full pelt to prevent Battiston having a clear shot at goal, and just after the substitute had made contact with the ball, Schumacher jumped into him, clattering him to the ground just inside the box as the German's knee and hip made devastating contact with Battiston's head. He lay flat on his back, his clenched fist hovering above his chest before dropping lifelessly. Two of his teeth lay on the turf around him. It didn't look good.

Ten minutes after coming on, Battiston left the field on a stretcher, drifting in and out of consciousness. The French players gesticulated angrily at the referee, rightfully claiming that they should have a penalty and that Schumacher should see red. But, like most of the millions watching on TV, Dutch referee Charles Corver hadn't seen the incident, his eyes instead drawn to watching Battiston's shot drift just wide of the post. There would be no penalty. There would be no red card. There wouldn't even be a yellow. Schumacher played on.

Despite this harrowing incident, France remained the side in ascendancy. They pushed further forward in search of a winner. As the game crept towards 90 minutes, despite it being nearly 11pm, the temperature inside the stadium was still a sweltering 35ºC. And the French had used their last sub to replace Battiston – they wanted it over there and then.

The full-time whistle arrived before they could get over the line, 20-year-old right-back Manuel Amoron having rattled the crossbar just moments before. Then in extra time, and in spite of Battiston's injury, the match cemented itself as one of the World Cup's best.

Nothing much changed in the first half of the extra 30. France redoubled their efforts to break down the German defence, and just two minutes in succeeded with a stunning goal. A free kick from the right wing ballooned off the head of Wolfgang Dremmler and came down invitingly for centre-back Marius Trésor, gifted a bizarre amount of space on the penalty spot. With the ancient maxim 'put your foot through it' ringing in his ears, Trésor produced a lethal volley and fired the ball high into Schumacher's net. *Les Bleus* finally had their breakthrough.

West Germany needed to change something. In the 97th minute, manager Jupp Derwall rolled the dice on his not-yet-fit talisman Rummenigge. The substitution hardly had the desired immediate effect, as 60 seconds later Alain Giresse rifled a shot in off the post from the edge of the box. France were 3-1 up, and it looked for all the world like they were heading into the final.

They slowed their pace of play, looking to protect their convincing lead. Thousands of French fans rejoiced in chanting 'Ole!' every time their team made a pass. But they couldn't keep Rummenigge quiet for long. He deftly turned in a Littbarski cross just before the midway point to get West Germany back in the game.

Die Mannschaft came on strong as the second period of extra time got under way, with France tiring and hoping to see out the win. They could barely see out three minutes as the Germans decided to one-up Trésor's stunner from earlier and score an even better goal. Littbarski was released down the left wing, going out wide to try and find a way around France's blue bus at the back. He pinged a cross over to the far post for Horst Hrubesch to head the ball back towards the centre of the box. There, Klaus Fischer, his back to goal, was waiting to pounce. The forward contorted his body in an instant to acrobatically leap into an overhead kick. French keeper Jean-Luc Ettori could only watch as the ball flew into his top corner; 3-3.

The tide had well and truly turned. Not only were West Germany now level, they used the remaining ten minutes to pin an exhausted France back further and further in pursuit of a winner. Fischer came closest, unleashing a long-range effort that sailed just wide of Ettori's post. This time, France did manage to hold on to what they had. The match, for the first time in World Cup history, was heading for a penalty shoot-out.

The Germans are nowadays rightly feared for their fantastic record from 12 yards. But in 1982 their only previous experience came from the final of the Euros six years prior, when they were beaten by Czechoslovakia, a certain Antonín Panenka dinking the ball over Sepp Maier to give his side the title. France, meanwhile, had never participated in a competitive shoot-out.

The first five kicks were flawless, leaving France 3-2 up. Then the Germans blinked first. Uli Stielike's tame penalty was saved comfortably by Ettori, who today would likely have been penalised for coming off his line too early. But Didier Six spurned the chance to give *Les Bleus* a two-goal cushion, rolling an even lamer effort into the grateful grasp of Schumacher. Littbarski made it 3-3, before star men Platini and Rummenigge both converted their efforts to take the shoot-out to sudden death.

The demise of French hopes of making the final certainly was sudden. Left-back Maxime Bossis, like Six before him, rolled a weak effort towards goal and Schumacher guessed right. Hrubesch stepped up and calmly dispatched West Germany's final kick. They were into the final. The French players collapsed in devastation.

Despite the sensational footballing rollercoaster that had been played out in Seville, the Battiston incident was the thing most focused on in the aftermath. 'We have been eliminated brutally,' lamented France manager Michel Hidalgo. Battiston had been taken straight to hospital after his injury, where it was discovered alongside the lost teeth that he had broken three ribs, damaged his spine, and briefly slipped into a coma. In his post-match interview, Schumacher was told that Battiston had two teeth knocked out. His response was almost as brutal as the original challenge, retorting, 'If that's all that's wrong with him, I'll pay for the crowns.'

In fairness to the German keeper, on finding out how seriously injured Battiston was, he visited the Frenchman in hospital to apologise personally. That didn't stop him coming top in a French newspaper poll a year later asking who the most hated man in France was, beating Adolf Hitler into second place.

The French were understandably aggrieved, but two years later tasted glory by winning the European Championship on home soil, a rejuvenated Battiston a key part of the side. In later years, more attempts have been made to refocus memories of that night in Seville to the astonishing game of football that played out rather than Schumacher's one-man *blitzkrieg* on Battiston. Even Platini, who was terrified at the time that his team-mate might be dead, has shifted his focus. 'In the heat of the action, I felt a profound sense of injustice after Schumacher's foul, but now I remember that match as one of the most thrilling moments of my life,' he remembered. 'For me, no book or film or play could ever recapture the way I felt that day. It was so complete, so strong, so fabulous.'

1982: Resurgent Rossi and Tearful Tardelli

Sunday, 11 July 1982
Santiago Bernabéu Stadium
Madrid, Spain

Thanks to Schumacher and the Disgrace of Gijón, West Germany entered the final as everyone's least favourite team. There was overwhelming support for Italy – and hatred towards the Germans – among the Spanish supporters that made up the majority of the 90,000-strong crowd in Real Madrid's Bernabéu. More worryingly for them, Italy were their bogey team. Since the conclusion of the Second World War, they'd only managed to defeat the *Azzurri* once in eight meetings.

But just like their opponents, the Italians had started their tournament in underwhelming fashion. Drawn into a supposedly straightforward group alongside Poland, Cameroon and Peru, they hadn't even won a game on their way to qualifying for the next round. Three draws were enough to earn them second place behind Poland and a spot in the second group stage.

The task at hand was gargantuan. To reach the semis, they'd need to squeeze past reigning champions Argentina and tournament favourites Brazil. The South American giants had plundered 16 goals between them to that point. A big ask for an Italian side that had managed only two.

First up were Argentina, featuring a young Diego Maradona in their ranks. Like all great Italian teams, they defended bravely against an early onslaught of Argentinian attacks, before striking twice in ten minutes in the second half to give themselves a comfortable lead. The holders managed a late consolation but couldn't find an equaliser. The first half of the mammoth job on Italy's hands was complete.

Argentina imploded in their next fixture, losing 3-1 to the Brazilians. With that, Italy and Brazil's last clash in the group effectively became a quarter-final. There was one marked difference, though: Brazil, thanks to having beaten Argentina by one more goal than Italy had managed, could draw and still go through. Italy had to win.

This Brazil side was a fearsome one. Free-scoring and stylish, they possessed three of the best players on the planet. Zico was at his peak, bagging goals for fun. The elegant Falcão pulled the strings from the centre of midfield, while the enigmatic Sócrates was the brains behind it all, orchestrating the *Seleção*'s devastating attacks.

To stand any chance of making it to the semis, Italy needed to find something more than they'd shown so far. It came from a most unexpected source.

Paolo Rossi went to the World Cup not so much under a cloud as amid a hurricane of controversy and doubt. The prolific Juventus striker, who went to the 1978 tournament as a youngster and scored three times, had spent the last two years banned from football after being implicated in a match-fixing scandal. Ahead of the World Cup, he returned from his ban to play just three games for Juve and one friendly for the national side. The Italian press heavily criticised coach Enzo Bearzot for taking Rossi, branding him unfit and a waste of a plane ticket.

Rossi hardly repaid his manager's show of faith when the tournament began. He'd started all four of Italy's games prior to the Brazil clash, hadn't come close to scoring, and looked lost for large portions of each match. After a particularly poor performance against Cameroon he was branded 'a ghost aimlessly wandering the field' in one match report.

Still, Bearzot stuck with his man for the pivotal fixture against the Brazilians, though by this point it looked like sheer, dumb stubbornness. It wasn't. Rossi was the focal point of a momentous Italian victory, scoring a sensational hat-trick to give his side an unlikely 3-2 win in a scintillating game that twice saw Brazil equalise before Rossi struck the winner in Barcelona.

He was back firing on all cylinders, netting both goals as Italy swept aside Poland in their semi. By the time the final arrived, he was a terrifying prospect for defenders once more.

The first half in Madrid was typically nervy. Neither side was willing to commit too many men to attack, so goalmouth action was sparse. In the only major flashpoint of the first 45, Antonio Cabrini had a chance to give Italy the lead from the penalty spot but fired his kick wide. Still, at least they had the crowd on their side. Each German player's name was booed by fans when read out prior to kick-off, and every time Schumacher touched the ball you'd have thought you were at a pantomime, such was the hysterical hissing. Italy were effectively playing a home match in Madrid.

To the crowd's delight, the deadlock was finally broken in the 57th minute. The *Azzurri* took a short free kick quickly, catching the German defence off guard. Marco Tardelli shifted the ball out to the right wing and Claudio Gentile, who fired an inviting ball towards the six-yard box. Rossi stepped up yet again for his country, glancing in a header from close range. It was his sixth goal of the tournament, enough to win him the Golden Boot ahead of Rummenigge. Each of his strikes had come in those final three all-important matches.

West Germany's game plan shifted immediately now they'd fallen behind. White shirts flooded forward in search of a leveller. After ten minutes of consistent German attacking, with Italy happy to sit back and defend, an errant Paul Breitner pass towards the Italian box was intercepted by sweeper Gaetano Scirea. He set off on the counter, carrying the ball into the opposition half.

German defenders swarmed back as Italy passed it around the edge of the box, looking for an opening. Scirea, not known for his attacking ability, decided to stay up. He found Tardelli on the edge of the German area, the Juventus man dinking the ball across on to his left foot with his first touch, and with his second sweeping a delicious half volley through a raft of defenders and straight into Schumacher's net.

The Bernabéu exploded. But that was nothing in comparison to Tardelli's celebration. The midfielder was overcome with emotion, and ran towards the Italian bench pumping his fists and screaming 'Gol!' repeatedly. He shook his head almost in disbelief, his tear-filled eyes fiery and wild. It's one of the most iconic images in the tournament's history; a pure, unadulterated display of passion. 'I think in that moment I went beyond madness,' he later said.

The chances of a German comeback akin to the one they'd conjured against France truly died in the 81st minute when another counter attack produced a third goal for the *Azzurri*, Alessandro Altobelli slotting in easily inside the box. It was 3-0 and there was no way back for West Germany.

Breitner made it 3-1 with a consolation two minutes later, but there was no doubting Italy's dominance in the final. The King of Spain presented the trophy to 40-year-old goalkeeper and captain Dino Zoff, who had rolled back the years and been fantastic for his side throughout the tournament, becoming the oldest World Cup winner. Against the odds, Italy had their third title.

1986: The Unemployed Hero

Thursday, 12 June 1986
Estadio Jalisco
Guadalajara, Mexico

Just 16 years after its first visit, in 1986 the World Cup returned to Mexico, the North American nation becoming the first to host the tournament twice. It was originally destined for Colombia in 1986 but the country withdrew from hosting duties on economic grounds after FIFA expanded the tournament to 24 teams in 1982, requiring more stadiums to be built. Of the nations to step in, Mexico proved the most attractive, and the eyes of the football world turned once more in its direction.

For this edition, FIFA again tweaked the format, finally abolishing the unpopular second group stage in favour of a straight knockout. As well as the winners and runners-up from each of the six groups, the four best-performing third-placed teams would join them in a round of 16.

Brazil went into the tournament with high hopes and, as always, one of the favourites. Of their dominant midfield trio of Zico, Falcão and Sócrates, only the latter remained a regular starter. He still conducted proceedings with an effortless swagger from the heart of midfield, while the old legends around him made way for younger, fresher talent. But the loss of those three at their best left Brazil slightly weaker than they had been in 1982. They needed to band together if Mexico was to deliver them any success.

So it was far from ideal when, at a training camp in preparation for the tournament, Brazil manager Telê Santana sent promising young winger Renato Gaúcho home for returning to the team hotel late and, for want of a better word, hammered.

Renato's team-mates weren't happy, in particular first-choice right-back Leandro, who himself had been caught returning late but wasn't subject to the harsh treatment the youngster was. The defender, in a show of solidarity, withdrew himself from Brazil's World Cup squad. Santana's plans were falling apart before a ball had been kicked.

At least Édson, Leandro's back-up, was an adept and experienced full-back who Santana could rely on. He helped keep a clean sheet as the Brazilians edged out Spain 1-0 in their opening group match. Then, ten minutes into their second fixture against

Algeria, he pulled up with a knee injury. Santana brought on Falcão to play out of position in defence for the remainder of the match, but as Brazil only limped to a 1-0 win over the North Africans, it became apparent this was not a long-term solution. It was time to gamble on an entirely unknown quantity.

When Leandro left the squad and Édson stepped into the starting 11, Brazil needed another replacement right-back. There was not a wealth of adequate options to turn to, and eventually fate smiled on Josimar. The 24-year-old was, astonishingly, unemployed when he was called to join up with his national side, and initially thought the call-up was a prank. He'd last played for Brazilian mid-table side Botafogo, but hadn't kicked a ball competitively since his contract with the club had run out in March, three months before the World Cup. He didn't have a job. He had zero international caps. But he did have a spot on the plane to Mexico.

And now, with Édson ruled out, he also had a place in Brazil's starting line-up for their final group match against Northern Ireland in Guadalajara. Billy Bingham's side had to gun for an unlikely win to stand any chance of making it to the knockout stages, and actually created the first few chances of the game. Josimar and his defensive colleagues had to be alert, particularly whenever the dangerous Norman Whiteside was on the ball.

The fill-in right-back looked relatively comfortable making his international debut on the biggest stage of all, aside from a couple of occasions early on when he found himself bounding forwards out of position like an excitable Labrador when Brazil were on the attack. His side took the lead on 15 minutes and continued to push for more goals, keen to rediscover their attacking groove.

As half-time approached, Josimar received the ball on the right wing just inside the opposition half. He took two touches forward before slowing to look up at his options in the box. Striker Wálter Casagrande was in a fantastic position to sneak behind the Irish defence and nod in any potential cross. Josimar completely ignored him. You only make your international debut once. The rookie from Rio swung his right leg back like a lumberjack's axe and let rip with a diagonal thunderbolt from 30 yards. With laser-guided precision it flew straight into the top corner, past a dumbstruck Pat Jennings. The legendary keeper was celebrating his 41st birthday that day. Some present.

Josimar went off on his own personal lap of honour, arms aloft and running faster than he ever did in a game. This was the pinnacle. 'The Unemployed Hero', as the Brazilian press christened him, had scored an absolute screamer for his country at a World Cup. Nothing could beat that.

Except maybe doing it twice. Brazil went on to beat Northern Ireland 3-0 and next faced Poland in the round of 16. Josimar scored the second goal in a 4-0 rout. This one was of a different ilk, but every bit as captivating to watch, the Brazilian jinking past two defenders towards the byline before thumping in a shot from an inconceivable angle. It was yet another marvellous, inexplicable strike, giving the full-back his second goal in as many games. The only rational course of action from his position was to cross, but as he showed in the previous match, he wasn't a fan of crossing. Josimar and Brazil went on to the quarters.

After the tournament, he was an overnight celebrity in his home country. Botafogo re-signed him and he picked up another 13 caps for the *Seleção* over the next two years. An ill-fated move to Sevilla followed, and Josimar's career tailed off as the defender enjoyed his newfound fame by womanising and drinking and snorting everything in sight. 'The blondes came and the training went,' as he put it himself.

Josimar never could regain the heights of those two marvellous, magical moments in Mexico, and by the time the 1990 World Cup rolled around his association with the national team was dead in the water. But he did have one more part to play at football's greatest tournament, as Brazil prepared for their tantalising quarter-final with France.

1986: France, Brazil and an All-Time Classic
Saturday, 21 June 1986
Estadio Jalisco
Guadalajara, Mexico

The French went to Mexico looking to put the demons of four years earlier behind them. After hosting and winning the Euros in 1984, *Les Bleus* finally had a major title under their belt and arrived at the 1986 tournament as one of the favourites.

This was in no small part down to their quite sensational midfield, known as 'le carré magique' (the magic square). Essentially a diamond at the centre of a 4-4-2 formation, France had found perfect balance in the middle of the park. At the base, the bruising Luis Fernández broke up attacks with extreme prejudice and shifted play forwards, the tireless Jean Tigana would move the ball from defence to attack at speed, and the deft, technical talents of Alain Giresse and Michel Platini more often than not provided a killer blow to the opposition.

Yet at this point things had rarely gone to plan in France's long history at the World Cup, and 1986 proved no different as the European champions started slowly. They needed a late winner from the young Jean-Pierre Papin to edge past debutants Canada, before the Soviet Union held them to a draw. A 3-0 win over Hungary wasn't enough to claim top spot in the group, and France finished second on goal difference. Instead of the Belgium side they'd battered 5-0 at the Euros, they'd be facing reigning champions Italy in the last 16.

Rather than the close, battling encounter pundits predicted, France controlled proceedings as they cruised to a comfortable 2-0 win. Just like Brazil, they were waking up at exactly the right time, ready for the two to face off in a monumental head-to-head quarter-final, producing heaps of drama and a healthy dose of genius as the 'Brazilians of Europe' faced off against the Brazilians of Brazil.

The South Americans were right at home from the start, having played all four of their matches so far in Guadalajara. France were undeterred, and from the off the match was end to end. Both sides were purring, Brazil in particular linking together in some flamboyant, fluid passing moves early on. Then, with just over a quarter of an hour gone, French keeper Joël Bats launched a goal kick deep into the Brazil half. Imperious centre-back Júlio César rose to guide the ball to Josimar, who controlled with his chest.

A few fast passes later, Brazil were nearing the French box. Josimar, who naturally had chosen to remain forward, found Müller. The Germanically named forward rapidly exchanged passes with Júnior twice, completely flummoxing the defence and giving his colleague the opportunity to lay the ball off to Careca on the edge of the box. He fired first time over the onrushing Bats and high into Frenchman's net. It was a stunning team goal, created from nowhere, and Brazil had the lead.

Fifteen minutes later they nearly doubled it, but Müller was only able to strike the post after receiving Careca's inch-perfect ball. After a period when it looked like Brazil might run riot, this moment seemed to be a catalyst for France turning the game on its head. Soon their mighty midfield was dancing up the pitch once more and Platini, celebrating his 31st birthday in style, tapped in a deflected cross five minutes before half-time. Brazil had conceded their first goal of the World Cup, and the scores were level.

The second half continued in the same exhilarating fashion but neither side could make the breakthrough. In the 70th minute Telê Santana decided it was time to unleash a half-fit Zico as Brazil pushed for a winner, and the substitution paid near-instant dividends. The ever-dangerous superstar threaded a superb through ball with the outside of his right boot to Branco, who had wriggled free in the box. Bats knew he had to do something. He charged out to meet his man, who in turn knocked the ball past the French keeper and waited for the contact. Bats couldn't stop himself and bundled into Branco. The Brazilians had a penalty.

Regular taker Sócrates stepped up and placed the ball. Then he promptly walked away and Zico, who'd only had three touches since coming on, approached. The ensuing effort was poor and Bats was able to save comfortably. Zico had given his nation the chance to win the game, then spurned that chance himself seconds later.

He again had the opportunity to win it five minutes before the final whistle. Josimar, deciding that he should probably cross rather than shoot on this occasion, delivered a lovely ball on to Zico's head, unmarked just six yards from goal. His header was strong but Bats took cat-like reflexes to the next level to save the effort from point-blank range. France survived Brazil's late onslaught, and the match headed for extra time.

There was to be no slowing down and waiting for penalties in this encounter, even if players were intermittently dropping to the ground with cramp. Still the sides went at each other, relentlessly attacking in a frankly mesmerising display of skill and sheer determination to win. And then, in the 116th minute, France were served up a bitter taste of déjà vu.

Brazil wasted a corner by taking it so quickly they'd barely had chance to get anyone in the box to attack it. Bats punched the ball out to Amoros and France broke quickly. Platini, with one lazy, stroked pass, left the entire Brazilian defence stranded as late sub Bruno Bellone, with fresher legs than anyone on the pitch, surged into the opposition half to meet it. As the forward bore down on goal, he was so clean through that TV cameras couldn't pick up a single Brazilian outfielder in the same frame as him.

Carlos sprinted out of his box to meet him, though admittedly with a lot less bloodlust than Toni Schumacher four years earlier. Bellone saw him coming and knocked the ball past him in order to round him and tap into an open net. France were about to win, until Carlos decided to take evasive action by diving in front of Bellone and with two hands pushed him off balance. Bellone stumbled over his feet as he attempted to regain control of the ball, but by this time Brazil had men back and were able to clear.

It was agonising for France, but at least Brazil would lose their goalkeeper ahead of the seemingly inevitable penalty shoot-out. Maybe it wouldn't come to that if France could score from the free kick when play was pulled back. But no. Romanian ref Ioan Igna waved play on. No free kick for France, and no card for Carlos – of any colour. Worse still, Brazil now looked to take advantage of the state of shock the French found themselves in, and marched upfield on the counter. Careca bombed down the right wing and put a low ball in across the box, presenting an open goal neatly on a plate for Sócrates. Maybe the Brazilian great felt sorry for France, because the usually balletic star tripped over his own feet and failed to make contact. It was going to penalties.

The French would have been immediately reminded of their harsh semi-final exit at the hands of the Germans four years earlier. For Brazil, it was their first taste of shoot-out drama. Sócrates volunteered to take their first kick. He'd converted a gorgeous penalty against Poland in the previous round with a one-step run-up and tried the same again, but Bats was wise to him and saved brilliantly to deny the idiosyncratic superstar scoring with his final kick in a Brazil shirt. Advantage France.

The next four penalties were flawless, including a moment of redemption for Zico, who finally saw one of his shots fly past the superb Bats. With France's third kick came Brazil's moment to feel aggrieved, justice for the earlier very directly served. Bellone, the man Carlos had so cynically denied, stepped up to face him once more. The Frenchman clattered his penalty against the post. Carlos had guessed right, but he soon wished he hadn't. The ball ricocheted away from goal and smacked into the back of the diving keeper, then trickled into the net. The rules state this is considered a miss and shouldn't count. But it happened so fast the referee let the goal stand. That, or he was making up for his earlier mistake.

Brazil scored their next penalty to make it 3-3, but France still had one kick in hand. Mr Reliable, Platini, stepped up for France and spooned the ball high over the bar, leaving fans and team-mates in disbelief. The French captain would have been the most relieved man in Mexico as he watched Bats produce yet another magnificent save to deny César from Brazil's next kick. Fernández put his away with aplomb to give *Les Bleus* the victory after a breathless, breathtaking afternoon that *The Observer*'s Hugh McIlvanney described as 'perhaps the most extraordinary contest in the history of the World Cup'.

The win set up a semi-final rematch with West Germany and the chance for France to right the wrongs of that night in Seville four years ago. But again the Germans triumphed after a much less dramatic encounter, winning 2-0. France went on to finish third, defeating Belgium 4-2 in the play-off. In the years that followed, age blunted the edges of France's magic square. Without them, the team entered a torrid era that saw them fail to qualify for the next two World Cups. That tremendous French team of the 1980s may never have made it to a final but they played their part in two of the tournament's greatest games.

1986: The Hand of God
Sunday, 22 June 1986
Estadio Azteca
Mexico City, Mexico

Speaking of great games, England fans of a certain vintage will have no problem remembering this particular clash the day after France and Brazil's epic battle, forever etched as it is in the minds of Three Lions supporters everywhere as a stark reminder that sometimes, football really isn't fair. But it's also a perfect example of the audacity, guile, and sheer determination to win of one Diego Armando Maradona.

The 1986 World Cup had been one of slow-burning hope for England. They'd started their campaign with a loss to Portugal followed by a disappointing goalless draw with Morocco, a game in which Ray Wilkins received a bizarre red card for throwing the ball towards the referee. A 3-0 win in their third group game against

Poland, courtesy a hat-trick from an in-form Gary Lineker (who would go on to claim the tournament's Golden Boot), saw them progress to the knockout stages, where Paraguay were comfortably dispatched by the same scoreline. There was a consensus that things were coming together for England at the right time.

Meanwhile, in the Argentina camp, in their captain Maradona they had the rather significant advantage of the world's best footballer. He was putting in weekly awe-inspiring performances for Napoli in Serie A ahead of the World Cup, but it was the national team – his one true footballing love – that he often saved his most spellbinding displays for. And he and Argentina had certainly raced out of the traps in 1986. He set up all three goals in their 3-1 defeat of South Korea in their opening match as they went on to win a group that also featured reigning world champions Italy. A 1-0 win against Uruguay in the last 16 set them on their way to the quarter-finals.

It was there that they would meet England. Naturally, given the context surrounding the game, passionate patriotic sentiments were running high in both nations. As soon as the tie was confirmed after England's last-16 victory over Paraguay, the Falklands War of 1982 loomed over the pre-match build-up. England fans present at that match chanted 'bring on the Argies, we want another war' before the full-time whistle had even been blown. Ahead of the tie, the *Daily Mirror*'s front page simply read 'HIGH NOON', just in case anyone wasn't already certain that the match was akin to a spaghetti western-style showdown. Meanwhile, in Argentina, a senior politician submitted an ultimately rejected request to FIFA for there to be a formal minute's silence for the Argentine soldiers lost in the Falklands before kick-off.

The parallels constantly drawn in the press of both countries between the conflict and what was simply a football match were so prevalent that the players began to get frustrated. Maradona, when asked for the umpteenth time ahead of the match whether the war would be in the minds of the players on the pitch, snarled, 'Look, the Argentina team doesn't carry rifles, nor arms, nor ammunition. We came here only to play football.'

However, even in a footballing context, these two had history. The last time they'd met competitively was at the 1966 World Cup in that infamously dirty quarter-final, after which Alf Ramsey had branded the Argentinians as 'animals'. Whether you put it down to the Falklands War or their footballing past, no love was lost between the two teams.

As such, Argentina coach Carlos Bilardo was leaving nothing to chance when it came to preparations. After seeing his team labour against Uruguay, he felt the cotton blue away shirts that Le Coq Sportif had provided were too heavy for the searing Mexican heat. He requested some lighter shirts, but the kit suppliers were unable to make any at such short notice. Instead, it was left to one of Bilardo's coaches to trawl the sports shops of Mexico City to try and find something suitable. He returned with a choice of two blue kits. Incidentally, it was *El Diego* himself who chose the kit Argentina would wear, quipping in his own inimitably egotistical way, 'That's a nice jersey. We'll beat England in that.' Argentine FA badges and Le Coq Sportif logos were hastily sewn on, and some makeshift squad numbers were ironed on to the backs.

No matter how much the players might have tried to position the focus away from the game being a war, come matchday the combative atmosphere was plain to see. Some Argentina fans wore shirts adorned with the words 'Las Malvinas son Argentinas' (the Falklands are Argentine) and burned Union flags, while England supporters goaded their rivals about the result of the war. Expecting crowd trouble during the match, the Mexican authorities had sent some 20,000 riot police and troops to control the event. But such a high volume of men in uniforms only added to the hostile feel as the game kicked off.

The first 45 minutes were cagey. Argentina dominated possession but England's defence held tight, with centre-back Terry Fenwick receiving a yellow card for flooring Maradona inside ten minutes. Aside from this, the Three Lions didn't pay any special attention to Argentina's star man, focusing on defending as a unit rather than man-marking any individuals. The players trooped in for half-time having provided a largely uneventful first half of football.

Conversely, the second half would provide enough drama to keep journalists writing about it for decades to come. The 51st minute gave us the moment that England fans have never quite gotten over; the photograph that stands to this day as one of the most recognisable in the history of the sport; the goal that has an entire Wikipedia page dedicated to it.

Some neat passing play culminating in an incisive run from Maradona saw him with the ball at his feet near the edge of the England box. He then attempted to play an uncharacteristically sloppy one-two with team-mate Jorge Valdano, who was unable to control the misplaced pass. Valdano flicked the ball up towards England midfielder Steve Hodge. In a moment that has surely been replayed in his mind a thousand times over, Hodge swung his left boot wildly at the ball to clear it, but fatally mistimed the kick. It looped up and into the box, where the onrushing Peter Shilton and Maradona were both waiting to meet it.

Now, logic suggests that in this situation, six-foot goalkeeper Shilton would comfortably deal with the ball ahead of Maradona, who was seven inches shorter than him. This, of course, didn't happen. The England keeper seemed to only hop slightly off the ground, while Maradona leapt high in the air. In fairness to Shilton, he may well have felt it would only take his miniature jump to reach above Maradona's head to knock the ball away. But Maradona didn't use his head. His arm stretched high above him, punching the ball beyond Shilton and into the net. Referee Ali Bin Nasser noticeably looked towards his linesman – Bulgarian Bogdan Dochev – but neither signalled for the goal to be disallowed.

England players raced towards the referee, protesting the handball. On commentary, Barry Davies initially thought they were complaining that the goal was offside. Meanwhile, Maradona had run off to the side of the pitch in celebration. It took a while for his team-mates to join him. He later explained, 'I was waiting for my team-mates to embrace me and no one came. I told them, "Come and hug me, or the referee isn't going to allow it."'

He needn't have worried. The goal stood and Argentina were 1-0 up. After the game, Maradona inadvertently gave the most famous illegal goal in football its name by describing it as being scored 'a little with the head of Maradona and a little with the hand of God'. In Argentina, people saw it as revenge. Not for the Falklands, but for what they deemed the unfair sending off of Antonio Rattín in 1966. The English media took a resolutely different stance. The back page of the following day's *Daily Mirror* featured a large photo of a celebrating Maradona, stamped with the word 'CHEAT', and described the goal as 'one of the biggest injustices' in World Cup history.

Fingers were pointed at the match officials. In his post-match interview, England manager Bobby Robson said, 'You don't expect decisions like that at World Cup level.' Referee Bin Nasser and linesman Dochev blamed each other for the missed handball. The former claimed that as he was nearer, Dochev should have signalled for the goal to be disallowed, while Dochev himself asserted that as a linesman he had to wait for the call of the senior official on the pitch.

This miscommunication proved very costly for England. The fact that neither Bin Nasser nor Dochev would officiate in a World Cup match again came as little consolation. Always one to stir things up though, Maradona visited Bin Nasser 30 years after the game to present him with an Argentina shirt and described him as an 'eternal friend'.

The Hand of God goal should never have stood; of that there is no question. Many in England will for ever remember Diego Maradona as a cheat for this reason – especially Peter Shilton. Others will recognise in him an unerring desire to win at any cost. Either way, it wasn't the goal that actually beat England that day. That would come less than five minutes later, and this time it would thrust Maradona into the limelight for all the right reasons.

1986: The Goal of the Century

Sunday, 22 June 1986
Estadio Azteca
Mexico City, Mexico

Sorry England fans. We're still at *that* game. The dust had yet to settle on Maradona punching the ball past Shilton beneath the sizzling Mexican sun, but Argentina's number ten was about to make headlines yet again.

After an extended period of England players haranguing the referee for missing Maradona's handball, play resumed. Despite their lead, it was again Argentina applying most of the pressure in the minutes immediately following the restart, clearly pushing for a second rather than resting on their laurels. Not that they were causing the England defence any problems; much like in the first half, Argentina's advances were met with a solid wall of defenders that wouldn't let them get anywhere near the 18-yard box.

That was about to change. A stray pass from Glenn Hoddle during a rare England foray forward gave Argentina possession near the edge of their own box. Within two passes, Maradona had received the ball, still inside his own half. What followed was nothing short of breathtaking as *El Diego* left a desolate path of beaten England players in his wake.

First to fall was Peter Beardsley, who Maradona jinked away from with his very first touch. England fans wouldn't have been worried though; Peter Reid, renowned for his brutal tackling and break-up play in the middle of the park, was next on the scene. One heavy touch was all it took and Maradona was away, leaving Reid to chase but ultimately never get near to catching him (Reid himself later quite accurately described his pursuit as 'like a kid racing his dad in the back garden, knowing he wouldn't be able to get close').

Within two seconds, Maradona was deep inside England's half. Terry Butcher came marauding forward but he committed to what was in truth so obvious an attempted tackle that even the most amateur of Sunday league footballers would have seen it coming. As such, the world's best player had little difficulty in slipping past him.

The unenviable job of being goalkeeper Shilton's last line of outfield defence against Maradona was left to Terry Fenwick. As he advanced just beyond the edge of his own box, he looked like he might actually get close to the Argentina captain. A stunning dummy put paid to that idea as Maradona ran at rapid pace towards the left of the goal, only to shift the ball to the right at the very last second. As he surged past Fenwick's shoulder, the England defender reached his arm out and looked for a moment as if he was about to perform a full-on rugby tackle. He clearly thought better of the idea; perhaps that yellow card he'd earned for flooring Maradona in the first half crossed his mind.

Finally, Shilton – the man who felt more wronged than any other on the pitch by what had happened four minutes earlier – had his chance to stop this footballing magician's mesmerising run. Rushing off his line, he was powerless to succumb to yet another bewitching dummy. Maradona opened his body to shoot on his left, leaving Shilton to commit to a save while he instead took an extra touch before poking the ball into a now-empty net. A back-pedalling Butcher scythed him down just after in a challenge that would surely have been a penalty had the ball not already rolled in. Maradona didn't care. He got back to his feet and sprinted off to the corner flag before collapsing to his knees; it was seemingly a goal so good that it knocked the man who scored it off his feet.

His reaction, though, was nothing in comparison to that of Víctor Hugo Morales, who was commentating for Argentinian television,

'Dear God, long live football! What a goal! Diegoooo! Maradonaaaa! I'm so sorry, it brings tears to your eyes. Maradona, in an unforgettable run, in a move for all time ... You barrel-chested cosmic phenomenon ... From what planet did you come to leave so many Englishmen in your wake, to turn the country into a clenched fist screaming for Argentina?'

The clip of Morales's commentary has become legendary in Argentina in its own right. The passion in his voice perfectly echoed the way many Argentinians felt about getting one over on the English. The poetry in his words and the sheer excitement in his tone reflected just what it meant. It's worth mentioning that Morales wasn't even Argentinian; he was from Uruguay, one of Argentina's biggest rivals. The majesty of Maradona's magic feet had made him forget that, instead leading him to wax lyrical about the little genius.

This, it seemed, was a goal that transcended rivalries and footballing boundaries. Even the aggrieved Bobby Robson, still angry about Maradona's first strike, conceded that his second was 'a brilliant goal' in his post-match interview. 'I didn't like it, but I had to admire it,' he said.

Robson's side had rallied towards the end of the match, and a Gary Lineker effort to make it 2-1 in the 81st minute gave them some hope, but Argentina would ultimately see the game out with minimal fuss to progress to the semi-finals. And bitter though they were, the English press acknowledged Maradona's sorcery too, with the *Daily Mirror* proclaiming that he 'showed why he is the greatest of them all'.

Like the Hand of God, Maradona's second goal was a moment that very quickly passed into footballing folklore. In 2002, it was overwhelmingly voted as the 'Goal of the Century' in a poll conducted by FIFA. The man himself later gave some rather dubious credit to the England players he scored it against. 'I don't think I could have done it against any other team because they all used to knock you down,' Maradona said of his English opponents. 'They are probably the noblest in the world.' This surely came as a great comfort to the players who tried and failed to stop him that day.

There is no doubting that the goal is *the* iconic Maradona moment in his native Argentina. Fans have made pilgrimages to the National Football Museum in Manchester just to view the shirt he wore in that game (it has been intermittently on display there since being donated by Steve Hodge – the England player who essentially assisted the Hand of God goal with his wayward clearance – who swapped shirts with Maradona after the match). In 2020, following his death, there were very serious calls for a still from his run that led to the goal to be featured on an Argentinian bank note, such is its significance there.

Eleven touches. Eleven seconds. That was all it took for Diego Maradona to score the greatest goal in World Cup – and probably all of football – history.

1986: Magic Maradona Inspires Argentina to Glory

Sunday, 29 June 1986
Estadio Azteca
Mexico City, Mexico

Maradona's virtuosity had seen Argentina safely into the semis. There, he put on a repeat performance against Belgium, scoring two fantastic – although nowhere near as headline-grabbing – goals to fire his team into the final with a 2-0 win. West Germany were waiting for them after defeating France. In a World Cup punctuated by sensational matches, the final followed suit.

That in itself was a surprise. The Germans, now managed by the legendary Franz Beckenbauer, were an ageing team that didn't seem to possess the killer instinct they had on their run to the final four years earlier. Unlike the Argentines who romped through with convincing grace, their campaign had been underwhelming. They'd only managed second in their group behind Denmark, had just about squeezed past Morocco in the last 16 with a last-minute winner, and needed penalties to beat Mexico in the quarters after a borefest of a game. It was only in the 2-0 semi-final win over

France that they'd looked dangerous. As such, Argentina were heavy favourites.

West Germany's approach as the game kicked off in front of 114,600 spectators in the Azteca was typically stolid and pragmatic. Beckenbauer had given special instructions to Lothar Matthäus to focus his attention on Maradona, and the Argentine genius was largely suffocated in the early stages of the game, subject to some very full-blooded tackles each time he came into possession.

Midway through the first half, Maradona received the ball on the right wing near the German box, and managed a cheeky back-heel pass before being clattered to the ground cynically. He found José Luis Cuciuffo, a centre-back inexplicably wearing the number nine shirt who'd forayed forwards. He was subject to the same fate as Maradona before he could cross, and the referee awarded a free kick.

The magnificent Jorge Burruchaga delivered a swinging ball to the far post, where defender José Luis Brown was waiting. The centre-back, whose ancestry derived from Scotland and Ireland, was without a club when taken to the World Cup to replace the great Daniel Passarella, who missed out with a sudden illness. Brown rose highest to head in his first and only international goal, giving Argentina the lead in football's biggest match.

Aside from this, the rest of the first half was largely uneventful. When Argentina doubled their lead in the 55th minute through Jorge Valdano, the final showed no signs of matching some of the tournament's earlier games for drama. The South Americans were well on their way to a second World Cup crown, and were doing so without breaking a sweat. But you never can write off the Germans.

Two minutes after Norbert Eder prevented Burruchaga from making it three from close range by nicking the ball off his toe, West Germany had a moment of respite with a corner kick up the other end. With 74 minutes gone, Rudi Völler rose to meet Andreas Brehme's delivery and nodded across goal, where captain Rummenigge slid in to nab one back for *Die Mannschaft*.

There was still time, and Beckenbauer's men started to attack with a renewed intensity now the deficit was reduced to one. Five minutes later they had another corner from the same side. Brehme went over to take it again. Argentina hadn't learned from their earlier mistake because the play was near-identical. A high ball was met in the air and headed towards goal. Völler was waiting this time and flicked in an equaliser off his immaculate perm.

With ten minutes to play, the game had exploded into an end-to-end battle and the stakes couldn't have been higher. In the stands, Argentina fans stood deflated, typified by coach Carlos Bilardo's revelation that he felt 'dead inside' when the goal went in. They were so close. Luckily for them, their players' reaction was markedly different. *La Albiceleste* flooded men forwards to reclaim what they felt was rightfully theirs.

Just a few minutes after Völler's strike, the ball pinballed around a congested midfield. Finally it fell to Maradona on the halfway line. As three German players surrounded him, the little genius decided there was no time for pleasantries. He didn't fancy getting clattered to the ground again. So instead he hit it first time, stroking the ball precisely into the path of Burruchaga, who was surging through the midfield and defence towards the German goal.

With a wealth of space ahead of him, Burruchaga took two heavy touches and sprinted rapidly. He was far too fast for an onrushing Toni Schumacher to reach and commit another act of GBH on. With the keeper stranded, Burruchaga finished coolly, rolling the ball into the far corner. Argentina had the lead once more, and the Azteca erupted.

Had the Argentinians learned their lesson? In short, no. Still they pushed for more goals. They knew no other way to play. Maradona nearly grabbed one for himself when he jinked through the defence with 60 seconds left on the clock, but was felled before he had chance to shoot. Even from the ensuing free kick he didn't hold back and had a go at goal, forcing a good save from Schumacher.

Ultimately, West Germany had nothing left. Argentina won the World Cup for a second time after a truly phenomenal finale. There were jubilant scenes, including a handful of fans who managed to evade the rather forceful Mexican police to celebrate on the pitch.

The trophy was presented to Maradona, the man who had done more than any other had ever done to earn a winner's medal. He'd won twice as many fouls as any other player and attempted three times as many dribbles. Most importantly, of his side's 14 goals in the tournament, he'd scored five and assisted five. His performance throughout had been nothing short of artful, delivering moments of high drama, controversy and brilliance in equal measure – a perfect distillation of everything that makes football so great. Mexico '86 was truly Maradona's World Cup.

1990: Cameroon Shock the Holders

Friday, 8 June 1990
San Siro
Milan, Italy

After those two deliriously exciting World Cups in the 1980s, a new decade saw Italy welcome the tournament to its shores for the first time since Mussolini had exerted his influence over the event back in 1934. Italia '90, despite being so fondly remembered by England fans for their own team's exploits, was less of a rollercoaster spectacle. In fact, with an average of just over two goals per game, it ranks as the lowest-scoring edition of the World Cup so far.

But football isn't all about goals, necessarily, and the 1990 tournament had a handy knack of delivering some quite remarkable stories and shocks. The Republic of Ireland qualified for their first World Cup under Jack Charlton and went all the way to the quarter-finals, defeating Romania in a memorable penalty shoot-out in the process. There was the unlikely story of Salvatore 'Totò' Schillaci, who went to his home World Cup with Italy as their fifth-choice striker and returned with a Golden Boot. And then there was Cameroon, who started their epic tale in the very first match against reigning champions Argentina.

The Indomitable Lions were giants of African football throughout the 1980s. In that time, they'd reached the final of the Africa Cup of Nations three times, winning twice. In their only World Cup appearance, in 1982, they'd been unlucky to miss out on a spot in the knockout stages after drawing all three of their matches, including a 1-1 scoreline with eventual champions Italy.

Still, despite their pedigree back home, the overwhelming prediction was that they'd be swept aside with minimal fuss at the World Cup. This was still a team largely comprised of players from the French second division, and they were suffering an ill-timed spell of poor form ahead of the tournament. Cameroon's president Paul Biya considered this so alarming that he intervened himself, asking talismanic 38-year-old striker Roger Milla to reconsider his international retirement and help the team in Italy. This brought with it its own problems when several senior players voiced their discontent about the country's leader having a say in football affairs. Things were messy, and when the world sat down to watch the opening match of Italia '90, it was expecting a cricket score.

Bordeaux goalkeeper Joseph-Antoine Bell, one of the team's few genuine stars, had been one of the most vocal critics. He also said in an interview published the day before the game that his country would stand no chance against Argentina, even with him between the sticks. When it came to matchday, he wasn't. Dropping such a divisive personality seemingly worked wonders for the squad's belief. 'We absolutely wanted to win this match,' remembered Emmanuel Maboang, who came off the bench that day. 'We had no doubt, because we knew each other so well. We said that, apart from Maradona, the rest of the team were beatable.'

During the pre-match warm-ups on a hot Friday evening in Milan, many of the Cameroon players stopped what they were doing when the Argentina team emerged for their own preparations, in order to take photographs with Diego Maradona. 'He was our idol,' said Maboang.

The Cameroonians' fondness for Maradona clearly dissipated as soon as the game kicked off. It became apparent that their Russian manager Valeri Nepomnyashchy had a game plan to deal with the world champions: namely, kick them off the park at every opportunity.

From the get-go, the Africans set about roughing up their opponents to make the game difficult for them in every way possible. Naturally, Argentina's captain came in for special attention. 'Cameroon neutralised Maradona, mainly by kicking him,' wrote Matthew Engel in his match report for *The Guardian*.

The strategy was working. At half-time the scores remained goalless and Cameroon had been good value for it, too. Sure, they were heavy-handed. But they had not simply dug in to prevent Argentina scoring. They rushed forwards incisively on the counter whenever they got the chance, and had come closest to breaking the deadlock with a speedy, direct passing move that required a clearance off the line to prevent them going one up. They were very much in this game.

Disastrously for Cameroon, their chances took a huge hit on the hour. Striker Claudio Caniggia was released down the right wing for Argentina. The Indomitable Lions gave chase and midfielder André Kana-Biyik stumbled into Caniggia, tripping him in the process. French referee Michel Vautrot was quick to brandish a red card. It was a harsh, devastating decision to give for a challenge that had zero intent. Cameroon had committed plenty of fouls worthy of punishment that day, but Kana-Biyik's wasn't one of them.

With Cameroon down to ten men, those dreaming of an unthinkable upset started instead to wish for an unlikely draw. However, as the clock ticked past 67 minutes, they proved that miracles do happen. Argentina had started to bite back in the second half. A foul down the left touchline gave the Cameroonians a free kick adjacent with the 18-yard box.

They sent only two men up to attack it, but that was all they needed. One of those, Cyrille Makanaky, arrived first to the ball in and scooped it high into the air. It proved a rather unorthodox assist. François Omam-Biyik, younger brother of the dismissed André, leaped with Olympic athleticism high above the Argentinian defenders. He couldn't get much power on his header, but managed to direct it towards goal all the same. It caught Nery Pumpido off guard and the goalkeeper lay with his face in the turf after seeing the ball slip through his gloves and into the net. Cameroon had the lead. And they were going to do whatever it took to hold on to it.

Their defiant defending kept the Argentines at bay until the 88th minute. Cameroon had inched forward, hoping to score the match-sealing goal but Caniggia recovered the ball on the edge of his own box and started forward. With space in front of him, he darted to the halfway line, whereupon defender Emmanuel Kundé tried to scythe him down. Caniggia evaded Kundé, so Cameroon tried again. The Argentina forward hurdled another brutal attempted foul but was off balance as he ran on to try and spare his nation's blushes.

Third time was the charm for Cameroon. Benjamin Massing, already on a yellow card, sacrificed himself to save his country's win. He sprinted across Caniggia's path to stop him. Assault would be putting it mildly. Massing effectively tried to take Caniggia's legs off, and was so enthusiastic in his challenge that his own boot flew off in the process. He received a second yellow from Vautrot and walked, though the attack on Caniggia – who, incidentally, was fine – was worthy of five straight reds.

He'd done his bit though. Nine-man Cameroon held on to secure a truly remarkable World Cup win over their illustrious opponents, and at the final whistle the staff and substitutes streamed on to the pitch as though they'd won the whole thing.

The crowd were ecstatic too. The Milanese supporters weren't fans of Maradona thanks to his exploits with Napoli, and so jeered at the Argentina captain every time he touched the ball, and celebrated and cheered fanatically for the Africans. Afterwards, Maradona said he must have 'cured the Italians of racism' because 'the whole stadium was shouting for Cameroon'.

It turned out to be just the start of a sensational campaign for the Indomitable Lions. They topped the group and made it to the quarter-finals. Milla struck four times throughout the tournament as he became the World Cup's oldest goalscorer and delighted fans with his corner flag-dancing celebrations, firmly installing Cameroon as every neutral's favourite team. Thanks to their record-breaking efforts, Italia '90 was a seminal moment for African football, and it hasn't looked back since.

1990: Netherlands, Germany and an Almighty Spat

Sunday, 24 June 1990
San Siro
Milan, Italy

In a World Cup largely punctuated in the group stage by defensive tactics, there was one notable exception. Franz Beckenbauer, leading his West Germany side in a second World Cup, had revitalised *Die Mannschaft*. He introduced a wave of young blood to the squad while retaining the likes of Völler, Brehme and Matthäus. The result was a perfect mix of experience and new talent, and the Germans ran riot from their first match.

They opened their campaign with 4-1 and 5-1 wins over Yugoslavia and the United Arab Emirates respectively, the new striking partnership of Völler and Jürgen Klinsmann scoring five of those goals. A 1-1 draw with Colombia in a relaxed final match was enough to see them comfortably top their group. *Der Kaiser's* men were looking lethal.

On the flip side, the Netherlands were enduring an underwhelming tournament. They arrived in Italy as European champions having won the competition in 1988. What's more, they'd not been to the World Cup in 12 years, so their star-studded team with the likes of Ronald Koeman, Marco van Basten and

Ruud Gullit were expected to prove a point and perform well. But things just hadn't clicked. Shortly before the tournament, the players led a revolt against unpopular manager Thijs Libregts, who was replaced with Ajax coach Leo Beenhakker at short notice instead. The disarrayed Dutch only passed through the groups by virtue of three draws against England, Ireland and Egypt.

As one of the best third-placed teams in the groups, the Netherlands were guaranteed a last-16 fixture against one of the six group winners. And wouldn't you just know it, it was the old enemy.

Despite the fortunes of the two sides going into their clash being markedly opposite, you never could write the Dutch off when playing the Germans. This was the kind of match that everyone wanted to see; a face-off between two great rivals who had produced moments of magic and high drama against each other in the past. Just two years earlier at West Germany's home Euros, the Netherlands had defeated them in the semi-final in Hamburg courtesy of a late Van Basten winner, before going on to beat the Soviet Union in the final in Munich in front of a despairing German crowd. West German efforts to get revenge in qualifying for the 1990 World Cup had also proved fruitless, the sides playing out two hard-fought draws as both earned spots at the tournament. It didn't matter how out of sorts the Netherlands were. They always turned up against Germany.

The match was also played against the backdrop of especially bad blood between the two nations, even by their hot-tempered standards. In their home leg of those aforementioned qualifiers, Dutch fans in Rotterdam unfurled a savage banner reading 'Matthäus-Hitler', comparing the German captain to the Nazi dictator. This unsurprisingly drew a furious reaction from German fans and players alike. Their 1990 game at the San Siro was certain to be volatile.

This encounter began openly, both sides creating early chances. And predictably, both the *Oranje* and *Die Mannschaft* indulged in their fair share of tasty challenges, too. Then, in the 21st minute, Frank Rijkaard lunged into a tackle that set off a scarcely believable chain of events.

Völler controlled a long ball fabulously on the left wing and jinked past two orange shirts to open up the pitch before him. Rijkaard, sensing the danger, decided to take action, and ploughed into the German's leg before he could go any further. It was a cynical one, but an understandable strategic move considering the danger Völler posed.

What wasn't understandable was Rijkaard's reaction to receiving a thoroughly deserved yellow card for the foul. The Dutchman argued briefly with referee Juan Carlos Loustau before running off past Völler and spitting with flawless aim into his perfect perm. The pair exchanged verbals as West Germany waited to take the free kick and Völler accosted Loustau, inviting him to examine the string of phlegm now dangling from his hair. The Argentine official clearly didn't fancy it, and instead booked the German for dissent.

Much more followed. Völler attacked the ensuing free kick but was unable to get a proper contact on the ball and stumbled to the ground, whereupon Rijkaard rushed over to taunt him and even tried to drag him up by the ear. Yet again, the two found themselves in another argument, with Klinsmann rushing over to restrain Völler. Loustau had had enough. A mere 77 seconds had passed between Rijkaard's initial challenge and both him and Völler seeing yellow for a second time. They were off.

As the German stood with his hands on his hips, looking to the skies in search of an answer for how exactly he'd found himself in this position, Rijkaard couldn't resist one parting shot. He ambled over casually to his rival, paused for a second at his side to hock up the contents of his throat, and then spat once more into Völler's curls, who turned to him incensed as Rijkaard jogged off for an early bath. Völler had been subject to the ultimate disrespect – and picked up a red card for himself in the process.

The crowd inside the San Siro exploded into a furnace as both sets of fans bayed for blood. For a second they looked like they might get it when Völler sprinted towards Rijkaard, who was trudging off towards the changing rooms. He looked for all the world like a man possessed with anger, about to exact a punishing retribution on his aggressor. But in a second, those hoping for fisticuffs were disappointed as Völler took the high road and simply ran past the Dutchman and down the tunnel.

Over on Irish TV, co-commentator Eamon Dunphy rather amusingly took the edge off the situation, proclaiming, 'That's bad news for Rudi Völler and even worse news for his hairdresser!' Oddly, though, the edge had been taken off the game somewhat, too. Perhaps players calmed down slightly after seeing the referee would be taking no prisoners, and the flashpoint between Völler and Rijkaard remained the only moment of pure aggression in the match. A lively, attacking affair between the ten-man teams in the second half ended in a solid 2-1 victory for the Germans, who went on to the quarters. Justice had been done in the result, if nothing else.

The aftermath saw 99 per cent of attention directed towards spitgate and the match itself largely ignored. On ITV, pundits waxed lyrical about the state of the modern game. It was revolting. Disgusting. A stain on the sport. Ireland boss Jack Charlton, doing a quick turn on the box before his own side's last-16 match the following day, put it more simply, 'I'd have chinned him.'

As for Völler and Rijkaard, the German remained a class act throughout. Rijkaard apologised, described his actions as inexcusable, and Völler accepted instantly. If that wasn't proof enough of their reconciliation, the pair even posed for an advert for a Dutch butter company years later, resplendent in a pair of cream dressing gowns while enjoying a breakfast together. This one had a happy ending after all.

1990: Gazza's Tears
Wednesday, 4 July 1990
Stadio delle Alpi
Turin, Italy

Even without the suspended Rudi Völler, West Germany dispatched Czechoslovakia in the next round to make it to the semis. Another storied clash awaited them, this time against Bobby Robson's England.

An uninspired group stage had given way to a sensationally dramatic run through the knockouts for the Three Lions. They needed a last-gasp stunner from David Platt in extra time to beat Belgium in the last 16, before coming up against that giant-slaying Cameroon side in the quarters. Again they had to go the distance, with two Gary Lineker penalties earning them a 3-2 victory after 120 minutes.

As it often does, expectation was building back home. New Order's 'World in Motion' was riding high atop the charts. Lineker was leading the line with aplomb, even if he had soiled himself in the first game against Ireland. And the country was falling in love with a young, energetic Geordie called Paul Gascoigne. One night in Turin, against the old foes, he earned a place in English hearts for ever.

But first, it's worth remembering that England fans were astonished the team had even gone this far in the first place. A dismal campaign at Euro '88 saw Robson's side lose all three games and a barrage of caterwauling in the press for his head on a spike. Even in qualifying they'd only managed second place behind Sweden to earn their place at Italia '90.

When they got to Italy, it was against the backdrop of a dark period in English football. Hooliganism had been rife through the 1980s, and English fans had run riot at the Euros, so much so that it was decided to maroon the team on the island of Sardinia for all three of their World Cup group games, where Italian authorities felt they'd be better able to control England supporters. What's more, after the Heysel Stadium disaster in 1985, English clubs had been banned from European competitions, effectively isolating football in the country from the rest of Europe. The best players, both English and otherwise, went elsewhere. This was reflected in Robson's World Cup squad, which comprised more players from Glasgow Rangers than from any one English club.

Yet something was brewing out in Sardinia. The squad was fostering a togetherness rarely seen in England sides. TV viewers back home saw Gazza's clownish antics, frolicking with team-mates at the poolside. He wasn't bad on the pitch either, a particularly memorable moment coming in the group game against the Netherlands when he turned Ronald Koeman inside out and left him for dead. By the time the semis arrived, the nation was gripped in a state of uncompromising football fever.

Over 26 million viewers sat down to watch the match. And they were not disappointed. It was the opposite of cagey, an astonishing end-to-end display of attacking intent. At the heart of England's play was Gascoigne, berating team-mates for the ball at every given opportunity and surging forward with directness. When Brazilian referee José Roberto Wright blew for half-time, the score was still 0-0, but it had been a breathless, bombastic 45 minutes.

English hearts sank on the hour. West Germany had a free kick 22 yards from goal and Tomas Haessler laid it off to Andreas Brehme. His shot took a huge deflection off Paul Parker and looped agonisingly over Peter Shilton. England were behind after a devastating slice of bad luck.

Predictably, England turned the screws to push for an equaliser, and nearly succeeded instantly. A Gascoigne free kick was swung in superbly for Stuart Pearce, who could only guide his header just wide of Bodo Illgner's post. Then Chris Waddle saw a solid claim for a penalty waved away by Wright. They were getting closer.

As the clocked ticked past 80 minutes, the breakthrough came – and well deserved it was, too. Parker pumped a searching long ball into the box where a crowd of green German shirts attempted to clear. It was a case of too many cooks and they made an almighty hash of it. Lineker pounced. With one touch he kneed the ball away from the mass of bodies, and with another he swept a pinpoint shot into Illgner's bottom-left corner. The English fans in Turin roared cacophonously, and one supporter watching on telly back in north London ran through his glass patio door. It was yet another late show from the Three Lions but they were back level. A third successive period of extra time was looming.

West Germany rallied in the first moments of the additional period, Klinsmann twice coming close to restoring their lead. The Germans were on top and England were being stretched. With time nearing 100 minutes, Gazza's moment of agony arrived. He overran the ball in midfield and lunged enthusiastically to recover it before an onrushing Thomas Berthold could break. But he wasn't quick enough. Berthold beat him to the ball and Gascoigne slid into his trailing leg.

Immediately, panic spread across both Gazza's and thousands of England fans' faces. The imperious midfielder had already picked up a booking in the last 16 against Belgium, and two yellows meant a suspension. Instantly Gascoigne raised both of his hands in apology to the referee and ran over to Berthold, seemingly expressing his sorrow to him personally. Gazza's case wasn't helped by the German defender, who had rolled over in apparent agony approximately four million times before coming to a rest. Gascoigne later revealed that he hadn't ran over to apologise – Berthold was screaming, and the Geordie superstar didn't want the ref to hear, so he attempted to squeeze his lips together to muffle the sound.

His efforts were in vain. After a seemingly endless wait, Wright produced the dreaded yellow that would rule Gazza out of the final, should England get there. The 23-year old was visibly devastated. Cameras focused on him as his bottom lip began to quiver and tears welled up in his eyes, as he saw the chance to play in football's biggest game dissipate in front of him. 'I couldn't hold it back,' Gascoigne later wrote in his autobiography. 'I just wanted to be left alone.' Lineker, one of the first to comfort Gascoigne, recognised the state he was in, and was famously caught on camera mouthing 'have a word with him' to manager Robson on the touchline.

In what remained of extra time England had two more opportunities to win, Waddle hitting the post and Platt seeing a goal disallowed for offside. But they couldn't do enough. For the first time, England would be taking part in a penalty shoot-out.

And that's where it all ended; 1990 would be the beginning of England's long-standing hate affair with spot-kicks. It all started well enough. Lineker's, Peter Beardsley's and Platt's opening penalties were flawless, but so were Brehme's, Matthäus's and Riedle's. It didn't exactly help England's cause that 40-year-old Shilton only seemed to dive after the ball had already hit the back of his net. Then Pearce hit one straight at Illgner to give the Germans the advantage. Olaf Thon converted another, leaving England's fate in Waddle's hands. There was a stinging irony in this; Waddle had only stepped into the penalty line-up to replace Gascoigne, who was so emotionally drained that he felt it best to withdraw. Waddle skied it. West Germany were through.

England were within touching distance of the final and saw it all fade away before them. It hurt, and those involved were bitter. 'The only genius Germany showed was from the penalty spot,' said Terry Butcher. 'We battered them,' as Gazza more succinctly put it. England had played brilliantly, there was no doubt. But at the very least, it didn't go unnoticed back home. That summer in 1990 saw England's love for the beautiful game very much reignited, and the players were welcomed home in the age-old tradition as heroic losers, with thousands of fans greeting them euphorically at Luton Airport.

Gazza had recovered by then, laughing happily on an open-top bus as he posed with a pair of plastic breasts. He couldn't have known that his blubbing before the world was to be his last memorable act on the biggest stage. England failed to qualify in 1994, and the mercurial talent was considered even too mercurial for faith-healing devotee Glenn Hoddle to pick him in his squad for the 1998 tournament.

As for the Germans, they went on to face Argentina in a match widely acknowledged as the worst World Cup Final ever. Even Maradona couldn't conjure any magic as his depleted side fell to a 1-0 loss courtesy of a late Brehme penalty. West Germany, in their third final in a row, were world champions for the first time since 1974.

1994: Diana Ross Auditions for England Penalty Duties

Friday, 17 June 1994
Soldier Field
Chicago, USA

It had to happen eventually. In 1994, for the first time, football's biggest show rolled into the U S of A. FIFA had decided that it was time for the sport to make its case before the capitalist centre of the world. It was a controversial move, not least because three-time champions Brazil had also put forward a bid to host. There was also the small matter that the sport's greatest centrepiece was about to arrive in a country that didn't even have a national league – the North American Soccer League had folded in 1984. But cash beats heritage, and soccer went stateside.

In an attempt to encourage attacking play and improve upon the low-scoring tournament in Italy four years earlier, FIFA rang some changes. Of these, most notable were the awarding of three points for a win rather than two in the group stage, and the abolition of the rule that allowed goalkeepers to pick up the ball from a back-pass, the latter move being introduced worldwide in 1992. In fairness to the governing body, whether it was down to their tweaks or not, USA '94 proved a dramatic spectacle.

The circus began long before holders Germany – now unified – took to the pitch to take on Bolivia in the first match. On US TV, lengthy segments were dedicated to explaining how football actually works before proceedings began. And then of course there was the opening ceremony. No one puts on a show quite like the Americans, and the chequebook had clearly been used to full effect to enlist a galaxy of stars to welcome football to the country. President Bill Clinton gave a speech, Oprah Winfrey was called in on hosting duties, and musical guests included Daryl Hall and Diana Ross.

But just like America's rather awkward relationship with football, the ceremony itself proved a tad cringeworthy. After a long, choreographed routine showcasing various cultural cornerstones of each nation involved, it was time for the host nation to make its presence felt. Oprah introduced pop sensation Ross, and then promptly fell off the stage. It was a sign of things to come.

Ross appeared at one end of the pitch dressed head-to-toe in a red suit, as the opening strains of her mega-hit 'I'm Coming Out'

171

echoed around Chicago and the rest of the world. The swarm of dancers on the field before her parted as if Ross was a 20th-century Moses, and the singer began to jog towards the goal at the other end. Running and 'singing' proved difficult, as audiences around the globe observed that the perfect vocals were loud and clear despite the fact that Ross was holding the microphone nowhere near her mouth.

It was a disaster class in miming. But the next bit was surely going to be easy. Ross arrived at the other end of the pitch, where a football was waiting for her six yards from a specially erected goal. The keeper did his best Bruce Grobbelaar impression as Ross readied herself. Then bang: she pea-rolled the ball far left of the goal.

Far worse than Ross's gaffe was the ill-conceived plan for what would happen next. As the ball whimpered off and out of sight, the goalposts split in two and collapsed while an explosion sound effect played out, as if the sheer force and might of the goal Ross was supposed to score shattered the stanchions with its ferocity. The Chicago crowd jeered. It was a moment of pure comedy.

Commentating for the BBC, Alan Green described it as 'a dubious omen'. Could the razzamatazz of the States and the beautiful game ever be easy bedfellows? Certainly, the match that followed couldn't compare to the entertainment provided during the opening celebrations, with Germany playing out a rather dreary 1-0 win over their South American counterparts. Many viewers in the US switched over to watch some fella called OJ Simpson in a car chase with police.

But as the matches continued, the United States got the tournament it needed to put football on the map there. USA '94 ended up being a rollercoaster World Cup crammed with highs and lows, and fans got behind it in numbers. To this day, it remains the highest-attended World Cup. And in 1996 the country finally had a national league again with the formation of Major League Soccer.

As for Diana Ross, she'll have been relieved that hers wasn't the penalty miss to make the most headlines that year. That came with the final kick of the tournament a month on. She wasn't quite done with performing at sporting events alien to her, though. The following year, she inexplicably sang during the final of the 1995 Rugby League World Cup at Wembley. Fortuitously, on that occasion, they didn't ask her to kick a drop goal.

1994: Diego's Last Dance
Tuesday, 21 June 1994
Foxboro Stadium
Foxborough, USA

Of the stories flying around in the run-up to the 1994 World Cup, none was more compelling than that of Diego Maradona. Shortly after losing the final in Rome in 1990, Maradona returned to Napoli, where he was already a club legend. But even in that haven where he was treated as a hero, trouble was brewing. His later years in Naples were marred by a scandal regarding fathering an illegitimate son, swirling rumours connecting Maradona to the mafia, and ever-increasing cocaine use. To avoid testing positive for the drug and thereby receiving a ban, Maradona would regularly and without warning withdraw from the Napoli squad, citing stress.

With his playing time sporadic, the Argentinian legend gained weight, while his club's supporters grew frustrated and angry at his patchy appearance record. Then things came to a head in 1991. Maradona was finally caught for his cocaine abuse and handed a lengthy 15-month playing ban. With the player past 30, it looked like the end. *El Diego* left Napoli under a cloud and returned home.

Once his ban expired, he spent an underwhelming season with Sevilla and then went back to Argentina again, signing with Newell's Old Boys. His lengthy spell out of regular action meant he had featured just twice for his country since the 1990 final, and he even missed out on the 1993 Copa América despite being eligible once more. The international career of football's biggest name was fizzling out with a whimper.

Argentina, meanwhile, looked in fine fettle without Maradona, and won both the 1991 and 1993 editions of the Copa. But things started to turn sour when it came to World Cup qualification. A difficult campaign saw them on the brink of missing out altogether, before scraping a play-off spot against Australia. They had one last roll of the dice, and the whole of Argentina hollered for their number ten.

Manager Alfio Basile not only obliged; he returned Maradona to the starting line-up and made him captain for the two-legged fixture. It wasn't quite a fairytale, but with his leadership Argentina got the job done, winning 2-1 on aggregate and earning a spot at the World Cup.

173

Despite this, Maradona was still too overweight to be playing at the highest level, so embarked on a rigorous training regime to get himself back into shape and ensure he could cut the mustard at USA '94. Then he pulled out of the squad altogether, stating that too much pressure was being put on him, and then opening fire on the assembled press outside his house with an air rifle when they demanded an explanation.

Of course, he reversed his decision. Diego's demons and the tumultuous period he'd endured since Italia '90 had been well publicised the world over. When he lined up as captain for Argentina's opening match against Greece in Foxborough, all eyes were on him.

The new Maradona was different. He lacked the pace and energy of the previous incarnation. But his stupendous footballing awareness was still there, and four years on there he was, still dictating Argentina's play and driving them forward, albeit with clever one-touch passes and visionary movement rather than the raucous, romping dribbles of old. At half-time, *La Albiceleste* led the Greeks 2-0 courtesy of a Gabriel Batistuta double.

On the hour, Maradona announced that he was well and truly back. A rapid passing move scythed through the Greek defence and ended with Maradona on the edge of the box. He swung a lethal left boot at the ball and saw it fly into the top corner. It was a screamer, leaving the keeper rooted to the spot.

Maradona was elated and ran towards a TV camera near the corner flag, all the while howling in celebration. It's an image that's become nearly as iconic as him punching the ball past Peter Shilton. The Argentine magician looked demented, with bulging eyes, dilated pupils and that animalistic wail emanating from him.

Argentina won 4-0, Batistuta completing his hat-trick. But no one was talking about that. Maradona's return dominated the post-match reaction. 'The Resurrection of Maradona' read the headline in *La Gazzetta dello Sport*. He featured in his side's next game, playing the full 90 minutes and assisting the winner as Argentina fought from a goal down to beat Nigeria 2-1. After the final whistle, there was the strange sight of a medic leading Maradona off by the hand. He'd been chosen for drug testing. And clearly officials wanted him in the testing room before he had contact with anyone else.

That was how arguably the World Cup's greatest player bowed out. News trickled through in the days following the game that

Maradona had tested positive for ephedrine, a banned substance often used to aid weight loss. FIFA slapped him with another 15-month ban. The most enthralling international career of any footballer ever was over.

Attentions turned back to that goal celebration against Greece. Sheer passion alone doesn't do that to someone, and at the time the world raised its eyebrows at what might be going on behind the scenes. Now, it knew for sure.

Maradona was enraged in the aftermath. 'They've cut off my legs,' he said of FIFA. He was resolute that he hadn't taken anything illegal, but his case was weakened somewhat when the press learned he'd been working with Daniel Cerrini, a former bodybuilder who'd been hired to help Maradona shed the fat in Buenos Aires ahead of the World Cup. Cerrini had himself been involved in a bodybuilding doping scandal that involved the taking of ephedrine.

Without their captain, who regardless of how he achieved it had looked in form in the first two matches, Argentina floundered. They lost to Bulgaria in their final group game before crashing out in the last 16 to Romania. The country went into mourning, both for their team's early exit and for the ignominious implosion of their hero. Maradona went largely without blame back home, with most instead choosing to point fingers at FIFA and other organisational bodies.

After his second ban was up, *El Diego* had a brief stint back at Boca Juniors, but 1994 had proved a national trauma. The fairytale was so close; the troubled superstar returning against all odds to captain the team on a glorious World Cup campaign. The sad truth was that it was never possible. Maradona had let himself go far too long ago to get back into playing condition by any natural means. World football would have to find a new star.

1994: A Tragic Own Goal
Wednesday, 22 June 1994
Rose Bowl
Pasadena, USA

USA '94 was a chaotic World Cup. It was a tournament of comedy and controversy, of earth-shattering shocks on and off the pitch. But it was also one of tragedy, when one desperately unlucky player paid the ultimate price for a mistake on the field of play. Colombia qualified for the tournament with a swagger. The nation was mired in an era of crime and poverty. Fighting between guerrilla groups and the government was common, and the city of Medellín was plunged into a state of emergency following the murder of notorious drug baron Pablo Escobar. Bombs exploded, cars were burnt out and gangland murders spiked. But *Los Cafeteros* – their national football team – were providing a much-needed distraction.

Football, as in much of South America, is like a religion to Colombians. However, they rarely had anything to shout about on the international stage. Argentina, Uruguay and Brazil dominated things in that part of the world. Even Bolivia, Peru and Paraguay, with their considerably smaller populations, had managed at least one Copa América title. But not Colombia.

Finally, in 1994, Colombians had a team to invest real hope in. There were genuine stars in the team like Freddy Rincón, Faustino Asprilla and the enigmatic Carlos Valderrama, whose sensational curly mop was almost as celebrated as the player himself. Their romping qualifying campaign for the World Cup ended with an earth-shattering 5-0 win over Argentina in Buenos Aires. They were so good that day, Argentine fans stood to applaud Colombia for minutes after the match, while their own team had to sneak out the back door. Ahead of the tournament, Brazil legend Pelé was one of those to tip Colombia for big things, suggesting they would make the semis at least. Excitement and expectation in the country had never been greater.

They were strong favourites to win their opening match, against Romania. But the European side had an effective game plan. They sat back and suffocated the silky, attacking play of their opponents, then hit on the break at every opportunity. It was enough to see them claim a comfortable 3-1 win, with the magnificent Gheorghe Hagi lobbing keeper Óscar Córdoba from near the touchline for the second goal.

Colombia were deflated. This was not meant to happen. Guileful hackers managed to replace the welcome messages on the TVs at the team's hotel with ominous threats to the players in Spanish. In the run-up to their second match, against hosts USA, the squad and manager Francisco Maturana were subject to more death threats. It was with this heavy psychological burden that they went out to face the Americans in the Californian sunshine.

Despite the tension, Colombia went into all-out attack mode from the get-go. 'We attacked from all angles, but the ball wouldn't go in,' remembered striker Adolfo Valencia. With 34 minutes on the clock, the fateful moment that forever changed the face of football in the country arrived.

At the centre of it all was Andrés Escobar. The stoic, respected 27-year-old centre-back – no relation to drugs kingpin Pablo – was admired in Colombia both on the pitch and off it. He played his club football for Atlético Nacional in Medellín, where he'd been a key part of the side that tasted Copa Libertadores glory in 1989. Ahead of USA '94, his impressive performances had earned him a contract offer from Italian giants AC Milan, where he planned to go after the World Cup. A fervent advocate of peace in his homeland, he wanted to portray a new face of Colombia – one distanced from the violence and drug cartels that lingered in the memory. Tragically, he instead became a symbol for all that was wrong in the country.

The USA launched a rare attack that saw John Harkes running at the Colombia goal down the left. He played a low, early ball into the box, looking to find Earnie Stewart, who'd lost his man near the back post. It never reached Stewart. Escobar intervened. He had to; leaving the ball would have left it to run through to the American striker, who'd have a free shot on goal from close range. The Colombian defender stretched to try and poke the ball out for a corner but he could only nudge it past a flailing Córdoba, who'd rushed to the other side of his goal to close Stewart's shooting angle. Escobar had given the hosts the lead.

The Americans grabbed a second just after half-time, and Valencia's late strike for Colombia wasn't enough. They'd lost once more. That 2-1 defeat effectively ended their World Cup, leaving them needing a miraculous turn of events beyond their control to still make it out of the groups. Despite a rallying 2-0 win over Switzerland in their final match, this hugely talented Colombia side were out.

The reaction in the country was one of devastation and anger, and a smattering of riots broke out. Escobar was saddened, and upon his return home he felt moved to pen a column in Colombia's biggest newspaper, *El Tiempo*. 'We have only two options: either allow anger to paralyse us and the violence continues, or we overcome and try our best to help others,' he wrote. 'Life does not end here.'

Agonisingly, it did. Just a week after Colombia's final match, Escobar decided he needed to leave the demons in the past and get on with living his life. He felt it important to show his face to his fellow Colombians, to outline that his mistake was just that and he wouldn't allow it to govern his future. He went to a bar with friends in his home town of Medellín, a city in which Escobar had done so much to help disadvantaged children get into football.

There, they enjoyed some drinks, reflected on the tournament and looked forward to what Escobar's imminent move to Italy may hold. Always a man of the people, the defender chatted with locals and bought drinks for revellers. But as the night wore on, a group of gangsters began to chide Escobar for his own goal. As the situation grew more dicey, he decided it best to return home, and went out to his car in the car park around 3am. The four men followed him, whereupon one produced a gun and opened fire. Escobar was shot six times, with his assailant reportedly shouting 'Gol!' each time he discharged another bullet. The player was pronounced dead at hospital 45 minutes later.

In the aftermath, a bodyguard connected with a powerful cartel that had apparently lost big money betting on Colombia in the World Cup was charged with Escobar's murder. The outpouring of grief and rage across the country was universal. Over 100,000 mourners lined the streets for Escobar's funeral procession, throwing flowers and football shirts in the path of the hearse carrying his coffin.

Years later, Escobar's national team manager Maturana suggested that the player had not been killed for football reasons, and rather had been in the wrong place at the wrong time. But it's hard to imagine him being gunned down had the ball not trickled off of Escobar's foot and into Córdoba's net that day in Pasadena.

It would take seven years for the national team to draw a line under those traumatic events of 1994. In 2001 Colombia hosted the Copa América, despite security concerns originally causing the tournament to be cancelled. The governing body reversed its decision and the Copa went ahead, with Colombian fans packing stadiums with colour and passion, showing a much more positive side of the downtrodden nation. They went on to win the whole thing. Those most fanatical, beleaguered supporters finally had something good to celebrate.

1994: The Angriest Substitution Ever
Friday, 24 June 1994
Citrus Bowl
Orlando, USA

For the first time since the 1930s, no home nations qualified for the World Cup in 1994. With a summer festival of football to enjoy but no UK representatives, many British fans looked elsewhere for a team to root for. Attentions turned to Jack Charlton's Republic of Ireland side. His squad was packed with familiar faces, with every player plying their trade in either England or Scotland. What's more, the Irish FA and Charlton's very loose definition of what made a player Irish meant that of the 22 players in his World Cup squad, a whopping 15 weren't born in Ireland. As such, the Boys in Green found themselves with a legion of temporary supporters. And those watching at home certainly weren't disappointed for entertainment.

That shouldn't have come as a surprise. Ireland's qualifying campaign had been packed with drama until the final seconds. With a chance to secure top spot in their group in the last match, Charlton's men faltered north of the border in Belfast and could only manage a 1-1 draw with Northern Ireland in a charged game against the backdrop of The Troubles. It left them needing one of Spain or Denmark, who at the same time were facing off in Seville, to win – if the sides drew, they'd both qualify at the Republic's expense.

The tension was gigantic. Spain were winning 1-0 with five minutes to go, and Denmark were throwing everything at them to get the goal that would see them to the World Cup instead of Ireland. At the final whistle in Belfast, Charlton was asked by a TV reporter if he wanted to watch the last moments of the game. 'Do I bollocks,' he responded heartily. It was too nerve-racking. The Spanish held on, sparking jubilant scenes. Defender Alan Kernaghan burst into tears, and a 22-year-old Roy Keane ran around screaming and hugged captain Andy Townsend. Ireland were going to their second consecutive World Cup.

They were handed a tough draw in the groups, against Mexico, a Norway side who had just topped England's qualifying section, and three-time champions Italy. They'd be starting their campaign with the hardest fixture of them all, against the *Azzurri* at Giants Stadium in New Jersey.

179

The encounter proved one of the finest moments in Ireland's footballing history. Italy were one of the tournament favourites, boasting a formidable defence featuring Franco Baresi, Paolo Maldini and Alessandro Costacurta, not to mention the prodigious attacking talents of Ballon d'Or holder Roberto Baggio. Despite this, it was Ireland who landed the first blow. Ray Houghton scored with a sublime volley in the 11th minute to give the Irish the lead. After that, the game plan was all-out defence, and Paul McGrath turned in a sensational display at the back to keep the Italians at bay. Charlton's men had pulled off a miracle, and he laughed happily at full time looking like everyone's grandad on holiday in a short-sleeved shirt, tie, and awkward white baseball cap.

Another win would seal their spot in the knockouts. Next up was a flight south to face the Mexicans in Florida. Charlton, never one to crack the whip, ensured a jovial mood in his camp by allowing the players to visit the many waterparks of Orlando in their downtime. They also made liberal use of a help-yourself Guinness tap conveniently located on their floor in the hotel where they were based. Confidence and morale couldn't have been higher going into the clash with Mexico.

Less than ideal for Ireland were the conditions they'd be playing in. For the match in Orlando that day, the mercury rose to over 43°C, temperatures that their opponents were much more accustomed to. It showed. Mexico put in an assured performance to race into a 2-0 lead after 65 minutes. With his side up against it, Charlton decided to ring the changes. And that's when things really did reach boiling point.

Big Jack opted for a double substitution. Steve Staunton made way for Jason McAteer, while Tommy Coyne came off for Tranmere Rovers striker John Aldridge. Except when a frazzled Coyne took his place on the bench, no one had replaced him – the fourth official stretched out an arm to prevent Aldridge from making his way on to the pitch. Play was continuing, and Ireland only had ten men.

It transpired that an overly zealous FIFA delegate had snatched away the form detailing Aldridge's substitution to check it, meaning the fourth official hadn't received confirmation and couldn't let him on. To say Aldo blew a gasket is an understatement. The 35-year-old striker, originally from Liverpool, launched into a foul-mouthed, four-letter tirade at anyone who would listen. He employed an exhaustive thesaurus of expletives which he used to hurl at the official who'd made the cock-up, before he had to be restrained from attacking him. 'I just lost it,' Aldridge later said. 'Words came out that I didn't even know I had in my vocabulary.'

Meanwhile, Charlton himself was having his own argument further up the touchline. His frustration was plain to see as he too set off on an obscenity-laden rant at officials. X-rated verbals in Scouse and Geordie accents flew around Florida. And rather unfortunately for the pair, an opportunistic cameraman chose to cut to the chaotic pitchside scenes rather than the action on the field of play. The world got front-row seats to their explosion of fury.

Aldridge eventually got on to the pitch after nearly six minutes of waiting, making sure to lambast the fourth official once more as he made his way into the game. Charlton's double change turned out to be an inspired one. McAteer delivered a ball for Aldridge to head home on 84 minutes.

Mexico held on for a 2-1 win, while Aldridge and Charlton were both handed expensive fines from FIFA. The latter also had to watch from the stands as Ireland played out a goalless draw with Norway in their final game. But as it turned out, Aldridge's goal proved pivotal. Remarkably, all four teams in the group finished on four points with a goal difference of zero, but Aldo's late header meant Ireland went through in second place on goals scored. Their journey ended in the last 16 after falling to a 2-0 loss to the Netherlands. But they wouldn't have got there at all were it not for that switch against Mexico. It might have cost them an arm and a leg, but the substitution had been worth waiting for after all.

1994: Salenko's High Five

Tuesday, 28 June 1994
Stanford Stadium
Stanford, USA

The fall of the Soviet Union in 1991 brought with it a raft of brand-new international teams entering qualifying for the first time. With the USSR dissolved, countries like Lithuania and Latvia could play as national teams in their own right. And then of course there was Russia. The side in the 1990s boasted nowhere near the talent of some of the Soviet teams that had gone before, but there were hopes that a new era for the country would bring with it a united, successful national team.

They were handed a boost in the qualifying draw that saw them enter by far the easiest of the UEFA groups. The only side that looked threatening were Yugoslavia, who were subsequently banned as part of UN sanctions enacted due to the Yugoslav Wars. It looked for all the world like Russia would have an easy run at making it to the World Cup.

But behind the scenes, a scandal was brewing. The Russian Football Union controversially replaced popular manager Anatoliy Byshovets, who'd coached the team to gold at the 1988 Olympics, with the unforgiving Pavel Sadyrin. The players were slow to take to the establishment's man, and Russia were unconvincing throughout their qualifying campaign, with the press in the country particularly critical of the team after two low-scoring wins against minnows Luxembourg and Iceland in Moscow. They were doing enough to make it to the finals, but they certainly weren't inspiring much hope in the process.

They faced their closest rivals Greece in the final qualifier. Both nations were already guaranteed a spot at USA '94, but the match would decide who would go there as group winners. Russia were expected to win but again things didn't go to plan, with the Greeks running out 1-0 victors in Athens.

There was outrage both in the dressing room and outside of it. Sadyrin quickly pointed the finger of blame at the small handful of genuine stars he did have, citing the fact that the likes of Manchester United's Andrei Kanchelskis and Inter Milan's Igor Shalimov played outside of Russia, and their heads were instead focused on the lucrative opportunities Europe's top leagues could afford them. The players were further incensed when furious Football Union president Vyacheslav Koloskov stormed in and admonished them for their performance. When Sadyrin sided with Koloskov rather than sticking up for them, they knew it was time to do something.

Back at their hotel, the players discussed a course of action. They wrote a defiant open letter directed at president Boris Yeltsin, which was published in various Russian newspapers. In it, they criticised both the Football Union and Sadyrin, describing his techniques as dictatorial and outlining that they felt Russia would be doomed to fail at the World Cup with him at the helm. They called for Byshovets to be reinstated. All in all, 14 of Sadyrin's players signed the very public critique. It was damning.

The powers that be did nothing. Sadyrin remained in charge, and as the World Cup approached, more and more players withdrew their support for the changes they had demanded, not wanting to lose their chance to play on football's biggest stage. Only five continued in their defiance, including those star men Kanchelskis and Shalimov.

As such, Russia arrived at USA '94 noticeably lacking in firepower. All five of the absentees were wingers or strikers. When asked of them ahead of their opening match, Sadyrov was typically dismissive. 'They don't exist as far as I'm concerned,' he said.

With his main attacking forces unavailable, Sadyrov turned elsewhere. Oleg Salenko, a 24-year-old striker for Spanish mid-table side Logroñés who only made his debut as a substitute in that loss to Greece, was one of those who unexpectedly ended up with a spot on the plane to the States. He'd previously earned a cap for Ukraine in a friendly, but the chance to play at the World Cup was too tempting, and he switched allegiance. In the five caps he notched up for the national team ahead of the tournament, he drew a blank in every match. The omens weren't good.

Salenko made a cameo off the bench in Russia's opener against Brazil, which they lost 2-0. He featured from the start in their next match, against Sweden, and scored his first international goal from the penalty spot to put his side 1-0 up early on, but the Swedes rallied to win comfortably 3-1. The country's first World Cup as Russia was fast becoming a disaster.

Then the final group game happened, against Cameroon in Stanford, and ensured that Salenko would at the very least leave the United States with some memorable records as souvenirs. With the possibility of qualifying as one of the four best third-placed teams, Russia were not yet dead and buried, so went into the match against the Africans with an attacking plan to rack up as many goals as possible to improve their goal difference. Salenko was the beating heart of that plan.

The Russians raced into a 3-0 lead by half-time, with Salenko scoring all three to complete a first half hat-trick. The third, from the spot, was a masterclass in penalty-scoring nonchalance, with the striker casually caressing the ball into the bottom corner. The term 'stroking the ball home' had never been more fitting.

As the second half began, there was time for Roger Milla to extend his own record as the World Cup's oldest goalscorer, nicking one back for Cameroon at the sprightly age of 42. It proved to be only a brief respite from Russia's goal-getting *blitzkrieg*. On 72 minutes Salenko scored a fourth, hammering a cross into the top corner first time. Three minutes later he had a record-breaking fifth. An incisive ball behind the Cameroon defence found Salenko free in the box, and he clipped a delicate finish past the onrushing goalkeeper. He scored every goal with his first touch.

Russia won 6-1, with substitute Dmitri Radchenko adding another late on. Ultimately the boosted goal difference wasn't enough as results in other groups went against Russia to leave them just outside the best third-placed teams. But Salenko had written himself into the history books; no one had scored five goals in a single World Cup match before and nobody has done it since.

More good news for Salenko was to follow, and another record too. He ended up sharing the Golden Boot with Hristo Stoichkov for his six goals, and became the only World Cup top scorer to not make it past the first round. A bittersweet record, perhaps, but one to tell the grandchildren about all the same.

Salenko's exploits in the US earned him a big move to Valencia, but his career was from then on blighted by a string of injuries. Astonishingly he never played for Russia again. He came in, played eight games in seven months, and signed off with a World Cup Golden Boot. As international careers go, Salenko's was pretty efficient.

1994: A Bulgarian Underdog Story

Sunday, 10 July 1994
Giants Stadium
East Rutherford, USA

The group stages at USA '94 had provided a plethora of shocking, fascinating moments and stories. But as the tournament entered the knockout rounds, proceedings returned predictably to the form book. Italy defended, Argentina cheated, the Netherlands imploded, and the Germans won. The reigning champions, while not particularly convincing in the groups, had a habit of getting the job done, and had played in four of the last five World Cup finals. They edged past Belgium 3-2 in the last 16, and with Jürgen

Klinsmann firing on all cylinders, it looked like they were destined for the latter stages once more.

After their win at Italia '90, then-manager Franz Beckenbauer suggested that the now-unified Germany would only be stronger going forward. 'I'm sorry for the other countries,' he said, 'but now that we will be able to incorporate all the great players from the east, the German team will be unbeatable for a long time to come.' New coach Berti Vogts didn't exactly flood his squad for 1994 with eastern talent, but the additions of Matthias Sammer and Ulf Kirsten undoubtedly made his side a more formidable beast than before.

The quarters saw Vogts's Germany pitted against a team that upset all the odds to get to the World Cup in the first place: Bulgaria. The old Eastern Bloc nation had a decent team. A rule during the country's communist days prevented players from playing outside of Bulgaria until they were 28, but this was relaxed after the collapse of the USSR. Now, they had players dotted around Europe's top leagues. They also had the talismanic Hristo Stoichkov, the Barcelona striker who was capable of producing moments of dumbfounding genius.

Still, they were handed a tricky qualifying group featuring rising stars Sweden and a French side packed with some of the world's best, and making it to USA '94 looked to be a monumental ask. However, after France fell to a shock home defeat to Israel in their penultimate qualifying game, the door was opened for the Bulgarians. The only slight snag was that to make it to the World Cup they'd have to win their last match, against France in Paris.

No one gave them a shot. Looking at the line-ups from that night, it's easy to see why. *Les Bleus'* side was a lethal mix of established stars and the nucleus of the team that would do great things in 1998. Eric Cantona, Marcel Desailly, Laurent Blanc, Emmanuel Petit, Didier Deschamps and David Ginola all featured in the pivotal game at the Parc des Princes. And what's more, Gérard Houllier's men only needed a draw.

The game began predictably, with early French pressure paying off after half an hour as Cantona volleyed his side ahead from close range. Five minutes later Bulgaria equalised from a corner, Porto striker Emil Kostadinov heading the sides level. But no matter how much the Bulgarians pushed for the goal that would send them to the World Cup as the match wore on, France held firm.

As the clock ticked towards 90 minutes, Ginola had possession near the Bulgarian corner flag. Surely that was it; he'd play for time and shield the ball until the final whistle. The ever-classy virtuoso decided that holding on for a draw wasn't for him and inexplicably fired a wild cross far beyond the box to gift Bulgaria possession. They broke up the pitch quickly. A chipped ball found Kostadinov surging into the box. From a tight angle, he walloped a volley towards the French goal. It was perfect. The ball crashed into the underside of the bar and bounced in. They had won it with practically the last kick.

On TV back in Bulgaria, the commentator screamed 'God is Bulgarian!' over and over. In his post-match interview, Stoichkov was typically icy. 'They played for a draw and never went looking for a win,' he said. 'They didn't deserve to qualify and we hit them where it hurt most.'

Even so, the underdogs from qualifying became the underdogs at the tournament proper. In the five World Cups they'd previously made it to, Bulgaria had never won a game. It certainly seemed like that wouldn't be changing any time soon when they were battered 3-0 by Nigeria in their opener. They managed their first finals win by beating Greece 4-0 in their next match, but a spot in the knockouts still seemed unlikely, with Stoichkov and Co needing to get something against two-time champions Argentina in their last group game.

However, the now Maradona-less Argies were unsettled, and it gave Stoichkov cause for confidence. 'Without him they wouldn't even win playing with twice as many players,' he said before the match. His self-assuredness was echoed by his team-mates. Bulgaria were in cruise control as they eased their way to a 2-0 win and a last-16 clash with Mexico, which went to penalties. The Mexicans must have been taking tips from Stuart Pearce and Chris Waddle, because they missed their first three spot-kicks to send Bulgaria into the quarters.

That was where they met Germany. True to the theme, Bulgaria were again given no chance against *Die Mannschaft*. Belief was at an all-time high in the Bulgarian camp though, and the players were in relaxed mood in the build-up. The day before the game, they were pictured drinking beers and smoking cigarettes around their hotel swimming pool. German preparations were markedly different, as Vogts took his players, head to toe in some quite stunning Adidas training gear, out for a run halfway up a mountain.

As kick-off approached, Bulgaria's defensive enforcer Trifon Ivanov told coach Dimitar Penev that the game would go to plan in his own inimitable way. 'With my bloodthirsty look, they will be scared to death,' he reassured his manager. 'Rudi Völler will fall to the ground when he feels my breath.' In fairness to Ivanov, he probably takes the crown as the most downright terrifying player ever to feature in a World Cup, with a bone-chilling beard and mullet combo that made him look like a Bond villain's brutish bodyguard. Back home, he used to ride around in a tank in the countryside where he lived for fun, so his assertion that the Germans might be a little wary of him was probably correct.

The first half was a scintillating contest, both teams attacking with gusto. Bulgaria hit the post, then Klinsmann saw a header from point-blank range brilliantly saved by captain Borislav Mihaylov. The score remained goalless when half-time came, but the match was electrifying. And the outsiders were giving as good as they got.

Devastatingly, in the opening moments of the second half, a mistake at the back cost Bulgaria dearly. While clearing a cross, Yordan Letchkov foolishly left a trailing leg for Klinsmann to crash into. The striker – not exactly renowned for staying on his feet – was felled, and Germany had a penalty. Lothar Matthäus stepped up to bullet it past Mihaylov and give his side the lead.

This was a crushing blow. It allowed Germany to effectively shut down the game, and Bulgaria struggled to find the impetus or creativity to craft an equalising chance. Their opponents looked the more likely to score again, and Völler saw his potentially game-clinching strike on the rebound ruled out for offside.

Penev's men still had that one magical, unpredictable force that was Stoichkov. Nicknamed *El Pistolero* (the gunslinger) in Spain for his explosive ability to turn a match on its head, Bulgaria were going to need him to pull off an unlikely comeback. With 15 minutes left the forward had the ball 25 yards from the German goal and was going nowhere. He managed to tempt Andreas Möller out of the defensive unit, then twisted his body as Möller approached, drawing the foul. All part of the plan, it seemed. Because when he stepped up to take the free kick seconds later, Stoichkov lifted a thumper over the wall and straight into the net beyond Bodo Illgner, who didn't move. All square.

Giants Stadium roared. The American supporters loved an underdog story just as much as any seasoned football fan. Momentum was now with the Bulgarians, and in the minutes after their equaliser they began to pin Germany back in their own half.

Bulgaria made a few short, sharp passes from a throw-in before the ball came to Zlatko Yankov, facing away from goal on the right wing. Yankov turned on his heel, sent his marker for a hotdog and fired a diagonal cross into the penalty area. The box looked deserted, until of all people Letchkov, who'd given away the spot-kick earlier, zoomed into the frame and leaped in front of his man. He dived bald head-first into the ball, which shot past Illgner.

The ground exploded. Back home, capital city Sofia erupted. Football fans around the rest of the world enjoyed a sweet dollop of *schadenfreude* at the Germans' expense. Bulgaria held on for a seismic win. They were in the semi-finals of the World Cup.

The fairytale didn't continue. They then played Italy who, led by an inspired Roberto Baggio performance, won 2-1. Stoichkov did grab Bulgaria's consolation goal though, tying him with Salenko on six goals and giving him a Golden Boot to go home with. At the end of the year, Stoichkov won the Ballon d'Or ahead of Baggio, too.

The party ended in the third-place play-off, where Sweden ran riot in a 4-0 win. By this point, it didn't matter. Bulgaria went to the World Cup as surprise qualifiers, with the main aim of finally winning a match at the tournament, and instead ended up going all the way to the final four, knocking out the reigning champions in the process. It was an unlikely dream and the players returned home as heroes.

1994: The Penalty That Went into Space

Sunday, 17 July 1994
Rose Bowl
Pasadena, USA

What a dramatic, captivating World Cup the USA had seen. It was only fitting that the world would be treated once more to an enthralling encounter in the final. Brazil were facing Italy in front of 94,000 spectators at the Rose Bowl in Pasadena, and it was a salivating prospect. The pair had dished up World Cup classics in the past. There was the 4-1 rout Brazil produced in the 1970 final, and the stunning 3-2 win the Italians conjured up on the way to lifting the trophy in 1982. Same again, please.

Except in 1994, the *Azzurri* and the *Seleção* didn't exactly play ball. The match was not one for the ages. But at its climax, it provided a moment of breathtaking theatre that reverberated around the world, ensuring that USA '94 ended in exactly the same way in which it began: with a missed penalty.

Italy started the tournament slowly. They followed up that shock defeat to Ireland with a 1-0 win over Norway and a draw with Mexico, meaning they only made it through to the knockouts in third place. The world's best player, Roberto Baggio, had been quiet for the Italians throughout the groups, his incomparable vision and ballerina's touch deserting him. Manager Arrigo Sacchi relied heavily on the likes of captain Franco Baresi and Paolo Maldini at the back to get results, and the former was now ruled out with a knee injury sustained in the Norway win.

In the last 16 the *Azzurri* faced surprise package Nigeria, who'd won the group featuring Bulgaria and Argentina. And again it looked like Italy were sleepwalking. Nigeria went ahead in the first half after an uncharacteristic defensive cock-up from a corner. Italy were evidently missing their captain and defensive marshal. Then Gianfranco Zola, who'd only come on eight minutes earlier as Italy pushed for an equaliser, was sent off in the 75th minute. Down to ten men, with time ticking away and a goal behind, the three-time champions were dead and buried.

Or so it seemed. Baggio chose this moment to finally come to life. The Divine Ponytail, so nicknamed for his very 1990s hairdo, showed why he'd been awarded the Ballon d'Or back in December. With two minutes remaining, Baggio drove a pinpoint finish from the edge of the box into the Nigerian goal to draw the sides level. Then in extra time, he helped win Italy a penalty after pulling out an audacious lobbed through ball in the box to Antonio Benarrivo, who was fouled. It was Baggio who took it, scoring for a second time and sending his country to the quarter-finals.

Spain were up next. *La Roja* would be nowhere near as accommodating if Italy yet again failed to turn up from the start. This time, they hit the ground running. Baggio was outstanding, linking up all of his team's attacking play so fluidly. His namesake Dino Baggio (no relation) malleted in a screamer from 30 yards midway through the first half to give Italy the lead, before Spain equalised on the hour. Step up Mr Ponytail once again. Clearly a fan of scoring with two minutes left, Baggio grabbed the winner on 88, dribbling mesmerisingly beyond Spanish keeper Andoni Zubizarreta and firing Italy into the last four.

Then there was that semi against Bulgaria. Baggio was the man of the match once more, scoring both goals as his side defeated everyone's favourite underdogs 2-1. Someone had flipped a switch as soon as Italy hit the knockouts because Baggio was suddenly emphatically unplayable.

Brazil's progression to the final was significantly less dramatic. They had their own superstar in the shape of Romário, who like Baggio had bagged five goals so far. This Brazilian side, managed by Carlos Alberto Parreira, was not in the same mould of the trailblazing Samba boys who had gone before. But they were clinical and efficient, winning each of their knockout games by a one-goal margin.

The final that unfolded between these two footballing giants was a stolid affair. Perhaps in part that was down to the furnace-like heat in California that day. 'If we go upfield we're not going to be able to get back,' midfielder Roberto Donadoni told Sacchi at half-time. As such, the ball was largely caught in midfield, with attacks coming at a premium. Italy had been handed a boost when Baresi, fresh from an operation to mend his knee injury, was named in the team for the first time since he'd had to come off against Norway. The imperious centre-back turned in one of the greatest performances of his hyperbolic career, barely allowing Romário a sniff.

Italy's main goal threat struggled too. Baggio picked up a knock in the semi-final and played with heavy strapping around his leg against Brazil to protect an injured hamstring. In normal circumstances, a player in this situation might be given a painkilling injection to get through the match, but not Baggio – he was allergic. If he was to perform in the final, the help he needed would have to come from a higher power. The player had famously converted to Buddhism earlier in his career, and before the game hundreds of Buddhists at a temple in Bangladesh joined together in prayer to ask that Baggio remain fit.

The bad news was, after that attritional 90-minute battle, the scores remained goalless. Baggio's hamstring would have to hold up for another half an hour.

The extra period continued in the same vein as normal time, the ball being held up in a congested midfield save for the occasional half chance. For the first time, the World Cup Final finished 0-0. And for the first time, it was going to penalties.

Baresi took first for Italy. He tarnished his otherwise flawless performance by skying it, but Gianluca Pagliuca spared his blushes by saving Márcio Santos's kick straight after. The next four went in, before Daniele Massaro saw his effort saved by Cláudio Taffarel in the Brazilian goal. *Seleção* captain Dunga then gave his side the advantage. The Divine Ponytail stepped up. He had to score.

Baggio had been nothing short of dazzling in dragging Italy to the final. Without him, they'd have stood no chance of making it. If Italians could have picked any player in the world to take that penalty, they'd have picked him. He placed the ball and eyeballed Taffarel. Baggio looked glacial. Calm. Confident. He stepped back for his usual long, near-straight run-up, the one that had helped him score the winner against Nigeria. On commentary, Barry Davies opined, 'The man who really has brought his team to the final now has to save them.' Bang.

The ball flew high over the bar and into the stands, sending Brazilian players and their fans back home into a frenzy as they claimed their fourth World Cup. They'd had a long 24-year wait since last becoming world champions, and this was catharsis for the missed opportunities of that fantastic side that fell short through the 1980s. But the headlines weren't Brazil's.

Baggio stood rooted to the spot, dejected. It was so cruel, so unfair. In that one kick, the memories of his brilliance over the previous weeks would be washed away, for the time being at least. 'I still dream about it,' Baggio wrote in his autobiography. 'It was the worst moment of my career.'

At home, Baggio was rightly celebrated. Expectations for the tournament had been low, and Italians understood that they couldn't have got so far without him. Cold comfort, maybe, but recognition all the same.

Four years later, Baggio won a penalty late on in Italy's opening group game against Chile at the 1998 World Cup. With his side trailing, it was a must-score, and Baggio was tasked with taking it. He bent over with his hands on his knees as he steeled himself. That familiar long run-up was the same, but this time he looked nervous, like the weight of four years of frustration and bitterness were playing on a loop in his head. And then he scored.

Jules Rimet (left) presents the trophy that bears his name to Uruguayan FA president Dr Paul Jude following his country's 4-2 win over Argentina in the first-ever World Cup Final.

Italian dictator Benito Mussolini (centre) poses with his victorious Azzurri *side after they won their second World Cup title in 1938.*

The USA team ahead of their seismic shock win over England at the 1950 World Cup in Brazil. Match-winner Joe Gaetjens is in the front row with the ball at his feet.

France's Just Fontaine scores one of his 13 goals at the 1958 World Cup, against West Germany in the third-place play-off.

The Bent-Legged Angel himself, Garrincha, sends Czechoslovakia's Ján Popluhár for a hot dog on the way to lifting the World Cup with Brazil in the 1962 final in Santiago, Chile.

Pickles the dog takes a trip to Downing Street after locating the stolen Jules Rimet trophy in 1966.

The great Pelé, the only man to win three World Cups as a player, poses with the trophy after Brazil's win in 1970.

The Netherlands' Johan Cruyff chases West Germany's Franz Beckenbauer during the 1974 World Cup Final in Munich.

Scotland's Archie Gemmill watches as the ball flies into the top corner after his sensational strike against the Netherlands in 1978.

Patrick Battiston lies unconscious on the floor after his clash with Harald Schumacher in 1982.

A tearful Marco Tardelli celebrates after scoring for Italy in the 1982 final against West Germany.

Diego Maradona rises with his fist in the air, ready to punch the ball beyond Peter Shilton during Argentina and England's quarter-final in 1986.

Frank Rijkaard aims an inch-perfect gob into Rudi Völler's curly locks in 1990.

Diego Maradona is led off by a nurse for his ultimately failed drug test at the 1994 World Cup in the USA.

Roberto Baggio's penalty sails over the crossbar and into orbit as he hands the World Cup to Brazil in 1994.

David Beckham sees red after fouling Argentina's Diego Simeone in 1998.

Roy Keane walks trusty companion Triggs after he was sent home from the 2002 World Cup for a foul-mouthed outburst at Republic of Ireland manager Mick McCarthy.

Disgraced referee Byron Moreno flamboyantly flashes a yellow card while officiating the controversial clash between Italy and South Korea in 2002.

The rather bizarre statue recreating Zinedine Zidane's headbutt on Marco Materazzi in the 2006 World Cup Final.

Frank Lampard's strike flies beyond Germany goalkeeper Manuel Neuer at the 2010 World Cup, a goal which ultimately wouldn't count.

Italy's Giorgio Chiellini holds his shoulder after being bitten by Uruguay's Luis Suárez in 2014, who holds his teeth in the foreground.

England goalkeeper Jordan Pickford stops Colombian Carlos Bacca's penalty as the Three Lions won a first-ever World Cup penalty shootout in 2018.

1998: Football 1 Politics 0

Sunday, 21 June 1998
Stade de Gerland
Lyon, France

France hosted the World Cup for a second time in 1998. The tournament was expanded once more, rising to 32 teams from 24. The format change proved FIFA's most lasting, with the top two teams progressing from each of eight groups of four to the knockouts. They also introduced the golden goal, which was significantly less enduring.

Naturally, more qualifying berths provided more opportunities for less-established nations to make it to the World Cup. The USA, enjoying a post-hosting boom in the sport, qualified comfortably, losing only twice on the road to France. Over in Asia, the fearsome partnership of Ali Daei and Karim Bagheri, who plundered an eye-watering 28 goals between them in qualifying, helped Iran make it to the World Cup for the first time in 20 years after beating Australia in a play-off. The pair of relative footballing minnows weren't expected to make any waves at the tournament. But when they were drawn in the same group, it set up an encounter that attracted the attention of the globe.

The political context to the match was stratospheric, more so even than when East and West Germany faced off in 1974. Relations between the countries had been non-existent for 20 years, since the Iranian Revolution. The US had backed the incumbent monarch Shah Mohammad Reza, who had disillusioned Iranians with his authoritarian, western-influenced policies. Even with the US's backing, the Shah was overthrown and exiled. His replacement, Ayatollah Khomeini, formed the Islamic Republic of Iran, the name by which the country is still formally known. Thousands died during the Revolution, and the Ayatollah labelled America as 'the great Satan' following his ascendancy to power.

Shortly after, the USA backed Saddam Hussein and Iraq in their invasion of Iran, prompting a bloody, eight-year long war. Iranians took 60 US citizens hostage in the American embassy in Tehran for over a year. The countries were ideologically polarised, and through the 1980s and '90s engaged in many high-profile military standoffs, despite never being fully at war. It was a cagey, nerve-shredding juxtaposition. And now they had to play each other in a football match.

In sporting terms, the match was vital, too. Iran and the USA had both lost their opening games, to FR Yugoslavia and Germany respectively, so needed three points to stand any real chance of making it through the groups. The pre-match coverage was not dominated by football, though. 'Many families of martyrs are expecting us to win,' said Iran striker Khodadad Azizi, referencing the thousands of lives lost in the Revolution and the Iran-Iraq War. 'We will win for their sake.'

His manager, Jalal Talebi, was keen to distance the match from politics. His personal story was an intriguing one. An Iranian by birth, he'd fled the war in 1983 and moved to California, and attempted to leave any talk of the two nations' divisions at the door during his pre-game press conferences. His US counterpart Steve Sampson did the same. But outside of the footballing sphere, there were different ideas.

Mujahedin-e-Khalq (MEK), an Islamic militant group opposed to the Ayatollah who both Iran and the US designated as a terrorist organisation, bought up some 7,000 tickets for the match. They planned a full-scale demonstration in the stands, hoping their banners and chants would put their political agenda on TV screens around the world. FIFA caught wind and indicated to camera operators where the group would be sat, instructing them in no uncertain terms to not give them any airtime. When MEK learned this, plans were mooted for a pitch invasion instead. To combat this, FIFA deployed 150 armed French riot police at the side of the pitch where the group was seated. Everything possible was done to ensure the match could be played without political interruption.

The Ayatollah got involved, too. Iran, drawn randomly as the away team, were by FIFA rules supposed to approach the American players to shake hands ahead of kick-off. Iran's leader quite fiercely informed the country's FA that this could not happen; he wanted to give the USA no concessions whatsoever. Officials came up with a unique compromise to ensure the obligatory pre-game show of sportsmanship could take place. Instead, the players posed for a joint photograph, arm in arm with one another, and the Iranians presented their American opponents with bouquets of white roses as symbols of peace.

The match itself was a competitive but good-spirited affair. An open, end-to-end contest saw the deadlock broken in the 40th minute by Iran's Hamid Estili, who fired a superb header beyond Kasey Keller. More memorable than his goal, though, was the celebration. Estili's strained expression as he ran, fists out by his sides, screaming passionately, was the perfect distillation of what the goal meant to Iran as a whole.

Iran grabbed a second to seal the win in the last five minutes, before Brian McBride struck a consolation for the States. Back in Tehran, the country was in frenzied jubilation. People danced in the streets long into the night, women removed their headscarves in celebration, and alcohol flowed. This was momentous given the strict Islamic laws preventing such things. 'The Revolutionary Guard didn't do anything about it because they were also so happy,' said Mehrdad Masoudi, an Iranian FIFA press officer who'd helped organise the pre-game photo. 'They were football fans first and Revolutionary Guards second.'

It was also Iran's first World Cup win. They hadn't managed one in their only previous appearance at the tournament in 1978. The fact it came against the US made it doubly sweet. Both sides were ultimately eliminated in the groups, but it didn't really matter. Their match in Lyon extended beyond football.

'We did more in 90 minutes than the politicians did in 20 years,' remarked US defender Jeff Agoos. Perhaps a slightly grandiose statement from a player who didn't play a single minute at France '98. He did feature 18 months later, when the goodwill built up in their World Cup encounter led to a groundbreaking friendly between the sides on US soil. It was 1-1 that time. Sometimes, football really is capable of transcending anything.

1998: Magic and Madness in Saint-Étienne

Tuesday, 30 June 1998
Stade Geoffroy-Guichard
Saint-Étienne, France

'After tonight, England vs Argentina will be remembered for what a player did with his feet.' So ran a prominent Adidas advert in English newspapers the day that the Three Lions were due to once more face a World Cup standoff with Argentina, in the last 16 at France '98. The sportswear giant chose Manchester United starlet

David Beckham as the poster boy for the ad, the slogan plastered across a photo of Becks looking like he meant business. The whole thing turned out to be eerily prescient.

England were back at world football's showpiece after missing out in 1994. Glenn Hoddle was now in charge of the national team and his players looked convincing in qualifying, topping their group ahead of USA '94 runners-up Italy. Expectation was high. Hoddle's men swept aside Tunisia in their opener in France, Alan Shearer and Paul Scholes grabbing the goals in a comfortable 2-0 win.

Beckham didn't feature at all in that match, despite coming into the tournament off the back of a stellar campaign for Manchester United that had seen him named in the PFA's Team of the Year for the second consecutive season. Hoddle had publicly criticised Beckham's focus as the reason for his omission, citing his Spice Girl fiancée Victoria Adams and his promotional work for various sponsors as distractions. The England manager was not unfamiliar with controversial decisions. He'd taken a faith healer to France as part of the England staff, purportedly to help the squad mentally, and had decided not to select Paul Gascoigne for the tournament despite the Rangers midfielder being one of the side's best performers in qualification. Becks was just the latest in a string of maverick calls.

He missed out on the starting 11 in England's second game, too. Romania ran out 2-1 winners with Beckham featuring as a substitute. The media back home cried out for Golden Balls to play from the start in the team's final group match, a pivotal clash against Colombia. Hoddle finally obliged and Beckham was superb. After Darren Anderton had fired England ahead on 20 minutes, Beckham curled in a glorious free kick from 30 yards – his first goal for the national side – to help his team to a 2-0 win and a spot in the knockouts. 'I've always been focused on my football,' he said afterwards. 'That's always come first, before everything else. Nothing gets in the way.' Point taken.

After such a performance, Beckham was unsurprisingly straight into Hoddle's team for the last-16 clash with Argentina. *La Albiceleste*, managed by their old World Cup-winning captain from 1978 Daniel Passarella, cruised through their group, winning every game without conceding a goal. The encounter in Saint-Étienne would be the first time the sides had met in a competitive match since Maradona's Jekyll-and-Hyde showing in 1986. Fans in both nations were whipped up into a frenzy by hopeful, non-stop press coverage in the days preceding the game. The excited build-up proved warranted, as a pulsating classic unfolded.

The clash was overseen by Danish referee Kim Milton Nielsen. An IT manager by day, Nielsen made his presence known from the off. Within five minutes England keeper David Seaman clattered into Diego Simeone in the box. It was a stonewall penalty. Nielsen pointed to the spot, and Gabriel Batistuta dispatched the kick with his fifth goal of the tournament to put Argentina one up. It was a nightmare start for the Three Lions.

Fortunately, 18-year-old Liverpool *wunderkind* Michael Owen had clearly been studying the Argentinian playbook. Three minutes later, he surged into the box and leapt to the floor as two opposition defenders cut across him. Replays confirmed that Owen had executed a sublime dive. Nielsen was fooled and Shearer equalised emphatically from the subsequent penalty.

The brilliant, breathless start continued. With 16 minutes gone, Argentina pushed to regain their lead. Paul Ince wrestled possession back near the England box and knocked it forward to Beckham. He saw Owen making a run into the Argentinian half and clipped a flawless ball into his path. The teenager's touch was just as perfect, taking it in his stride near the halfway line and bearing down upon Carlos Roa's goal. Roberto Ayala lay in wait for him, but some furiously fast feinting from the England striker befuddled him. Owen drifted out right and Roa came off his line to close the shooting angle. But it was too late. The keeper was left stranded as a sensational finish arrowed over his head and into the far-left corner. It was, quite simply, a wonder goal.

The attacking play continued, but the remainder of the first half was less frenetic than the opening quarter of an hour. England held firm when Argentina advanced and searched to increase their lead at every opportunity, Ince nearly doing exactly that when he volleyed a screamer of an effort from 30 yards that zipped just over the bar.

As the half entered stoppage time, Argentina won a free kick just outside the England penalty area. Batistuta lined up to take it, a lengthy run-up suggesting he was about to hit a thunderbolt towards Seaman's goal. The wall readied itself. The Argentine striker bombed towards the ball and promptly ran over it, leaving Juan Sebastián Verón to nudge the simplest of passes into the box to Javier Zanetti, who somehow had managed to evade the entire England defence. He had a free shot at goal and rifled the ball into Seaman's top corner. 'We had worked on that for four years, but it was the first time it succeeded,' he said afterwards. Trust England to be the first to be fooled by the routine; 2-2.

Half-time only served to bring an unwelcome break to the rousing action, which resumed at pace from the beginning of the second period. Less than two minutes into the second half, Beckham went to collect the ball near the halfway line and was crunched to the ground by Simeone, who charged into him from behind. Becks lay flattened on his front on the ground, and Nielsen blew for a free kick.

Now, what followed has been subject to one prevailing question: why? England had won the foul and Simeone's challenge, while being full-blooded, was hardly a leg-breaker. As Beckham remained on the floor and Simeone walked backwards away from him, maybe that Adidas ad he'd appeared in flashed through his mind. Maybe he thought he better make sure the prophecy it foretold came true. Because inexplicably, directly under the ref's nose, he flicked up his right leg into the back of Simeone's knee, and was shown a straight red card.

Simeone made a meal of it and started appealing before he'd even hit the ground, and his team-mates surrounded Nielsen imploring him to send Beckham off. Of course they did; this was Argentina. But it was all so unnecessary. A brief flash of petulance that consigned England to practically a full half of football with ten men.

In fairness to England, they played in much the same fashion as they had in the first half, attacking at will despite being a man light. It even looked like they might have won it when Sol Campbell nodded in from a corner in the 81st minute and charged off feverishly shrieking in celebration. Nielsen ruled it out, and no one was really sure why. It later turned out the ref had seen a stray elbow from Shearer make contact with Roa. It could have been more disastrous were it not for Anderton, whose quick thinking managed to break up Argentina's subsequent counter attack just as it looked as though they might win it themselves, with half of England's players having ran off jubilantly after Campbell.

Extra time came and went and the teams still couldn't be separated. Penalties. In 1998, England fans were starting to suspect how this one might go. Since 1990 they'd had two more shoot-outs, both at Euro '96, where they'd beaten Spain before losing once more to the Germans. It was not an enticing prospect for Three Lions supporters. Certainly not against Argentina, who to that point had competed in six shoot-outs and won five.

Both opening kicks were scored, then a glimmer of hope that things might be different this time for England as Seaman produced a terrific save to deny Hernán Crespo. The optimism was brief, Ince seeing his penalty saved by Roa immediately after. The next five all went in, leaving extra-time substitute David Batty needing to score. Roa, a devout Seventh-day Adventist, observed the sabbath on a Saturday, and refused to play matches scheduled for that day. Unfortunately it was a Tuesday. He guessed correctly and repelled Batty's effort. England were out.

A euphoric Argentina passed through to the quarters, where they were eliminated by the Netherlands courtesy of a spectacular Dennis Bergkamp goal. In England, the aftermath led to widespread devastation. They'd turned in a thrilling display but had still come up short. For fans and press alike, there was only one man to blame.

The *Daily Mirror* ran with the headline '10 Heroic Lions, One Stupid Boy' the following day, and inside printed a dartboard adorned with Beckham's face. A group of fans in London went one further, burning an effigy of the midfielder, and he received numerous death threats. The reaction was widespread and savage.

Football has a knack for stories of redemption. Four years on at the 2002 World Cup, England having only qualified courtesy of a stupendous Beckham free kick in the last moments of their final match, the sides were drawn against each other once more, this time in the groups. Michael Owen pulled out his old trick against the Argies again and dived to win a penalty. Beckham, now captain, stepped up and buried it, along with the demons of Saint-Étienne.

1998: Where's Ronnie?

Sunday, 12 July 1998
Stade de France
Saint-Denis, France

There aren't many players who can claim to have been as integral to their team as Ronaldo was for Brazil going into the 1998 World

Cup. They might have been reigning champions. They might have been the bookies' favourites to retain their title. And they might have had a team peppered with superstars looking to take 'Samba football' back to the pinnacle of the game. But Ronaldo was the focal point; the all-conquering forward who would be Brazil's ultimate weapon.

He may only have been 21 at the time, but there's no understating just how important Ronaldo was for Brazilian hopes of winning a record-extending fifth World Cup. Long before the Ronaldo of the Cristiano variety was breaking records, *Il Fenomeno* was making his own history. He'd won back-to-back FIFA World Player of the Year awards in 1996 and 1997, and in as equally short a time had broken the world record transfer fee twice with moves to Barcelona and then Inter Milan. He was, simply, the man who would make great things happen for Brazil. As *The Guardian* put it, 'The hopes and dreams of a nation rested on his shoulders.' No pressure, then.

Despite Ronaldo and Brazil's giant stature as the tournament began, their World Cup didn't get off to the most convincing of starts, struggling past Scotland to claim a 2-1 win in their opening game. Brazilian worries faded somewhat after a comfortable 3-0 victory over Morocco in their second, only to swiftly return with a vengeance following a humbling 2-1 defeat at the hands of Norway. They still progressed to the knockout stages as group winners, but Brazil were rattled.

Worse still, Ronaldo had not been at his rampant best. Rumours persisted that he was struggling with a knee problem (something that would hamper his career in later years). As a result he couldn't always train, and Brazil were pumping their star player full of pain-relieving injections to get him through. There were off-the-field problems too. His national team had flown out his parents – who were separated – to support him in France, but decided to put them up in the same house. This would prove a distraction for Ronaldo, as he found himself repeatedly having to deal with his mother and father arguing.

Yet as Brazil began their knockout campaign with a last-16 tie against Chile in Paris, it seemed any off-field problems or knee niggles were a world away from Ronaldo's mind. He was back to his brilliant best, scoring twice as Brazil romped through to the quarter-finals with a 4-1 win. His excellent form continued as Brazil overcame Denmark and then the Netherlands to reach the final against hosts France. Their talisman was firing on all cylinders and looked unstoppable yet again. So you can imagine the shock that reverberated around the football world when, 72 minutes before kick-off in the final, Brazil submitted their team sheet – with Ronaldo on the bench.

This bombshell caused something of a media frenzy. John Motson, commentating for the BBC, described the scene, 'I've never had anything like this in my career. The scenes in the commentary boxes for the last 45 minutes have been absolute mayhem and chaos.' Back in the studio, presenter Des Lynam clearly thought the news so unbelievable that he decided to give the audience some proof, showing the official FIFA team sheet to the camera and highlighting that Edmundo would be playing as striker for Brazil, with Ronaldo relegated to the role of substitute.

People had suspected something wasn't right when the Brazil players didn't emerge from the dressing room to warm up. Rumours of what might have happened swirled. Had Ronaldo come down with a sudden illness? Maybe his knee problems had got the better of him. There were reports he was suffering from an ankle injury. Some even suggested that the whole thing was an elaborate way of unsettling the French team, and that Ronaldo would be substituted on very early in the game. Whatever it was, confusion reigned in the stands, TV studios and living rooms across the globe. Surely, *surely* the world's best striker couldn't miss the World Cup Final.

And then, shortly before kick-off, some more news filtered through. Brazil coach Mário Zagallo had reinstated Ronaldo in the team. Gary Lineker, who was interviewing David Ginola ahead of the match at the time, broke the news as 'the biggest wind-up in World Cup football history'. Over on French TV, pundits accused Brazil of gamesmanship, aimed at disturbing the focus of the French team. What had actually gone on behind the scenes?

Earlier that day at the Brazilian team hotel, the players had retired to their rooms to rest after lunch. Ronaldo, rooming with Roberto Carlos, had gone to bed, when he suddenly fell to the floor, shaking uncontrollably. Reportedly, Carlos initially thought his team-mate was joking, only to realise that what was happening was something much more sinister. Carlos ran to get help, first finding Edmundo, who in turn ran through the corridors waking his colleagues and the Brazil staff up to alert them of the situation.

Ronaldo was suffering a long convulsive fit. Midfielder César Sampaio was the first person to administer first aid, reaching into Ronaldo's mouth and grabbing his tongue to prevent him from swallowing it. Doctors soon arrived and Ronaldo came to after being unconscious for over three minutes. He was soon up and walking around, but the scene left the squad unnerved and worried, with Edmundo stating later that 'all the players were scared by what they saw'. As the Brazil team left the hotel to head to the Stade de France and the World Cup Final, Ronaldo was not with them, instead taking a trip to hospital for tests.

After three hours, Ronaldo arrived at the stadium with less than an hour left before kick-off. Reflecting on his short hospital stay years later, he revealed that after a variety of medical tests, there was 'no conclusion' regarding his condition. 'I was all right,' he said. 'It was like the convulsion had never happened.' Maybe this was the case for him, but it certainly wasn't for his team-mates. Their trip to the game had been a sombre one. Zagallo remembered that ordinarily, 'When Brazil leave for a match, all there is, is music. But on that day, this didn't happen. There was no music on the bus. Everyone, all the players, were asking about Ronaldo.'

When Ronaldo finally got into the dressing room, he found a team of players – usually brimming with confidence – looking shell-shocked and worried. But the more pressing matter was the fact that he was down to start the final as a sub. This, he would not accept. And he told his manager as much. 'I have to play. I'm fine, I'm OK,' he said to Zagallo. In turn, Zagallo turned to the Brazil team doctor, Lídio Toledo, 'I was waiting for the doctor to make a call. But he said nothing.' The manager, faced with the world's best footballer telling him he was fine and ready to play, restored Ronaldo to the starting line-up.

The match itself was one to forget for Brazil. The traumatic events earlier in the day had left their mark, and it didn't help that they were facing a sensational French side featuring an unstoppable Zinedine Zidane, who would score twice as they put Brazil to the sword 3-0 to claim their first World Cup crown. The entire Brazil team looked tense and fragile throughout the game. Brazilian journalist Ricardo Porto is adamant why this was the case, 'The team was not focused on playing. They were focused on looking at Ronaldo.' Indeed, there was a moment in the first half when Ronaldo was clattered by France goalkeeper Fabien Barthez, and numerous Brazil players were seen dramatically holding their heads in their hands, clearly nervous that any knock could potentially have dire consequences for their team-mate given what had happened to him earlier in the day. This was no frame of mind to be playing a World Cup Final in.

In the aftermath, conspiracy theories quickly surfaced. The most prevalent of these was the suggestion that Brazil sponsors Nike had forced Ronaldo to play, fearful that the financial cost of not fielding football's biggest star in football's biggest game would be significant. This was never proven, and Ronaldo to this day claims he was fit to play. It certainly wasn't one of his best performances. But just as it was for David Beckham, he'd go on to exorcise those demons in style four years later.

2002: The Saipan Incident

Thursday, 23 May 2002
Republic of Ireland team meeting
Saipan, Northern Mariana Islands

The World Cup broke new ground in 2002 as it landed in Asia for the first time. South Korea and Japan had submitted rival bids to host the tournament, but FIFA decided to kill two birds with one stone and told them they could host together or not at all. So the world's best players trooped to the Far East for a World Cup unlike any that had gone before.

The Republic of Ireland returned after missing out on France '98, having emerged impressively from a difficult qualifying group featuring Portugal and the Netherlands. Manager Mick McCarthy had a squad with genuine quality, not least thanks to the two Keanes, Messrs Robbie and Roy. The former, aged 21, was exciting fans with his impressive performances up front for a Leeds United side that had just finished fifth in the Premier League. The latter needs no introduction. The voracious, volatile Manchester United captain wore the armband for his country by this point, too, and was ready to eagerly lead the Boys in Green into battle at the World Cup.

But then, as the tournament approached, things started to go pear-shaped. The Football Association of Ireland sent McCarthy's team to the minuscule Pacific island of Saipan for preparations, purportedly to get the players acclimatised the hot, humid conditions in that part of the world. The trip started badly, and only got worse.

The squad arrived at Dublin airport for their lengthy journey, comprising three separate flights, and were faced with a long wait in a packed departure lounge. Players mixed with fans, journalists and holidaymakers – hardly the greatest way to focus ahead of playing in football's biggest competition. Then a comedy of errors developed when Ireland finally did make it to Saipan. The training pitches there were rock-hard and would have looked more at home on the moon than accommodating elite footballers. The FAI somehow managed to misplace all of the team's training gear, meaning they had to borrow kits and footballs from the locality. Then when someone did finally water the pitches, they got a bit carried away and flooded them instead.

Roy Keane, used to only the highest standard of professionalism as part of Alex Ferguson's Old Trafford setup, was outraged. He described the FAI's training camp as a 'third world approach to the game'. In fairness, it was shambolic. Some players were injured on the inadequate surface. Any hopes Ireland's captain might have held that his team could be a surprise package at the World Cup seemed to be blowing away in the wind.

He decided he'd had enough. After having taken McCarthy aside to express his concerns on two separate occasions, only to have them fall on deaf ears, Keane decided he was off. He told his manager that he was withdrawing from the squad. Team physio Mick Byrne managed to talk him down off the ledge, and he stayed in Saipan. But not for long.

Amid all of these private rows, rumours had started to swirl in the press back home regarding the tension in the Irish camp. Several stories had been printed critical of Keane, branding him an oversensitive moaner. To dispel these, he'd agreed to give interviews to the media prior to deciding that he was going to stay and play in the World Cup. Always a man of his word – and despite having now reaffirmed his commitment to Ireland – he honoured his promise and sat down with Tom Humphries of the *Irish Times*. And it was explosive.

Keane explained what had happened in his own terms, outlined why his nose had been put out of joint, then announced that after the World Cup he'd be retiring from the national side. He didn't reveal anything that he hadn't already addressed with McCarthy, but the fact he'd now done so in public didn't sit well with the Ireland manager, and an infamous team meeting followed when the article hit newsstands.

McCarthy lambasted Keane in front of the entire squad, holding up a copy of the interview and enquiring why he'd done it. An argument broke out and the pair exchanged insults, before the manager accused his captain of having feigned injury to get out of playing in an earlier qualifying match. This lit all of Keane's many fuses, and he embarked on a verbal tirade condemning McCarthy.

'You're a fucking wanker. I didn't rate you as a player, I don't rate you as a manager and I don't rate you as a person. You're a fucking wanker and you can stick your World Cup up your arse. I've got no respect for you. The only reason I have any dealings with you is that somehow you are the manager of my country! You can stick it up your bollocks.'

Say what you think, Roy. The room was shocked into stunned silence. Forward Niall Quinn described the rant as 'the most surgical slaughtering anyone has ever got'. Rather unsurprisingly, McCarthy held a press conference shortly after and announced that he'd sent Keane home.

Shockwaves reverberated around Ireland and beyond. The team would be without their best player for the World Cup. Press camped outside of Keane's house to record any crumbs of comment that the former Ireland captain might offer, and it became a nightly appearance on the evening news to see Keane out walking his ever-forgiving Labrador, Triggs, who became something of a celebrity in his own right. Taoiseach Bertie Ahern got involved and implored Keane and McCarthy to resolve their differences so Keane could feature in the tournament. But even Ireland's figurehead couldn't mend the situation, and the side embarked on their World Cup campaign without their star man.

Ireland performed unexpectedly well in the groups, qualifying for the knockouts in second place behind Germany. They were eliminated by Spain in the last 16 on penalties.

Irish fans largely held Keane responsible for the situation, feeling that he should have put his personal differences with McCarthy aside to focus on the team's World Cup hopes. The incident became one of almost mythological renown, and even inspired a musical, *I, Keano*, comedically reimagining those involved as members of a Roman legion preparing to do battle.

Keane eventually returned to the international fold in 2004, following the departure of McCarthy as manager. But the firebrand never made it to another World Cup.

2002: A Seismic Senegalese Upset

Friday, 31 May 2002
Seoul World Cup Stadium
Seoul, South Korea

Roy Keane wasn't the only star midfielder to hit the headlines ahead of the World Cup in South Korea and Japan. France's talisman Zinedine Zidane sustained a thigh injury in a warm-up game for the tournament, leaving a question mark over as to whether he'd be able to feature at all. It was a huge blow for Roger Lemerre's team, losing the man who had been so influential in helping *Les Bleus* to their championship four years earlier.

Still, this shouldn't pose *too* much of a problem. The 'Rainbow Team' – so nicknamed for their ethnically diverse squad – were all-conquering, and perhaps the best international team Europe had ever seen to that point, not to mention being ranked as the world's best side by FIFA. After their emphatic World Cup win on home soil, they followed it up by winning Euro 2000 in dramatic fashion courtesy of a David Trezeguet golden goal. They went to Asia as one of the favourites to retain their crown, and with a dazzling list of superstars too long to name in their ranks it was easy to understand why.

They'd been handed a pretty straightforward draw, too. Their group comprised Denmark, a Uruguay team with little star power, and debutants Senegal, who were up first in the opening match of the tournament. The West Africans' squad was almost entirely made up of players from the lower echelons of France's Ligue 1, and the country was largely thrilled simply to have made it to the World Cup.

But scratch beneath the surface, and the Senegalese weren't quite the pushover neutrals might have been expecting. The country had little footballing heritage but had just made it to their first Africa Cup of Nations Final in the winter, only losing to giants Cameroon on penalties. Much of the young squad would go on to earn big moves to the Premier League, and there was clear talent there. Regardless, a dominant French rout was universally expected.

Senegal's French manager Bruno Metsu had an inspiring message for his team ahead of kick-off. 'I know that tonight, after the match is finished, people will be talking about you right across the world,' he told them. 'Show me what you're capable of.' There was also the small matter that Senegal had previously been colonised by France, only gaining independence in 1960. The players had a point to prove.

Anyone expecting the West Africans to sit back and defend was grossly mistaken. It was thought that with France's considerable firepower, strike partnership Trezeguet and Thierry Henry both having just finished as top scorers in Serie A and the Premier League respectively, that Metsu's team would do anything they could to repel *Les Bleus*. But from kick-off, while the French looked threatening, Senegal for their part mercilessly attacked down the wings. Striker El Hadji Diouf was brilliant, the main focal point of his side's play.

On the half-hour mark, the soon-to-be Liverpool forward was released down the left wing. He was entirely on his own, and when Frank Leboeuf approached to dispossess him it looked like Diouf's run might come to nothing. He dummied superbly to push forwards toward the byline. His options in the box were sparse, and he fired a low ball aiming to find Papa Bouba Diop. Emmanuel Petit touched it towards goalkeeper Fabien Barthez, who spilled the ball out across his goal line. Diop, who was already on the floor by this point after stretching to try and meet Diouf's cross, managed to compose himself to scoop the ball into the open net. Senegal, against all expectations, had the lead.

The midfielder sprinted off to the corner flag in celebration, an iconic moment that's been replayed countless times on World Cup best-of programmes. It was unorthodox. He removed his shirt, placed it on the ground, and danced round it with his team-mates. Not quite as legendary as Roger Milla jiving with the corner flag, but a memorable, seminal moment for African football.

Of course, they still had an hour to keep the French and their fearsome attacking arsenal at bay. At times, the Senegalese goal led a charmed life as France pushed incessantly for an equaliser. Henry and Trezeguet both hit the woodwork, and keeper Tony Sylva produced some remarkable saves to deny *Les Bleus*. Senegal held on for a 1-0 win. They'd achieved the impossible.

The full-time whistle brought with it emphatic celebrations, as the players danced on the pitch with Senegal flags. One man who stayed grounded was coach Metsu. 'We have got to make sure we come down off our cloud and get our mind straight for our next two games,' he said in his post-match interview. 'It won't mean anything to get a good result against France and then go out of the tournament with three points.'

His players listened. Draws against Denmark and Uruguay followed, ensuring their progression to the last 16. Another sensational performance ensued as Metsu's men defeated Sweden 2-1 via a Henri Camara golden goal to earn a spot in the quarter-finals and equal the best showing from an African side at the World Cup. It ended there for them as they found themselves on the wrong end of a golden goal against Turkey. But they'd well and truly demonstrated their footballing credentials before the world, and were welcomed back to Dakar as heroes.

France's campaign went from bad to worse. Henry was sent off in the goalless draw with the Uruguayans that followed, before Denmark put the final nail in the coffin by beating the French 2-0 in the final group game. A half-fit Zidane was rushed back into the team for that clash, but couldn't make the difference. He wasn't quite done with making World Cup headlines and had a last tilt at glory four years later in Germany. Meanwhile, the curtain went down on France's 2002 title defence without the team scoring a single goal.

2002: South Korea, Italy and the Worst Referee Ever

Tuesday, 18 June 2002
Daejeon World Cup Stadium
Daejeon, South Korea

Senegal's win against France in the tournament curtain raiser set the tone for a World Cup of shocks. Particularly eye-catching was co-hosts South Korea's unlikely run to the semi-finals. But on their way to the final four, they featured in a controversial last-16 match against Italy that raised questions about the competition's integrity, and especially that of the man in the middle, Ecuadorian referee Byron Moreno.

Moreno grew up in Ecuador's capital Quito and was obsessed with football. However, the youngster was never interested in being a player. He idolised referees. And while it might be hard to imagine any teenager in this day and age going to bed beneath a poster of Howard Webb, for Moreno it made sense. His father had a job within Ecuador's football federation, rating and assessing the performances of officials. He grew up surrounded by the laws of the game, and so it felt natural for him to pursue a career as a man in black. After a few years refereeing in Ecuador's top flight, he earned the ultimate honour: a call-up to be one of the officials at the 2002 World Cup.

By this point, Moreno was a feared figure back home, officiating with a take-no-prisoners attitude. He once sent off seven players in one match and was eager to bring his no-nonsense style to the world stage. His first match at the tournament went by without incident as he oversaw the USA's 3-2 win over Portugal in the groups. But then he was assigned to that last-16 tie between Italy and South Korea.

Italy had a strong team in 2002 and were expected to go far. They'd stumbled slightly in the groups, only mustering second place, but if the *Azzurri* could get things together at the right time they were dangerous. South Korea were breaking new ground under the management of Dutch coach Guus Hiddink, having made it to the knockout stages for the first time. Despite the home advantage, the Italians were overwhelming favourites to win and reach the quarters.

Step up Moreno for his moment in the sun, turning in one of the worst refereeing performances the World Cup has ever seen and making himself public enemy number one across all of Italy.

Italian fans were already disillusioned with officiating prior to their clash with South Korea. They'd seen four goals disallowed through the group stages, and many supporters sympathised with manager Giovanni Trapattoni, who felt his side would have clinched top spot were it not for so many decisions going against them. Things were about to get a whole lot worse.

As the teams trooped out ahead of kick-off, South Korean supporters in the stands held up cards spelling out 'Again 1966', referencing their neighbours' famous 1-0 win over Italy that consigned them to an early exit from the World Cup in England. The South now wanted to make their own history against the *Azzurri*.

And to be fair, Hiddink's men went toe-to-toe with their illustrious opposition from the off, pressing relentlessly and looking to attack wherever possible. Within four minutes they'd won a penalty. Christian Panucci ragged Seol Ki-Hyeon's shirt and pulled him down in the box, leading Moreno to point to the spot. It was just about the last thing the Ecuadorian got right in the game. The Koreans couldn't take advantage of their deserved spot-kick, Ahn Jung-Hwan seeing his effort saved superbly by Gianluigi Buffon.

It was Italy who struck first, taking the lead thanks to a bullet Christian Vieri header from a corner. The remainder of the first half passed by rather smoothly, South Korea pushing for an equaliser and Italy reverting to type and getting back in numbers to defend their lead.

Moreno seemed to take leave of his senses during the half-time interval, because when he returned he embarked on a string of downright bizarre decisions, all of which went against Trapattoni's side. At the beginning of the second period Alessandro Del Piero found himself wrestling for possession with Kim Tae-Young inside the Korean box. Kim quite blatantly threw an elbow into the striker's face, leaving him visibly shocked. It looked for all the world like a penalty and a red card. Moreno's call? Free kick to South Korea.

As the game ticked towards 90 minutes and the Koreans pushed further and further up the pitch searching for a leveller, Moreno failed to spot Paolo Maldini getting booted in the head while defending a corner. Shortly after that, the attacking pressure finally paid off. With just two minutes remaining Seol drove a shot beyond Buffon after Italy failed to clear a cross and sent the game into golden goal extra time.

Moreno failing to send Kim off and award Italy a penalty earlier turned out just to be the hors d'oeuvre. As the sides slogged through the additional period Moreno started to look off the pace. The extra minutes were clearly taking their toll on the rather rotund ref and he frequently found himself behind the play as the ball pinged from end to end. With the first 15 coming to a close, Francesco Totti wriggled free in the box and advanced towards a shooting position. Song Chong-Gug decided it was an all or nothing moment, clattered into the Roma striker and sent him crashing to the ground.

The referee, who seemed to be miles away at the time, blew his whistle and lolloped urgently to where the incident had taken place. The hearts of 40,000 South Korean fans in Daejeon and millions across the country sank. Italy were going to have the chance to win it with one kick from the spot.

Or not. There would be no penalty for Italy. In fairness, it was by no means a stonewall spot-kick. There'd been definite contact, but the choice not to award it was less controversial than the decision he'd made in overlooking the elbow on Del Piero earlier. What was a lot more contentious was the fact he decided to book Totti for diving, which was clearly not the case. Worse still, Totti was already on a yellow card. He was off.

Italy were incensed and remonstrated at length with Moreno, who just seemed to smirk smugly and dismiss them. Nothing was going their way, and now they'd lost perhaps their most creative force to boot. It looked like salvation might finally have arrived when Damiano Tommasi put the ball in the net on 110 minutes, only to see it incorrectly chalked off for offside. As he ran back up the pitch he actually laughed, such was the ridiculousness of the decisions going against his team.

That's not to take anything away from South Korea, who put in a spirited, shrewd performance. With the game hurtling towards penalties, striker Ahn Jung-Hwan, the man who'd missed his spot-kick at the start of the match, rose high above Maldini to meet a swinging ball into the box. He played his club football at Perugia in Italy, and had just endured a poor campaign that only saw him score once all season. In Daejeon he equalled that tally and powered a lethal header beyond Buffon. It was the most golden of goals. The stadium went into raptures. South Korea had matched the North's feat and sent Italy packing.

An estimated three million people partied long into the night on the streets of Seoul. It was a seminal moment for football in the country. Things only got better a few days later when the side defeated Spain on penalties to make it to the semis. The story would end there as they lost 1-0 to Germany, but Hiddink's men had gone above and beyond what even the most hopeful fan might have thought possible.

For Italy, the post-mortem centred on only one man. 'No other team in the entire history of the World Cup has suffered so many injustices,' wrote the *Corriere della Sera* the following day. Tales abounded that Moreno must have been paid off, so bad was his performance. Some suggested FIFA had instructed him to help South Korea to win because it would be financially beneficial to have the hosts go far in the tournament. No evidence of this was ever found and Moreno strenuously denied all allegations, but it didn't matter. He'd become the most hated man in Italy overnight.

Politicians talked about him in the Italian parliament and labelled him a disgrace. A popular band wrote a song called 'Drop Dead Moreno' in which they implored him to get hit by a train. A seaside resort in Sicily named a particularly unpleasant block of public toilets after him. This was pure and unfiltered loathing.

FIFA received an astonishing 500,000 complaints about Moreno's officiating from all around the world – not just Italy. All the while, the Ecuadorian continued to enrage supporters by describing the match as 'one of the best performances of [his] career'. Amid all the hullabaloo, FIFA thought it best to send him home.

Back in Ecuador, Moreno was welcomed back with open arms, and even ran for mayor in Quito. Scandal soon followed, though. During a game he oversaw in the capital between LDU Quito and their biggest rivals SC Barcelona, and with the home team trailing in front of his mayoral electorate, Moreno added on an inexplicable 13 minutes of added time and awarded a penalty to Quito, who went on to score twice and win. For this, he received a lengthy ban and never returned to top-level officiating again.

His story reached a rather dark end in 2010 when he was caught smuggling six kilos of heroin in his underpants through JFK Airport in New York and was sent to prison. Italy fans rejoiced. Buffon commented, 'Six kilograms of drugs? He had them in 2002, but not in his underwear. In his system.' According to them, albeit in a very convoluted way, justice had been done.

2002: Brazilian Brilliance and a Disgraceful Dive

Sunday, 30 June 2002
International Stadium Yokohama
Yokohama, Japan

Brazil went to the Far East with a point to prove. After that crushing defeat in the 1998 final in France, Brazil responded the following year by winning the Copa América. But then things started to go off the rails. They were unconvincing in qualifying and crashed out of the 2001 Copa at the hands of lowly Honduras. By the time the World Cup rolled around, they were on their fifth manager in four years, Luiz Felipe Scolari. It looked dangerously like this golden generation of players might pass by without winning that fifth World Cup title that Brazil fans so dreamed of.

The squad Scolari took to Asia read like a who's who of the world's best. Seeing Rivaldo, Cafu, Ronaldinho and Roberto Carlos on the team sheet was the stuff of nightmares for the opposition. Such a glittering list of names hadn't helped Scolari in the Copa, though, so it was anyone's guess as to what kind of Brazil side would turn up at the World Cup.

When they found themselves 1-0 down to Turkey at half-time in their opener, things didn't appear promising. But the *Seleção* turned in a resolute second-half performance to turn things around. Ronaldo, back in the international fold despite not having played a single second across Brazil's entire qualifying campaign due to injury, had a moment of personal redemption to equalise on 50 minutes, before Rivaldo slotted home a somewhat dubious penalty late on to win it. Defender Alpay Özalan was shown a second yellow for the incident and the match finished in a tense, volatile atmosphere.

Brazil found a way, even if they had needed South Korean ref Kim Young-Joo's help. The story didn't end there, though. As the game entered its final seconds, Turkey were erratically searching for an equaliser. The Brazilians had managed to win a corner up the other end of the pitch and looked to close the game out. Enter Rivaldo.

The wizard-like Barcelona forward had grown up in abject poverty in the favelas of Recife, and due to malnourishment was bow-legged and had lost most of his teeth. Brazilian clubs rejected him through his early teens, considering him too physically weak to make it as a professional footballer. Yet against all odds he'd risen to the pinnacle of the game, even claiming the Ballon d'Or in 1999. His was a true Cinderella story. And then he did something that made everyone forget all that and saw him labelled a cheat for the rest of his career.

He went over to take the corner and hovered around the corner flag, having left the ball on the pitch. It was classic gamesmanship to waste a few precious seconds. That's par for the course. However, when Hakan Ünsal lightly kicked the ball towards Rivaldo in an attempt to hurry him up, the ball glanced off his thigh. The Brazilian collapsed to the ground holding his face, and in an Oscar-worthy performance writhed around until Kim showed Ünsal a red card.

The entire Turkish contingent were outraged, as were the South Korean fans in attendance at the game in Ulsan, who roared into a chorus of boos upon being treated to a slow-motion replay of the incident on the big screens. Rivaldo was fined by FIFA afterwards for unsportsmanlike behaviour, but that was the end of the matter. Ünsal still had to serve his suspension and Rivaldo doubled down on his actions afterwards. 'Obviously the ball didn't hit me in the face,' he told reporters. 'But I was still the victim.'

After coming through that, Rivaldo's incredible legacy suitably tarnished, Scolari's men went from strength to strength, scoring nine goals in the next two group games against China and Costa Rica as they qualified for the knockout stages with a 100 per cent record. A 2-0 win over Belgium in the last 16 followed, sending Ronaldo's personal tally to five goals in four games. He was well and truly back to his brilliant best.

Next up in the quarters were England, who posed a sterner test and even took the lead through Michael Owen. Rivaldo equalised on the brink of half-time, then David Seaman and his horrific ponytail had a moment to forget when Ronaldinho's dinked free kick from a ludicrous angle caught the Arsenal shot-stopper off guard and looped into the net behind him. Brazil were through to the semis and it all seemed rather easy.

Then who should they face in the last four but Turkey. The team united in the wake of what they perceived to be an unjust result against the Brazilians and, in only their second World Cup and their first since the 1950s, had embarked upon an unlikely run to the semis. And they were gunning for revenge.

Ronaldo, meanwhile, began to fear the injury problems that had plagued him for the last two years might be returning when he picked up a knock in training. The news of this was leaked to the press, and ahead of the Turkey game Brazil's superstar striker was dreading having to answer questions about it, fearing the extra focus on his fitness issues in the media might influence Scolari's team selection. He had a unique solution. Ronaldo turned up for his pre-match press conference having shaved all of his hair off save for a crassly cultivated semi-circle on the front of his head. The press promptly went into meltdown quizzing him about his new haircut rather than his potential injury.

The forward was straight into the starting 11 and proved the difference for the *Seleção* once more as Brazil overcame Turkey 1-0 in a hot-blooded encounter. The South Americans were into their third successive World Cup Final, and the chance for Ronaldo and Co to banish the painful memories of France was one game away.

Their opponents for the all-important match in Yokohama were Germany. In 2002 they were perhaps the perfect example of the clinical German efficiency so often associated with *Die*

Mannschaft. Now managed by old striker Rudi Völler, they'd bullied their way into the final with a physical, unrelenting style, conceding just once in the process. Between the sticks was the fearsome Oliver Kahn. The Bayern Munich keeper had been flawless throughout the tournament, collecting five clean sheets and looking immovable at the back. Brazil would need a vintage Ronaldo performance to break through.

They got one. After a first half that saw both sides rattle the woodwork but no goals, Ronaldo – still sporting an ungainly wedge of hair on his forehead – came to life. On 67 minutes, in a moment of horribly cruel irony, Kahn made his first and only mistake of the World Cup to gift Brazil the lead. The goalkeeper attempted to hold on to a long shot from Rivaldo but spilled the ball into the path of Ronaldo, who was following in. He tapped it into an open goal; 1-0 Brazil.

That man again sealed the win ten minutes later, rifling a devastatingly accurate finish into Kahn's bottom-left corner. Brazil lifted the World Cup for a record fifth time, and Ronaldo took home the Golden Boot along with his winner's medal having struck eight times across seven matches. Any doubts about his fitness had been cast aside. Any suggestions that he might falter once more in football's biggest game had been incorrect. *Il Fenomeno* was back, and Brazil owed World Cup number five to him.

2006: Third Time Unlucky for Graham Poll

Thursday, 22 June 2006
Gottlieb-Daimler-Stadion
Stuttgart, Germany

The World Cup returned to Europe in 2006, with Germany on hosting duties. More puritanical fans were delighted to see the tournament return to what they considered a traditional footballing nation. That, or they were just happy that they wouldn't have to wake up at 6am to watch Slovenia versus Paraguay.

The proceedings in Germany once the play kicked off were pretty familiar, too. All of the biggest footballing countries made it through the groups. England had high hopes then got knocked out on penalties. And there was some rather colourful refereeing. In a World Cup where cards were dished out like confetti, it was English official Graham Poll who grabbed the most headlines.

Poll travelled to Germany as one of the most experienced referees at the tournament. He'd overseen a match at the previous World Cup, and was considered one of the main names in contention to take charge of the final come the end of the month.

A referee's role is a peculiar one. The biggest achievement an official can hope for at the end of the game is that precisely no one is talking about them. Poll oversaw two matches in the first rounds of fixtures without incident. It was job done as far as he was concerned, as both games passed without him making any contentious calls or obvious errors. He certainly hadn't hurt his chances of being awarded some big ties as the tournament went on. Then Poll was assigned to the final group clash between Croatia and Australia, and everything changed.

The match was delicately poised. The Socceroos, under the management of South Korea's hero from four years ago, Guus Hiddink, had recorded their first World Cup victory courtesy of some late Tim Cahill heroics in their opener against Japan, before losing to defending champions Brazil. Croatia also lost to Brazil but could only manage a draw against the Japanese. It left them needing a win to progress. Anything else would see Australia through to the last 16.

This was a match of special pertinence beyond football. Many Croatians had fled the country while it was part of Yugoslavia and moved to Australia. Of the Socceroos' 2006 squad, eight of the players had Croatian heritage, including legendary midfielder Mark Bresciano and captain Mark Viduka, whose cousin Luka Modrić was on the bench for the opposition. It added a unique edge to the occasion.

The significance of the game should not have affected Poll, who in his lengthy career had refereed FA Cup and UEFA Cup finals. However, he started the clash in inauspicious fashion. After ordering Australia to retake the kick-off for no apparent reason, he incited the ire of the Croatians inside two minutes by pulling the play back for a free kick when they felt they had the advantage. However, Poll was vindicated somewhat when Darijo Srna walloped an absolute screamer over the Aussie wall and straight into the top corner. Croatia had an early lead.

A very open first half ended with Poll awarding Australia a penalty for handball. His decision was bang on the money. Replays showed that defender Stjepan Tomas had his arm high in the air, his outstretched fist grazing a cross that had just been whipped into the box. Craig Moore dispatched the spot-kick and Australia were level. And it looked like Poll had moved past his early wobbles.

The early stages of the second half brought an agonising moment for Australian keeper Zeljko Kalac. The shotstopper was very much a stand-in for his country, behind established number one Mark Schwarzer. But Hiddink decided to give Kalac the nod for the all-important Croatia game, feeling he'd perform well against the country of his heritage. That wasn't quite the case. Croatia captain Niko Kovač fired a low, speculative effort straight at Kalac from range, but the goalkeeper fumbled it horrifically and saw it bounce over him and into his own net. The Europeans had the lead once more. Fortunately for Kalac, his own cock-up was far overshadowed by that of another later on.

On the hour, Poll booked Croatian centre-back Josip Šimunić for blocking off Harry Kewell as he romped towards the box. Then he inexplicably waved away another Australian shout for a penalty when Tomas reproduced his antics from earlier and punched the ball away as it flew into the penalty area. The Socceroos were incensed, but play continued.

The match descended into chaos. Australia threw everyone forward searching for that equaliser that would send them through to the last 16, while Croatia defended their lead vigorously and with little regard for the rules of the game. On 79 minutes Australia had their leveller, Kewell volleying the ball home from close range after Croatia failed to clear a cross.

As the teams fought for their World Cup lives, Poll found himself with his hands full. He flashed deserved red cards to Dario Šimić and Brett Emerton two minutes apart, bringing both sides down to ten men as they battled away.

Poll struggled to keep a lid on things, and even let the fact that Srna pushed him after he sent off Šimić slide. As the seconds ticked down, Croatia had Australia pinned back deep in their own half but managed to clear to Viduka on the halfway line. Poll's old pal from earlier, Šimunić, had been left as the last man back and decided to take extreme action, hauling Viduka to the deck. The ball pinballed into the path of onrushing Joshua Kennedy, who looked to have a free run at the Croatian goal. In the most glaring case of 'in for a penny, in for a pound' ever, Šimunić hacked him down from behind before he could go any further.

The English official stopped play. Šimunić was about to get his marching orders. He was already on a yellow, and in truth the two fouls he'd just committed within seconds of each other were both worthy of a booking anyway. Poll produced the yellow card and Šimunić stomped off. Except he didn't troop off the pitch; he just carried on playing. The referee had forgotten to show him the red card.

Commentary teams the world over rambled in bemused astonishment at how Poll could have made such a basic error. Šimunić didn't exactly keep his head down after that, and Poll showed him a *third* yellow at the end of the game for dissent. Finally, this time, he did follow it up with the overdue red. The match finished 2-2 and Australia went into the knockouts.

The game had been a harrowing one for Poll, who saw his chances of refereeing football's biggest event go up in a puff of smoke. He chose to jump before he was pushed and asked FIFA not to consider him for any more matches at the World Cup. The governing body obliged, presumably without much effort to convince him otherwise.

In his autobiography the following year, Poll revealed that he'd accidentally noted Šimunić's second yellow card beside Australia's number three in his little black book. He offered the explanation that the Croatian centre-back's accent had confused him. To be fair, Šimunić was born and raised in Canberra and spoke English with a broad Aussie twang. That didn't deter fans back in England, who upon his return to the Premier League serenaded Poll with chants of 'three is the magic number' and brandished yellow cards with the number three daubed on them. Football's a funny old game.

2006: The Battle of Nuremberg

Sunday, 25 June 2006
Frankenstadion
Nuremberg, Germany

Graham Poll's gaffe aside, 2006 really was a quite brutal World Cup. It holds the record for both the most yellow and most red cards shown at any edition of the tournament. This was in part blamed on FIFA president Sepp Blatter, whose directive to referees to adhere to the laws of the game as strictly as possible seemed to result in harsher decisions throughout the competition.

There was one game in particular, though, that would have seen even the most lenient official flashing a barrage of cards. The belligerents were Portugal and the Netherlands, who met in a bloodthirsty last-16 clash that came to be known as the Battle of Nuremberg.

In the blue corner were Marco van Basten's Netherlands. They'd had a straightforward if uninspiring campaign in the group stages, finishing second to Argentina. The most entertaining moment of their World Cup run to that point had come in the stands during their first match, in Leipzig, when a large group of Dutch fans sporting special orange lederhosen provided by beer company Bavaria had been prevented from entering the stadium because Budweiser was the official beer of the World Cup, not Bavaria. Rather than miss the game, they watched in their underpants.

In the red corner, Luiz Felipe Scolari was back, this time managing Portugal. They'd suffered a crushing disappointment losing in the final of their home Euros in 2004 to outsiders Greece, so were looking to make amends in Germany. With potentially the country's greatest team, featuring the likes of Luís Figo, Ricardo Carvalho, Deco, and some kid called Cristiano, Portugal had romped through the groups, winning every match.

It was certainly a fascinating match-up, two historic footballing nations going head to head at the World Cup for the very first time. But there was no reason to suspect there'd be any special animosity in the fixture. Until the game kicked off, that is, and the pair set about each other like drunken thugs in a pub car park.

Mark van Bommel set the scene, cynically tripping Ronaldo less than two minutes in. The Dutchman received the first of many yellow cards in a match where Russian referee Valentin Ivanov must have been concerned that he'd get a repetitive strain injury. It didn't take long before he was again reaching for his pocket. Five minutes later, Ronaldo was the victim once more as Khalid Boulahrouz was added to the book for planting his studs high on the Portugal star's thigh. Replays confirmed he was lucky to come away with just a caution.

With the Netherlands clearly deciding that brutality was the way forward, Portugal resolved to play them at their own game. After 20 minutes they collected their first booking, Maniche going into the back of Van Bommel and sending him to the ground. He felt hard done by but recovered quickly enough to strike the game's only goal three minutes later, evading the Netherlands defence superbly and firing a devastating finish beyond Edwin van der Sar. It was a fleeting moment of genuine quality in a match that then fast descended into all-out war.

The first casualty was Ronaldo. An accumulation of heavy tackles on the Manchester United forward saw him sustain a knee injury that forced him off after half an hour, with Simão taking his place. The next to go was Portugal's Costinha, except no one would be replacing him when he left the action. Already on a yellow for a crunching tackle he'd made earlier, he saw the match's first red in first-half stoppage time. He was actually dismissed for a handball, but the savagery would only resume after the interval.

Van Bommel, the man who'd opened proceedings in such ferocious fashion, became Portugal's primary target. Petit saw yellow for felling him early in the second half, then in a melee while play was stopped, Figo headbutted him. For a second it looked like the Dutch hardman might flatten Figo, before deciding against it. After the game, Scolari defended his captain in enigmatic fashion, stating, 'Jesus Christ may be able to turn the other cheek, but Luís Figo isn't Jesus Christ.' However, it was a biblical-scale miracle that the Portugal skipper only managed to pick up a yellow, his sneaky Glasgow kiss happening behind the back of Ivanov. The 'football' continued.

Van Bommel might have thought better of exacting revenge on Figo, but Boulahrouz wasn't above it. As the two challenged for a loose ball down the wing, the Dutch wing-back threw an accurate elbow into Figo's face. Ivanov showed him a second yellow, the teams now both reduced to ten men.

The barbarism and bad blood flowed on. Deco, enraged that the Netherlands hadn't returned the ball to Portugal after they'd put it out so a player could get treatment for an injury, heartily slid in on Dutch centre-back Johnny Heitinga, who was marauding forwards. Deco became the latest name in the book, and the anger spilled over on to the touchline, with staff from both sides tangling in a pitchside scuffle. It was sheer pandemonium.

Five minutes later, the little Portuguese magician walked. Deco picked up the ball to prevent the Netherlands taking a quick free kick in their pursuit of an equaliser and Ivanov sent him off, leaving Portugal with nine.

The cards continued to flow remorselessly, ending finally with a second yellow for Giovanni van Bronckhorst in the 95th minute. The dismissed players, minus Costinha, were caught by television cameras sat on some stairs away from the pitch, looking like shellshocked toddlers consigned to the naughty step. Finally the havoc was brought to a close, and Portugal went on to infuriate England in the quarters.

All in all, Ivanov showed a scarcely believable 16 yellows and four reds. Unsurprisingly, the tally stands as the most cards shown in a World Cup match. Blatter, ever the paradigm of virtue, decided to blame the whole affair on the referee, criticising Ivanov and stating that he 'was not at the same level as the participants'.

The Battle of Nuremberg typified what was a particularly ruthless World Cup, but the madness didn't end there. Five days later, Germany and Argentina brawled as the hosts defeated the South Americans on penalties, then Wayne Rooney was sent off in England's quarter-final with Portugal for stamping on Ricardo Carvalho, exploding in the face of club team-mate Ronaldo, who worked his persuasive powers on the referee. But the most shocking, flabbergasting, what-the-hell-have-we-just-seen flashpoint was reserved for the final itself.

2006: Zizou Loses His Head

Sunday, 9 July 2006
Olympiastadion
Berlin, Germany

Every now and then, a footballer capable of transcending team loyalties comes along. These one-in-a-million players command the attention of the world with their sheer trailblazing brilliance. Love them or hate them, you can't help but be drawn into watching them at every possible opportunity, captivated by the mere possibility that you might witness some magic. Zinedine Zidane was very much one of those players.

In a trophy-laden career spent largely between Juventus and Real Madrid, Zizou established himself through the late 1990s and early 2000s as quite simply the best midfielder in the business. Nothing seemed to be beyond him. For France, too, he'd been the lynchpin of success. Zidane scored twice in the World Cup Final in 1998 before playing an integral part in their Euros win two years later. He was considered so pivotal to *Les Bleus* that his absence due to injury at the 2002 World Cup was cited as the main reason France performed so poorly. It didn't matter what team he was in – Zidane was always the main man.

After a shock exit to Greece in the quarter-finals of Euro 2004, Zidane decided to hang up his international boots for good. The French golden era had come and gone; time for a new age to be ushered in. The fresh crop weren't exactly setting the world alight though, and found themselves struggling in qualifying. A run of three straight goalless draws at home to Israel, Ireland and Switzerland was particularly worrying.

Manager Raymond Domenech decided to call up the old guard. He asked Zidane to come back and be his captain. Zizou duly obliged, and along with the returning Claude Makélélé and Lilian Thuram, helped France climb from fourth in their qualifying group to the top spot. *Les Bleus* were heading to Germany.

Meanwhile, Zidane made another announcement: the World Cup would be his last act as a footballer. No more acrobatic volleys. No more swaggering through defences like they weren't there. No more slicing entire teams apart with one pinpoint pass. He was retiring from the sport completely, this time for good. But not before one last shot at glory.

France started the tournament poorly, with back-to-back draws against Switzerland and South Korea. Zizou berated his team-mates for spurning opportunities, clearly desperate to give the world one last show, but wasn't much better himself. *The Guardian* tore into him in its report after the Korea match, describing him as 'slow and sloppy' and warning, 'This was not the Zidane we will recall or want to recall.'

What's more, he'd managed to get himself suspended for the final, make-or-break group game against Togo, picking up yellows in each of France's two matches so far. Without him, the French managed to edge the African minnows 2-0 – coincidentally on Zidane's 34th birthday – and squeezed into the knockout stages behind Switzerland.

A question mark hung over the captain's head, with many suggesting he shouldn't even get back into the team for the knockout stages. Domenech kept the faith and restored him to the starting line-up for a monstrous last-16 tie against Spain. A match on the sidelines seemed to have done wonders for Zidane's form. He assisted one and scored another as the French came from behind to beat Spain 3-1 and earn a spot in the quarters. It was just the kind of vintage performance fans had been hoping for.

His renaissance didn't stop there. He set up the only goal in the next match as France defeated reigning champs and tournament favourites Brazil, before scoring a crucial penalty in a 1-0 win in the last four against Portugal. Zidane was looking unstoppable, and in the process he'd somehow managed to drag France into the final.

Italy lay in wait. Like France, the *Azzurri* had not been among the pre-tournament favourites, but in true Italian fashion had been defensively magnificent, conceding just once on the way to the final. Led by the supreme Fabio Cannavaro, who at 5ft 9in gave hope to even the most diminutive of centre-backs, Italy had enjoyed some last-gasp drama throughout the knockouts, beating Australia in the last 16 thanks to a 95th-minute penalty, before vanquishing hosts Germany in the semis with two goals in the last two minutes of extra time.

An unpredictable game in Berlin was guaranteed. The recent history of the sides added some fascinating context, too. The pair hadn't met since that dramatic Euro 2000 final when France edged the Italians through a David Trezeguet golden goal. FIFA had by now abandoned that short-lived extra-time experiment, but Italy were keen for revenge.

First blood, however, went to the French. Italy centre-back Marco Materazzi, who was never far from the limelight over the course of a frantic match, was harshly penalised for clipping Florent Malouda in the box inside seven minutes. Argentine referee Horacio Elizondo pointed to the spot, awarding France a very soft penalty.

No prizes for guessing who stepped up to take it. Zidane shifted on the spot and eyeballed Gianluigi Buffon in the Italian goal. The pressure was astronomical. Here he was with a chance to put his side ahead, in his last game for France; his last game full stop, on the biggest stage that world sport can provide.

Mere mortals might have wilted. Not Zizou, who languidly approached the ball and chipped a ludicrously audacious Panenka into the underside of the crossbar, where it bounced safely over Buffon's line. Zidane sprinted off calmly, having just put France ahead in the World Cup Final in the coolest way possible.

Ten minutes on the sides were back level, Andrea Pirlo whipping in a corner for that man Materazzi to rise highest and power a header beyond a flailing, helpless Fabien Barthez.

After that explosive start, the game became attritional with the majority of goalscoring opportunities coming from set pieces. Luca Toni had the ball in the net after nodding in a Pirlo free kick but the goal was disallowed for offside. With neither team capable of grinding the other down, the final headed for extra time.

The first half of the additional period belonged to France. Zidane, now in the twilight of the twilight of his career, was still running the show. Franck Ribéry looked like he might restore his side's lead when he made a mazy run into the box, but fired his shot wide. Then with a minute remaining Zidane himself came within a hair's breadth of making it 2-1, glancing a superb header towards goal and forcing Buffon into a quite sensational save. He couldn't have come closer to writing a glorious ending for himself.

Tempers became more fraught as the seconds wore on. Five minutes into the second half, Italy broke quickly up the pitch. Alessandro Del Piero charged at the French defence, but in his eagerness he fouled Makélélé in the process. France went to take the free kick quickly, but Elizondo stopped them. Something had happened up the other end of the pitch.

The referee, spectators and TV cameras had all been distracted by Italy's counter attack. Audiences the world over were bemused as to why a break in play had been ordered. The only indication as to what might have happened came from Materazzi, who lay in a crumpled heap on the floor. Cameras somewhat ominously focused on Zidane, who was hovering sheepishly nearby. And then came the replays.

The Italians had just thwarted a French attack, and Materazzi and Zidane exchanged words as they made their way back up the pitch. *Les Bleus'* captain jogged ahead of the Italian centre-back, but turned on his heel to face him, Materazzi appearing to have shouted something after him. From nowhere, the red mist descended. With just ten minutes left and a penalty shoot-out beckoning, Zidane planted a vicious headbutt into the Italian's chest, and the mouths of billions watching around the world dropped to the floor.

The referee and linesmen had been nowhere near the incident when it happened, and for a second it looked like Zidane might get away with it. But then Spanish fourth official Luis Medina Cantalejo rang the death knell of Zizou's career. He'd seen everything and dutifully informed Elizondo. The red card appeared, and Zinedine Zidane left the football pitch for a final time. Domenech waved his arms about animatedly like a Gallic Monsieur Bean, but it was no use. Zidane trudged off with his head down, straight past the World Cup trophy and into the dressing rooms.

The inevitable shoot-out followed. This was not something the Italians would have been particularly enthused by, having exited three of the last four World Cups on penalties, including that agonising final defeat to Brazil in 1994. But France were without their designated taker, the man who could provide such a calming influence to his team-mates. The *Azzurri* scored five faultless penalties, and Trezeguet's miss for France proved the difference. Italy lifted the World Cup for a fourth time.

In the wake of the match, questions whirled regarding what Materazzi might have said to so enrage Zidane. Unsubstantiated newspaper theories made scurrilous claims that the defender had made racist remarks, but Materazzi later revealed that the incident began when Zidane gloatingly offered to give him his shirt. The Italian responded, 'I'd prefer the whore that is your sister.'

With that, the greatest midfielder of his generation ran head first into ignominy. Sections of the French press condemned Zidane. *L'Équipe* got emotionally philosophical, asking, 'What should we tell our children, for whom you have become an example for ever?' Rumours abounded that certain members of the French camp were furious with Zidane, and blamed him for their loss.

When the squad returned to Paris, Zizou needn't have worried about what kind of reaction he'd get from fans. Supporters chanted his name raucously and French president Jacques Chirac delivered a glowing speech celebrating his career and achievements for *Les Bleus*. Put plainly, France may not have even been at the World Cup without him, let alone a whisker away from winning the whole thing, and those who mattered most recognised that.

In the ensuing years, Zidane has been quizzed about the incident numerous times. His anger towards Materazzi hasn't cooled, and in 2010 he said he'd 'rather die' than apologise to the Italian.

His legacy remains intact. In 2012, a gigantic, 5m-high statue of Zidane was unveiled in the French capital. It wasn't of him mid-shot, striking that awe-inspiring volley against Bayer Leverkusen in the Champions League Final. It wasn't of him heading home either of the goals he scored in France's World Cup Final win in 1998. It wasn't even that gutsy Panenka in 2006. Instead, that bullish head-butt was immortalised in bronze, with a screaming Materazzi cast midway through falling to the ground. For a player who never did things by the book, it may well have been the perfect ode.

2010: Time for Africa
Friday, 11 June 2010
Soccer City
Johannesburg, South Africa

When bidding for the 2010 World Cup opened, FIFA announced their plans to take the competition to a fifth different continent, confirming that they'd only be accepting bids from African nations. In 2004, Sepp Blatter revealed that South Africa's Nelson Mandela-backed campaign had won. Football's biggest party was heading for the Rainbow Nation in an event of huge importance to both the country and Africa as a whole.

African football had come a long way since the days of Zaire booting away free kicks. In 2010, a healthy chunk of the world's top players hailed from the continent, and respect for the African game was at an all-time high. Hosting the World Cup brought things full circle, from the humblest of beginnings to inviting the planet's best to play on their shores.

The move wasn't without controversy, though. The country's preparedness was called into question, while animal rights activists baulked at plans to slaughter a cow at each host stadium in a traditional South African blessing of good luck. Media outlets, particularly in European nations, criticised the security of South Africa and suggested the tournament would be unsafe for fans. One typically sensationalist *Daily Mail* article told of 'grisly murder scenes' and 'victims boiled alive'.

As it happened, the most unpleasant thing waiting for supporters came in the form of a long, plastic horn. The freshly renovated Soccer City in Johannesburg was to host the curtain-raiser, South Africa's opener against Mexico. The stadium carried great symbolism. Mandela had made his first speech upon being released from prison there in 1990, then six years later it played host as South Africa appeared in their first Africa Cup of Nations, which they then went on to win at the ground. It made sense that the arrival of the World Cup should be heralded there, too.

A colourful, all-singing, all-dancing opening ceremony preceded kick-off. Then, with the football about to begin, television viewers around the world adjusted their sets. A distracting, droning hum, akin to that a swarm of bees might make, echoed out of their speakers. No amount of fiddling with the volume settings was going to fix it. The world was being introduced to the vuvuzela.

The South African instrument was a popular fixture of football matches in the country, and it was going nowhere. Fans in the stadiums delighted in tooting the irritating horns to their heart's content from the first second of the opener to the last second of the final. So commentary teams spent the next month wrestling with the noise, no match report passed without a mention of the bothersome buzzing, and fans argued about watching matches with the TV on mute. France captain Patrice Evra even blamed his side's poor performance in a 0-0 draw with Uruguay later that evening on the instrument.

As it turned out, the humming sounds coming from the stands were just about the most interesting thing during a sterile first half that saw very few chances. The hosts, managed by Brazil's 1994 World Cup-winning manager Carlos Alberto Parreira, struggled for possession, and the festival atmosphere among the 84,000-strong crowd inside Soccer City was dampened. The first African World Cup was starting with a whimper.

Thankfully, the match exploded into life in the second half. With Mexico having pinned back all 11 *Bafana Bafana* players deep inside their own half, a stray pass gifted the South Africans possession. A sharp passing move saw the hosts work the ball into the Mexican half. Kagisho Dikgacoi, a bit-part midfielder at Fulham, looked up and spotted winger Siphiwe Tshabalala sprinting beyond the Mexico defence and into a gaping hole down the left flank.

One perfectly weighted pass later and Tshabalala, the man with surely the most satisfying name in World Cup history, was in. However, between the chasing centre-back Ricardo Osorio and onrushing goalkeeper Óscar Pérez, the shooting angle was tight. Like Thierry Henry in his prime, Tshabalala took one glimpse at the postage stamp in Pérez's top-left corner and promptly fired the ball straight into it.

Soccer City went into raptures. So did Peter Drury in the commentary box. 'Goal *Bafana Bafana*!' he screamed. 'Goal for South Africa! Goal for *all* Africa!'

Mexico had to go and ruin the party, Rafael Márquez slotting what was, in truth, a deserved equaliser ten minutes from time. After a moribund opening 45, the second period had been a bright, breathless spectacle, and South African fans had seen enough to get them excited.

Sadly, the high hopes crashed down to earth with a thump in their next game when Uruguay swept them aside 3-0. That all but ended their World Cup, leaving them needing to beat the French, hope Mexico lost to Uruguay, and pray for a six-goal swing to finish in second. It wasn't likely.

You never know, though. France had a full-scale meltdown in Africa. After that goalless draw with Uruguay, Mexico rolled them over in a 2-0 win, a game in which an awful Nicolas Anelka was hauled off by Raymond Domenech at half-time only to tell the coach, 'Go get fucked up the arse, you dirty son of a whore.'

Anelka was swiftly sent home, much to the ire of the rest of the squad. They did what the French do best and went on strike, refusing to train under Domenech. In this atmosphere they came into the game with South Africa. The *Bafana Bafana* couldn't engineer a hefty victory to qualify for the knockouts on goal difference but they did run out 2-1 winners against the beleaguered French in Bloemfontein, a remarkable result against the previous tournament's runners-up, and a standout moment in the history of the national team.

The fans celebrated a famous victory, and the team were praised for performing well in a difficult group. Commentators informed us that this was the first time that a host nation had been eliminated in the first round, but the vuvuzelas drowned them out. For a month, the World Cup belonged to Africa.

2010: Frank Lampard's Ghost Goal

Sunday, 27 June 2010
Free State Stadium
Bloemfontein, South Africa

Supporting England is a unique rollercoaster. Fans went into the 2006 World Cup with expectations at an all-time high and a squad brimming with the best players in world football. Then Portugal and penalties happened once again. Sven-Göran Eriksson left, and his assistant Steve McClaren took over. One failed Euros qualifying campaign later, and hopes for an English success at a major tournament were firmly in the toilet.

After that disaster, Italian great Fabio Capello was tasked with revitalising the Three Lions. His pragmatic approach to coaching wasn't always pretty but it got results. England qualified for the 2010 World Cup at a canter, scoring more goals than any other UEFA team. And just like that the rollercoaster was back on the ascent, optimism building for what could be a barnstormer of a tournament for England in South Africa.

The draw for the group stages reinforced English confidence. 'England. Algeria. Slovenia. Yanks.' read the front page of *The Sun,* the tabloid rag highlighting each of the first letters in red to spell out 'EASY'. It was practically a free pass into the knockouts, according to the media. The England coaster climbed further, reaching an apex of bookies slashing odds and James Corden collaborating with Dizzee Rascal to release a truly awful World Cup song.

And then, with that old-school English belief at its highest, the coaster juddered and threatened to descend. David Beckham, who'd been in sensational form throughout qualification, ruptured his achilles tendon, ruling him out of the World Cup. It juddered again, and England lost captain Rio Ferdinand a week before their opening match when Emile Heskey literally fell on him in training, knackering his knee ligaments.

Forty minutes into the Three Lions' first game and there it was: freefall. After uncharacteristically taking an early lead through stand-in captain Steven Gerrard, a low, bobbling Clint Dempsey shot rolled towards Rob Green in the England goal. The keeper got two firm hands behind the ball, just firm enough to deflect it behind him and into the net. Fans fumed, pundits pontificated, and England couldn't score again.

One draw down, and another to come, this time against Algeria, who hadn't featured at a World Cup since 1986. A rotund brown bird set up camp on top of the North Africans' net, and it wasn't disturbed. In a drab, dreary contest on manager Capello's 64th birthday, the teams played out a stinking 0-0 draw. As a parting gift, Wayne Rooney decided to launch into a rant to a passing TV camera at the final whistle, criticising the fans who had booed the team's coma-inducing performance. Good old England, always good for a laugh at the World Cup.

Finally some respite came in the last group game against Slovenia, when a 1-0 win thanks to a Jermain Defoe goal secured a spot in the knockout stages. It was just like one of those mini-slopes on a coaster, when the car climbs for a second only to drop once more, because Landon Donovan then went and bagged a 91st-minute winner for the Americans against Algeria. This consigned England to second place and a last-16 fixture against Germany.

The World Cup's true breakout star had his say and forecast doom for the English. Paul the Octopus, who earned a name for himself from his tank at a German aquarium by correctly predicting the results of his home country's games, selecting food from one of two boxes adorned with the flags of the teams involved, swiftly gobbled the grub from the German box. Weymouth-born Paul had betrayed England. The Three Lions' card was marked.

Supporters gulped as the match kicked off in Bloemfontein, and only had to wait 20 minutes to see a long goal kick from Manuel Neuer fly towards the England box and somehow mystify John Terry, leaving Miroslav Klose to run through, poke the ball beyond David James and make it 1-0.

They had a second 12 minutes later, and it all came so easily. England were split in two by some fast German passing, the ball eventually winding up with Lukas Podolski who fired a low shot across James's goal and into the bottom corner. The way things were going, a cricket score was on the cards.

Five minutes later came a real collector's item: an England attack. The Three Lions managed to win a corner, took it short, and eventually found the head of Matthew Upson, who nodded it in. Out of nowhere, England were back in it.

Remarkably, 56 seconds later, they looked to have levelled it. Deciding to make hay while the sun was shining, Capello's side surged forwards looking for an equaliser straight from the restart. A German clearance ricocheted off Frank Lampard and bounced invitingly in front of him. The legendary midfielder let rip with an instinctive finish on the edge of the box, which hit the underside of the bar and bounced far over Neuer's line. Capello pumped his fists on the sideline. Beer was thrown into the air in pubs across England. Lampard ran off, arm raised above his head in celebration, then looked back towards the referee. Realisation. The Chelsea man put his hands on his head. The referee hadn't given it.

As Neuer caught the bouncing ball and played on as if nothing had happened, England's players looked shellshocked. It could have been 2-2. It *should* have been 2-2. Meanwhile, the Germans were off up the other end, nearly making it 3-1 when Podolski fired a long, driven effort just wide of James's post.

Half-time brought angry, passionate dissection of the incident and freshened calls for FIFA to adopt goal-line technology. Sepp Blatter had consistently and inexplicably opposed it, but now, surely, he had to stand up and take notice. Decisions this poor should not be happening on football's biggest stage.

England crumbled in the second half. They were never quite able to put the injustice behind them, their momentum had evaporated, and *Die Mannschaft* took advantage. Two breakaway goals from a 20-year-old Thomas Müller made it 4-1. The Three Lions were out, and dubious decision or not, they'd been humbled.

The aftermath was marked by rage. Naysayers suggested that Lampard's strike would have been irrelevant anyway as Germany still would have won 4-2, missing the point entirely that levelling the match in such a fashion moments before half-time would have completely changed England's approach. Over in Germany, comparisons were drawn with Geoff Hurst's goal in the 1966 final. In their minds, justice had been done for that perceived indiscretion 44 years on.

Most importantly of all, FIFA and head halfwit Blatter were prompted to readdress the goal-line technology debate. Extensive testing was carried out in the intervening years, and by the 2014 World Cup the tech was in place.

After this, Lampard took a philosophical view. 'It changed the game for the better, so I'm pleased about that,' he said of the goal. His sentiments weren't echoed by the England fans who'd flown over 5,000 miles to witness it.

2010: One Hand Crushes a Continent

Friday, 2 July 2010
Soccer City
Johannesburg, South Africa

With six representatives at the 2010 World Cup – more than ever before – there was genuine hope that an African nation might produce something special at the tournament. Despite their valiant efforts, the hosts had exited in the group stage. That wasn't too much of a surprise: they'd been drawn in a tough group and at 83rd were by far and away the lowest-ranked African team in the finals.

However, when Nigeria, Cameroon, Algeria and Ivory Coast all crashed out in the groups, winning just once across their combined 12 games, the dream of an African side shocking the world on their home continent hung in the balance.

All hopes were pinned on Ghana, who were appearing at their second World Cup. Under Serbian coach Milovan Rajevac they'd become a disciplined, organised team. They also still had a sprinkling of African flair and stardust, the likes of Sulley Muntari, Kevin-Prince Boateng and Asamoah Gyan all capable of turning on the skill to tip the balance in Ghana's favour. In a tricky group featuring Germany, Serbia and Australia they'd finished second on goal difference, duly heading into the knockout stages as Africa's sole representatives.

Fans united behind them. Suddenly, Ghana were playing for the entire continent. South Africans in the stadiums joined with Ghanaian supporters and cheered for the Black Stars. It was a special, unifying phenomenon. Nowhere exploded with as much passion as Ghana's capital Accra, though, when the side edged past the USA in extra time of their last-16 clash to book a place in the quarter-finals.

Uruguay stood between Ghana and becoming the first African side to reach the World Cup semi-finals. The two-time champions also had a point to prove. Recent years had been unkind to them, and they hadn't been a major footballing power since their last title in the 1950s. A patchy record in the intervening years saw them fail to even qualify on six occasions. This was the furthest they'd gone at the World Cup in 40 years, largely thanks to the magnificent Diego Forlán. For both sides, the quarter-final carried huge significance.

Fans inside Soccer City were treated to a battling, topsy-turvy game full of theatre. Uruguay were renowned in 2010 for their physical style, bullying opponents into submission. But the Black Stars were prepared for that, and a combative match ensued. The South Americans dominated the early play, with Edinson Cavani glancing a lethal header towards goal from a corner, forcing Ghanaian shot-stopper Richard Kingson – who'd just spent the season warming the bench for Wigan Athletic – into a fine save.

Momentum shifted on the half-hour mark. From a corner up the other end, Ghana came close to taking the lead. Centre-back Isaac Vorsah rose unchallenged to meet Muntari's swinging delivery but fired his header just wide of the post.

The legions of African fans in Johannesburg roared on Ghana as they played their way into the game. The teams looked destined to be goalless at half-time, until, with 15 seconds remaining, Muntari let fly with a speculative, low, curved effort from 35 yards. It curled round a cluster of bodies, wrong-footed Fernando Muslera in the Uruguay goal, and bounced into the back of his net. Soccer City went into hysteria.

Ghana continued strongly at the beginning of the second half before conceding a free kick on the corner of their 18-yard box ten minutes in. For the second time in the game, the goalkeeper was wrong-footed, this time Kingson swaying one way and then the other as he struggled to read Forlán's superb, bending effort. The South Americans were level.

The ascendancy switched back to Uruguay, unrelenting in their pursuit of a winner. A little-known Ajax striker by the name of Luis Suárez was lively, shooting at will and pressuring Kingson into a flurry of saves. Ultimately the goal wouldn't come, and the match hurtled towards extra time.

Like it so often is, the additional period was characterised by cagey, cautious play, neither side willing to lose while trying to win. Until, as the final seconds ebbed away and a penalty shoot-out hovered on the horizon, Soccer City bore witness to one of the most exceptional, unjust climaxes to a match the World Cup has ever seen.

Ghana decided to go for it in the closing stages of extra time, but they couldn't quite do enough to beat Muslera with their torrent of quickfire efforts. With Portuguese referee Olegário Benquerença readying to blow the full-time whistle, the Black Stars had one last chance to whip a cross into the box when they won a free kick out on the right wing.

They did just that, Fulham's John Paintsil swinging the ball in. Boateng managed to flick it on, whereupon it pinballed around the box. A panicked Uruguay tried to clear frantically, while the Ghanaians swarmed to put the ball in the net. All hands to the pump, Suárez was back and defending on the goal line, and managed to block a Boateng effort with his feet. The ball ricocheted back out, prompting Dominic Adiyiah to head it towards goal.

With 120 minutes up, Suárez struck again. Adiyiah's goalbound effort flew past Muslera and looked destined to go over the head of the Uruguay striker on the line and send Ghana into the semis. But Suárez decided he was going to do anything to keep his team in it. With rapid reflexes, he threw his hands up in front of him and batted the ball away.

He knew what was coming. Benquerença promptly pointed to the spot and gave Suárez his marching orders. But at the very least he'd given his team a chance. Ghana had just seen the last four flash before their eyes, only to have it swatted away at the last second, putting incomprehensible pressure on the penalty that was to follow.

Suárez watched from the tunnel, his face buried in his shirt. Gyan stepped up. He'd been nothing short of sensational for Ghana throughout the tournament, scoring three goals – two from the spot – and leading the line heroically, even when chances were few and far between. If anyone deserved to put Ghana into the semi-finals, it was him. But he didn't. The penalty clattered into the crossbar and out for a goal kick. To make the whole situation even more distasteful for Black Stars fans, TV cameras cut to Suárez, who pumped his fists and beamed a big, toothy grin in celebration.

Karma didn't get to Uruguay in the penalty shoot-out that followed, either. Gyan bravely stepped up once more and dispatched Ghana's first kick, but two misses from captain John Mensah and denied match-winner Adiyiah sent the South Americans through.

It was a harrowing moment for Ghana. They felt completely robbed. For Suárez's part, he was quick to emphasise how glad he was with the action he'd taken, rubbing salt in fresh wounds. 'The Hand of God now belongs to me,' he declared afterwards. 'I made the best save of the tournament.'

At the very least, the old 'cheats never prosper' adage was proven partly true in the semis, when the Netherlands swept aside Uruguay to reach the final. Suárez featured in the third-place play-off, when the Germans proved too much to handle for the Uruguayans.

For Ghana's part, forgiveness was not forthcoming. 'He knows what he has done,' said Hans Sarpei, who played at left-back that day. 'We were crying and you see someone who has cheated us is celebrating. How can I forgive him? Never. Never ever.' That was a full ten years after the incident. Seemingly, Suárez is still one of the most hated men in West Africa.

2010: Tiki-Taka Takes the World by Storm
Sunday, 11 July 2010
Soccer City
Johannesburg, South Africa

If England fans thought they'd had a rough ride, spare a thought for Spanish supporters before 2010. A football-mad nation with two of the biggest clubs in the sport in Barcelona and Real Madrid, and a long list of illustrious players, they'd never even made it to the semi-finals of the biggest competition in football. *La Roja*'s history at the World Cup was a chequered tale of squandered opportunities, agonising near-misses and crushing disappointments. But all that was about to change.

Atlético Madrid legend Luis Aragonés took charge of Spain in 2004 after they'd crashed out of the Euros in the group stages. The talented squad, captained by Raúl, were expected to do great things, but once more the Spanish just didn't show up at a major tournament. At the World Cup in 2006, things looked more promising. Under Aragonés's stewardship Spain sailed through their group, winning every match and bagging eight goals. But then the last-16 clash against eventual runners-up France came along and Spain crumbled once more.

An under-fire Aragonés kept his job, and decided a radical new approach was needed to revitalise the national setup. Spain were always renowned for their fast passing play but previous incarnations of the national sides had also prioritised fire and physical effort, running through brick walls to get results. The problem was, those results never seemed to materialise.

With an exciting batch of young, talented midfielders bursting through the ranks, the manager switched the focus. He wanted to pass, pass, pass teams off the park, holding possession for as long as possible until an opening might appear, then make the opposition pay. And thus tiki-taka was born.

He unleashed it on the world at Euro 2008, and the world wasn't ready. Spain waltzed to the title, defeating Germany 1-0 in the final to send fans back home into delirium. But they wanted more. They wanted the World Cup.

Aragonés had consistently said he'd step down after the European Championship, and the man was true to his word. That left the incoming Vicente del Bosque to pick up where he left off. And he did exactly that. Clearly a fan of the old 'if it ain't broke, don't fix it' mantra, Del Bosque maintained Aragonés's tiki-taka style of play and Spain cruised into the 2010 World Cup, winning every single match in qualifying.

The world was taking notice. Spain arrived in South Africa as the bookies' favourites. Their embarrassingly fantastic midfield, comprising Barcelona enforcer Sergio Busquets, Real Madrid's ball-playing dynamo Xabi Alonso, and the dazzling, dizzying Camp Nou combo of Xavi and Andrés Iniesta, left every opposition defence quaking at the mere prospect of sharing the same pitch with them. Every defence, that is, except Switzerland.

Spanish hopes of an unencumbered romp to World Cup glory were left in tatters as the Swiss ran out shock 1-0 winners when the pair faced each other in their opening group game. That was it, as far as the Spanish press were concerned. The almost comedic old World Cup curse had returned to haunt Spain's greatest crop of players. *La Roja* were going to crash and burn on the biggest stage once more.

But Del Bosque's men were more resilient. Wins against Honduras and Chile followed, and Spain topped their group on goal difference, the undeniable David Villa stepping up and striking three of his country's four group-stage goals. Next up were old Iberian foes Portugal in the last 16, and Villa again proved the difference, registering the only goal in a 1-0 victory.

With surprise package Paraguay waiting in the quarters, Spanish fans were allowing themselves to dream and booking tickets for what would be a first World Cup semi-final. The match at Ellis Park, however, proved far from plain sailing.

The Paraguayans were dogged and organised, breaking up Spain's fluid, tricky play at will. And they should have been ahead. As the first half neared its end, Nelson Valdez had the ball in the Spanish net only to wrongly see his goal ruled out for offside. The teams went in for the break with the score locked at 0-0.

Early in the second half, madness descended. Gerard Piqué wrestled Paraguay striker Óscar Cardozo to the ground at a corner, only for Cardozo to see his ensuing penalty saved and held by Iker Casillas in the Spain goal. From the attack the keeper then launched, the Spanish broke quickly and Villa was hauled down in the Paraguay box. Another penalty. Alonso stepped up, buried it, and then was ordered to retake the kick due to encroachment by his team-mates. His second effort wasn't so successful, the South Americans' captain Justo Villar saving superbly to his left.

With that frenzy over and the match still goalless, it was left to Villa to once again play the saviour. His strike in the 83rd minute sent Spain into the semis, where a third successive 1-0 win, this time over Germany, was enough to schedule a date with destiny against the Netherlands in the final.

The match in Johannesburg was not one for the ages. The Dutch, exercising their full repertoire of brutality first exhibited during the Battle of Nuremberg four years prior, sought to grind Spain down with a stacked defensive unit and some eyebrow-raising challenges. The bookings flowed thick and fast. In the first half, Nigel de Jong did his best Bruce Lee impression and launched a flying kick into the chest of Alonso. English ref Howard Webb decided it was fair game and only showed a yellow.

The second half saw the best chance of the game go the *Oranje*'s way. Wesley Sneijder slotted an inch-perfect through ball to Arjen Robben, sending him one on one with Casillas, who produced a game-saving stop to keep the scores level. An excruciatingly tense match remained a stalemate after 90 minutes. The sides would need another half an hour to settle this one.

Late substitute Cesc Fàbregas had an opportunity to give Spain the lead at the beginning of extra time, only to see his effort brilliantly foiled by Maarten Stekelenburg in the Dutch goal. They looked to be through again in the second half of the additional period, Iniesta surging beyond a mass of orange shirts to meet Xavi's lobbed pass. Everton centre-back Johnny Heitinga dragged him back, leaving Webb with no choice but to flash the defender a second yellow card, making him the fifth man to be sent off in a World Cup Final.

Down to ten, the Netherlands looked to hang on for the lottery of penalties. But they couldn't keep the Spanish tide at bay for long enough. With four minutes remaining, Fàbregas found Iniesta free in the box, and he fired a low half-volley beyond Stekelenburg. Spain had won the World Cup.

The record books will tell you that Spain won by scoring the fewest goals of any side to lift the trophy. Their record in the knockout stages was a misleading run of four 1-0 wins. But none of that mattered. The whole country took to the streets. Fireworks exploded and car horns blared until daylight. It had finally happened. The perennial underachievers of international football were world champions.

2014: Suárez Takes a Chunk Out of Italy

Tuesday, 24 June 2014
Arena das Dunas
Natal, Brazil

For the World Cup's 20th edition, FIFA took the tournament back to where it all started in South America. Original hosts Uruguay didn't bid, so it was left to Brazil to take up the mantle. This was one for the traditionalists. The purest celebration of all things football, in the sport's most successful nation.

What a group stage we were treated to. Goals flew in at a rate of knots. The Netherlands battered Spain 5-1 in a repeat of the previous tournament's final, as the all-conquering reigning champions crashed out in the group stage. And England, Italy and Uruguay – with a staggering seven World Cup titles between them – were all drawn into a mouth-watering group of death that minnows Costa Rica promptly went and won with a game to spare.

It was in that same group that one of the World Cup's most colourful characters doubled down on the hate figure status he'd earned four years earlier.

By 2014, *everyone* knew Luis Suárez. When the supremely gifted striker wasn't banging goals in for a Liverpool side that had just come within touching distance of the Premier League title, he was making headlines for his off-the-ball antics. There was, of course, that handball against Ghana. But since then he'd embarked on a one-man mission of infamy. Shortly after the World Cup, while still with Ajax, he bit PSV midfielder Otman Bakkal, causing much outrage in the Netherlands. Then with Liverpool, he attracted the ire of the English press during a much-publicised racism row with Manchester United's Patrice Evra, before hitting the front pages once more for sinking his teeth into yet another opponent, this time Chelsea's Branislav Ivanović.

Ahead of the tournament, the Suárez PR machine whirled into action to assure the world that he was a nice guy, really. 'I want to change the bad boy image that has stuck for a bit because I don't think I am at all how I have been portrayed,' he said. 'That's not what I want to be remembered for. I want to do things right.'

So, could football fans expect a new incarnation of the divisive forward on the pitch in Brazil? In a word, no.

The striker missed Uruguay's first match through injury, and *La Celeste* struggled badly without him, falling to a humbling 3-1 defeat against the Costa Ricans. He made it back in time to put a dagger through England's hopes in their next game. Suárez glanced a header beyond Joe Hart in the first half to put his side 1-0 up, prompting England to fight for their World Cup lives. Wayne Rooney came close to levelling on numerous occasions, and should have equalised when Leighton Baines put the ball on a plate for him six yards from goal, only for the Manchester United man to fire it straight at goalkeeper Fernando Muslera.

Fifteen minutes from time he finally broke his World Cup duck. Remarkably the England legend had never scored at the tournament before, but tapped in from close range to briefly revive the Three Lions' campaign. But with five minutes left Suárez struck again to consign Roy Hodgson's side to a first group-stage exit since 1958. England captain Steven Gerrard must have thought he was back at Anfield because he headed a perfect through ball into the path of his Liverpool team-mate, who calmly dispatched it past Hart. With that blunder England were gone, and Suárez was looking lethal.

They'd need him to be at his brilliant best in their final, make-or-break clash with Italy. Only a win would do, with a draw seeing the Italians through to the last 16 on goal difference.

The game in Natal was a slog. The *Azzurri* were well aware that a draw would do them just nicely, and set up to frustrate Uruguay. Suárez was more infuriated than anyone, the striker spurning some golden chances to put his side ahead. As the game entered its 79th minute he showed everyone just how riled he was.

The South Americans were up in the Italian box in numbers, but saw yet another cross in thwarted by towering centre-back Giorgio Chiellini. As the ball drifted out towards the wings, Suárez and the defender came together, with both falling in heaps on the floor. Mexican referee Marco Rodríguez instantly blew for a free kick to Italy but no one was quite sure what had happened.

Then the replays came. The first few angles showed Suárez throwing his head into the Italian's shoulder, but it looked fairly innocuous. And then a close-up from behind the goal revealed the truth: he'd only gone and done it again. The Uruguayan had sunk his quite sizeable gnashers into Chiellini's flesh.

Suárez's own reaction was laughable. While on the deck, he held his teeth with a pained expression on his face, a truly pantomime charade of checking that they were all still there, and implying that he'd fallen, teeth first, into Chiellini. The extremely visible bite marks the Italian duly presented to the referee proved otherwise.

However, Rodríguez hadn't seen it. He'd only given a foul against Uruguay because he thought Suárez had pushed Chiellini. So no yellow or red appeared. The Uruguayan had gotten away with, for now at least.

Two minutes later, Uruguay had the goal that sent them into the knockout stages and subjected Italy to a group-stage exit for the second World Cup in a row. Captain Diego Godín shouldered the ball beyond Gianluigi Buffon to give Uruguay the win. At full time, the usually animated Suárez was relatively understated in his celebrations. Perhaps he knew what was coming.

The full force of FIFA came down heavy on Suárez after he'd completed his trilogy of masticatory assaults. They immediately banned him for nine international matches, all football for four months, and doled out a hefty fine to the player. Everyone had an opinion, almost universally condemnatory, from outrage in the *Match of the Day* studio to, rather bizarrely, a castigation from Bruce Springsteen.

Without their key man, Uruguay crashed out in their next game, against Colombia, in a match best remembered for a Golden Boot-bound James Rodríguez's sensational volley. The Uruguayans were, somewhat ironically, toothless up top, losing 2-0.

At the very least Suárez had near-universal support from his fellow countrymen. His international colleagues came out in droves after the incident to claim that nothing had happened, while the president of Uruguay, José Mujica, tore into FIFA for their handling of the situation and branded them 'a bunch of old sons of bitches'. Suárez, meanwhile, just claimed that he'd fallen over.

2014: The *Mineirazo*
Tuesday, 8 July 2014
Estádio Mineirão
Belo Horizonte, Brazil

You don't have to be an expert in the sport to grasp just how important football is to the people of Brazil. It's the beating heart of a nation of over 200 million people. And it certainly doesn't hurt that, historically, they've been bloody good at it. They've won the World Cup more than anyone else, each time sending the entire nation, from the impoverished to the bloatedly wealthy, into a frenzy of joy.

Yet for a nation that has enjoyed such footballing riches, it is an earth-shattering defeat that lingers most prominently in the national psyche. The *Maracanazo*, when Uruguay won 2-1 in Rio in 1950 to steal what would have been a first World Cup title for Brazil, remains a throbbing open wound. Every time the national side suffered through a difficult spell, the ghost of the *Maracanazo* would reappear in the press. The pain was passed down from generation to generation, to the point where a raft of Brazilian football fans whose grandparents weren't even born when it happened still harbour feelings of remorse whenever their home World Cup in 1950 is mentioned. But in 2014 they had the opportunity to put those demons to bed.

For Brazilians, the chance to finally taste the ultimate glory on home soil was intoxicating. For the players, however, it was a pressure cooker. Not only were they charged with consigning the misery of old to the past but they had to ensure it didn't happen again. As the legendary Zico put it, 'You looked at the faces of the Brazilian players when they walked on the pitch during the World Cup and it looked like they were about to compete in the Hunger Games.'

It looked like the situation might get too much for the *Seleção* even in their first game, when Croatia took the lead in São Paulo inside 12 minutes. But Brazil, managed by returning 2002 World Cup-winning coach Luis Felipe Scolari, got it together quick enough to turn things around. The talismanic Neymar netted twice and a late strike from Oscar secured a 3-1 win.

A drab 0-0 draw with Mexico followed, and again the Brazilian media started questioning the team's credentials. It's worth remembering that this Brazil side, besides Neymar and a handful of others, did not possess the same quality as some of the great teams that went before. They put the doubters on hold for long enough to trounce Cameroon 4-1 in their final group game, Neymar scoring another brace, and safely earned a spot in the knockouts as group winners.

There, penalties were needed to dispatch Chile, before an edgy 2-1 win over Colombia in the quarters. Brazil were far from convincing but they were getting the job done, and a crunch tie against Germany in the last four awaited. Neymar had been inspirational so far, and with him in their team they always stood a chance.

Therein lay the problem. With two minutes remaining of that physical, controversial quarter-final against Colombia, Neymar hit the deck after a meaty challenge from Juan Camilo Zúñiga. The game continued but he didn't get up. It looked bad. He left the pitch on a stretcher in tears – his tournament was over. Zúñiga's challenge left Neymar with a fractured vertebra. If Brazil were going to win the World Cup, they'd have to do it without their superstar.

The country's reaction was suitably emotional. 'Play for him!' screamed the front page of newspaper O Povo. Neymar wasn't going to be the only miss for the Germany game, either. Captain Thiago Silva had picked up his second yellow card of the tournament, meaning he'd be suspended. Brazil were torn apart by two gaping holes in their team.

This was not the ideal preparation for facing Germany, who under coach Joachim Löw looked capable of achieving something special. For a country with such a prolific winning record, the 18 years they'd gone without a major trophy was far too long. They looked bang at it in Brazil, opening their campaign with a 4-0 demolition of Portugal and comfortably topping their group, before emerging victorious against Algeria and then France on their way to the semis.

By the time the game arrived, Brazil were optimistic once more. The players spoke of being galvanised in the face of adversity. During a raucous rendition of the national anthem at the Estádio Mineirão in Belo Horizonte, stand-in captain David Luiz held up Neymar's shirt. The forward was watching from home, and the performance his team put in without him certainly wasn't a tonic.

Germany were ahead on 11 minutes, Thomas Müller volleying home from a corner at close range. It was farcical defending from Luiz in particular, who completely left his man to give Müller the freedom of the Brazilian box. Then veteran striker Miroslav Klose doubled the lead in the 23rd minute. Júlio César repelled his initial effort but couldn't prevent the ball from spilling back to the feet of Klose, who was left with an easy tap-in. It was an historic moment for the German, who broke Ronaldo's record to become the World Cup's all-time top scorer with his 16th strike.

Il Fenomeno's record going up in smoke was the least of Brazil fans' worries. Klose's goal sparked a seven-minute onslaught of sheer and utter domination. Practically straight from the restart, Toni Kroos made it three with a thumping effort from the edge of the box. Cameras cut to the supporters in the stands, thousands upon thousands of Brazilians sat with heads in hands, mouths agape. A minute later, he scored again. Cue the obligatory shot of a child in a Brazil shirt crying. Then Sami Khedira made it 5-0. It was harder for the cameras to find Brazil fans to focus on by this point, because half of them were leaving. Less than half an hour had been played.

Die Mannschaft were less ruthless in the second half, only scoring twice. Both came from substitute André Schürrle, his second the pick of the bunch, squeezing home a stunning finish from a ludicrously tight angle. To their credit, many of the Brazil fans still in the stadium stood and applauded.

There was time at the death for Oscar to salvage a single consolation goal, but the damage was long done. The 7-1 scoreline entered the record books as Brazil's joint-record loss, the previous hammering having come at the hands of Uruguay nearly 100 years ago, and the players were eviscerated, to a man burying their faces in the turf. A chorus of jeers rang out when the referee finally called time. If it'd been a boxing match it would have been ended an hour earlier.

The most comical representation of Germany's complete subjugation of Brazil came in the form of striker Fred's heat map. The majority of his touches had come in the centre circle from restarting the game so many times.

The Germans acted with humility after the final whistle, many going over to console their opponents. Löw expressed feelings of sympathy in his post-match interview and the players had agreed to celebrate any more goals they might score as understatedly as possible. Khedira later revealed that Löw actively asked his players not to humiliate Brazil during his half-time team talk. That ship had very much sailed.

The Brazilian national press was considerably less comforting. 'Shame!' read the front page of the sports newspaper *Lance!*. Luiz and Fred came in for special criticism. Meanwhile, on the streets, there were riots in São Paulo and fans set fire to Brazilian flags in Rio. This was another national trauma to add to the collection, and the press were quick to come up with a handy moniker: the *Mineirazo*.

The final five days later was less action-packed. A battling 0-0 between the Germans and a Lionel Messi-inspired Argentina went to extra time, when substitute Mario Götze scored the only goal, giving Germany their fourth World Cup crown. Brazil achieved a bit of catharsis when they beat Germany on penalties in the gold medal match at the Rio Olympics, with Neymar scoring the winning kick at the Maracanã. They're still waiting to put those ghosts to rest on the biggest stage of all, though.

2018: England Lift Penalty Curse
Tuesday, 3 July 2018
Otkritie Arena
Moscow, Russia

Shocks and oddities were the order of the day when the World Cup rolled into Russia in 2018. FIFA miraculously went back on their old technophobic ways and welcomed VAR to the tournament for the first time. Lionel Messi saw a penalty saved by Iceland's Hannes Halldórsson, who when he wasn't playing football earned a living directing music videos for his country's Eurovision entries. Belgium's Michy Batshuayi nearly broke his nose celebrating a goal by booting the ball into the post only for it to smack him plum in the face. Iranian left-back Milad Mohammadi attempted to take a front-flip throw-in. And reigning champions Germany went out in the group stage for the first time after a humbling loss to South Korea.

But all of that paled in comparison to the biggest peculiarity of all: England suddenly getting good at penalties.

Gareth Southgate's Three Lions weren't given a chance in Russia. The manager had only got the job after Sam Allardyce decided to commit career suicide when he became embroiled in a corruption scandal in 2016 and was hastily given the sack after one game in charge of the national team. Faith in Southgate's credentials weren't exactly unerring. His managerial experience to that point amounted to relegating Middlesbrough from the Premier League before leading England's under-21s to finish bottom of their group at the UEFA European Under-21 Championship in 2015.

England did qualify for the World Cup without losing a game, but that didn't hold much stock in either pundits' or fans' eyes given the poor standard of the qualifying group from which they'd emerged. At the very least, Southgate selected a talented young squad for the tournament, garnering praise for giving the next generation a chance to gain experience on the biggest stage. A lot of fans almost viewed 2018 as a free hit; England would exit early, and be better next time.

It certainly didn't look like it could get any worse when the Three Lions' tournament opener against Tunisia arrived. England looked off the pace and devoid of ideas, finding themselves stuck at 1-1 with the North Africans until the 91st minute, when captain

Harry Kane nodded in from close range at a corner. It wasn't particularly confidence-boosting, but at least they'd won.

Debutants Panama, who'd shocked even themselves by making it to the World Cup, were turned over by a comfortable 6-1 scoreline, Kane grabbing a rather fortuitous hat-trick after Ruben Loftus-Cheek's shot bounced off him while his back was turned and pinged into the Panama net. It was England's record win at the tournament, and the first kernels of hope started to pop. Sure, the opposition were hardly world-beaters, but England had played minnows before and never made the difference count. This time, they did.

The final clash was against Belgium, and both sides were already through. Southgate and his opposite number Roberto Martínez made sure in the build-up to dispel suggestions from the media that coming second in the group would actually offer a supposedly easier route to the final, and reassured reporters that their sides would be gunning for victory. Then they promptly made eight and nine changes respectively for the match no one wanted to win, but which Belgium did win 1-0.

Easier route secured, England faced Colombia in the last 16 in a nail-bitingly fractious match in Moscow. The South Americans decided physicality was the key to success, their more skilful side inhibited by the loss of their playmaker James Rodríguez to injury. Their game plan proved successful in the first half, stifling England's attacks and holding the score to 0-0 come half-time.

Shortly before the hour, England fans were dreaming of a first knockout stage win at any tournament for 12 years. Kane was wrestled to the ground as he attempted to meet a corner and American referee Mark Geiger pointed to the spot. The Tottenham man was ice-cool once more from 12 yards, burying his penalty straight down the middle. It was his sixth and final goal on the way to claiming the Golden Boot.

The tension built as Colombia pressed for an equaliser, while England searched for a second to put the game to bed. It just wouldn't come. As the match dragged into injury time, English fingernails were a thing of the past. And then the familiar feeling of deflation. With 93 minutes on the clock, domineering centre-back Yerry Mina rose highest to connect with Juan Cuadrado's corner and powered a header beyond his future Everton team-mate

Jordan Pickford. The nerve-shredding uncertainty of extra time beckoned.

The additional period was bitty and disjointed, with very few goalscoring chances. Danny Rose came closest, firing a cross-goal shot just beyond Colombia goalkeeper David Ospina's post. England searched more frantically than their opponents for a winner, perhaps sensing impending doom as the very real, very daunting prospect of a penalty shoot-out loomed larger. There would be no winner, though. It would have to be penalties.

Southgate understood more than most the agony a shoot-out can bring. It was he who missed the deciding kick when England faced off against Germany in the semi-final at Euro '96. The Three Lions' record in shoot-outs made for depressing reading: played seven, won one, lost six.

After the first five penalties emphatically hit the back of the net, England blinked first. There were those familiar pangs of hope slipping away as Jordan Henderson saw his poor effort saved by Ospina. Advantage Colombia. 'Oh no!' groaned Clive Tyldesley on commentary.

Then, something strange happened. The dying hope fizzled and flickered as Manuel Uribe missed the chance to capitalise on Colombia's advantage, hammering his kick into the bar. And then it burned brighter when Kieran Trippier smashed in his penalty to make it three each from the spot.

Colombia's last kick came next. Pickford produced a tremendous save to deny Carlos Bacca. It was the first time an England keeper had saved a penalty in a shoot-out in any competition for 20 years, since David Seaman managed the feat as the side crashed out to Argentina in 1998. Eric Dier now had the chance to win it for England. They couldn't, could they?

They could. Dier smashed his effort low beyond Ospina. The impossible had happened; England had won a penalty shoot-out for the first time since beating Spain at Euro '96, and the first time in the World Cup. The players mobbed Pickford in celebration. This was a seminal moment: two decades of penalty hoodoo vanished into thin air.

If he didn't before, Southgate now well and truly had the fans on side. Supporters chanted his name and Marks & Spencer sold out of the navy waistcoat he'd been sporting out in Russia. An eerily comfortable 2-0 win over Sweden in the quarters followed, sending England to their first World Cup semi final since 1990.

That was the end. Croatia were the opponents, and for a while, the final was within touching distance, Trippier firing England ahead in the fifth minute from a glorious free kick. But the Croatians levelled in the second half before winning it through Mario Mandžukić in extra time.

It felt like a wasted opportunity. But at the same time, England went to Russia with expectations practically non-existent, and made it to the final four. The FA were delighted, and awarded Southgate with a new contract soon after. And finally, that demoralising, disturbing, seemingly never-ending penalty curse had been lifted. Until it came back with a vengeance in the final of the Covid-delayed Euros three years later.

2018: Fantastic France and a Croatian Fairytale
Sunday, 15 July 2018
Luzhniki Stadium
Moscow, Russia

For England fans, Croatia's passage into the final was merely a devastating denial of the chance to play in football's biggest game. But theirs was a remarkable story in its own right. This small nation, that only gained its independence from Yugoslavia in 1991, and with a population of fewer than four million people, had made it all the way to the World Cup Final. It was nothing short of miraculous.

The team's slogan for the tournament, which was plastered across the team bus and a stack of official merchandise, was 'Little Country, Big Dreams'. And boy were they dreaming big in Russia. They'd had to beat Greece in a play-off to make it to the World Cup having finished second in qualifying to Iceland. At the finals they were drawn in a group with the Iceland side that had bested them on the way to the World Cup, plus Nigeria and Argentina. Making it to the knockouts looked like a big ask.

Their first game, on paper the easiest of the three, saw them take on Nigeria. They ran out comfortable 2-0 winners. But sterner tests were to come, starting straight away with a clash against the Argentinians.

Croatia promptly delivered one of the shocks of the tournament, steamrollering the two-time champions with three second-half goals to win 3-0. They were already into the last 16 when they faced Iceland in their last match, but that didn't stop them claiming yet another victory, 2-1 this time, sending the Croatians through to the next round with a 100 per cent record.

Manager Zlatko Dalić had his team purring. He'd had a nomadic coaching career prior to arriving at his national team, mainly taking charge of club sides in the Middle East. But now he was proving himself in the greatest arena of all. The team he'd built were resilient. When they went 1-0 down to Denmark in the last 16 after a matter of seconds, they equalised just a few moments later then went on to win on penalties. They needed spot-kicks again to sneak past hosts Russia in the quarters, overcoming a hostile, volatile atmosphere to do so. And then there was that semi with England, when they again came back from an early setback to win the game. They'd gone one better than the heroes of France '98, who in their first World Cup appearance as an independent nation finished third after losing to the French in the semis. Throughout, captain Luka Modrić was unplayable, dictating things from the centre of midfield with the composure and elegance of an orchestral conductor.

The final pitted Dalić's men against Didier Deschamps' France. *Les Bleus* were the overwhelming pre-tournament favourites, with a truly glittering squad playing for the world's biggest clubs. And while Croatia's team didn't exactly comprise nobodies playing in the Turkmenistan second division, it certainly lacked the lustre and star quality of their esteemed opponents. This was best evidenced by the fact that Andrej Kramarić, who featured in every game, had been deemed surplus to requirements at Leicester City just two years prior.

The French, despite the grand expectations of them, had been pretty uninspired in the group stages, only beating Australia and Peru 2-1 and 1-0 respectively before playing out a boring goalless draw against Denmark.

However the knockouts saw them come alive, defeating some of the world's best in the process. They began with a thrilling 4-3 win over Argentina, before Uruguay were seen off 2-0 in the quarter-finals. A 1-0 victory over that quality Belgium side that topped England's group saw Deschamps' team into the final.

Everything about the game looked like a mismatch. For all their pluckiness so far, surely this terrifyingly talented French side would be too much for the Croatians. What's more, all three of Croatia's knockout matches had gone to extra time, while none of France's had, meaning they'd played an entire game's worth of football more than their opponents. Add that to the fact that France had one more day of rest than Dalic's team and it made for a monstrous mountain to climb.

And in spite of all of that, Croatia turned up the heat on France to create one of the most entertaining finals in decades.

The underdogs came out of the traps much faster than their opponents, bossing the opening 15 minutes as thunder and lightning crashed around them in the Russian capital. It was against the run of play when France took the lead in the 18th minute, Mandžukić getting desperately unlucky when trying to clear an Antoine Griezmann free kick and instead glancing the ball into his own net.

Ivan Perišić levelled things ten minutes later. He collected the ball on the edge of the box and delivered a sublime half volley that blitzed past Hugo Lloris. It was a deserved equaliser for a side that spent most of the first half on top. For a while, Croatia looked like the champions-elect.

Then Lady Luck frowned on them once more. While defending a corner with seven minutes remaining before half-time, Perišić was penalised harshly for a handball while defending a corner, the ball coming at him rapidly from off Blaise Matuidi's head. In a World Cup where the use of VAR was widely praised, the technology saved its most contentious intervention for the biggest game of all. Argentine referee Néstor Pitana was implored to check the pitchside monitor and swiftly pointed to the spot. It felt harsh. Griezmann restored *Les Bleus'* lead and sent them in 2-1 up at the break, despite only having had a single shot to Croatia's seven.

Shortly after the restart, play was halted when a cluster of pitch invaders made it on to the pitch. Cameras cut to the onlooking Russian president Vladimir Putin, who looked like he'd just swallowed a wasp. Most of those who made it on to the field circled the players asking for high-fives, and a few obliged. Spare a thought for the man who asked Dejan Lovren to give him some skin, though. The irate Liverpool centre-back instead pushed him to the ground and tried to drag him off by his collar before a steward intervened.

That unwelcome interruption over, the toll of the extra minutes in Croatian legs started to tell, and their brave, defiant performance began to fade. Paul Pogba made it 3-1 just before the hour, then the sensational 19-year-old Kylian Mbappé evoked memories of Pelé, firing a lethal strike beyond Danijel Subašić to become the first teenager to score in the final since the Brazilian in 1958.

The score was not representative of the match; 4-1 felt incredibly unfair on Croatia. Perhaps France captain Lloris thought so too, because in the 69th minute he gifted Mandžukić the opportunity to cancel out his own goal from earlier by taking too long to clear the ball as the Croatian closed him down. There was a nicer ring to 4-2.

That was how it stayed. Deschamps became the third man after Mário Zagallo and Franz Beckenbauer to win the World Cup as both a player and a manager. It was redemption for the French, who were crushed two years earlier when they lost the final of Euro 2016 to Portugal in Paris. France were world champions for a second time.

Croatia, who fought so valiantly, returned home to over ten per cent of the population crammed on to the streets of Zagreb to welcome them as heroes, and having earned the respect and admiration of football fans the world over. They'd come so agonisingly close to achieving something that would have seen them pass into immortality, and shown smaller footballing nations that sometimes, with the right attitude and the right manager, anyone can fight at the top table in the sport. Dreaming big could pay off.

'You have to have a dream, an ambition,' Dalić philosophised afterwards. 'Then follow those dreams and ambitions. One day, maybe it will come true. In football, or in life in general. Never give up.'